MOUNTAINS, CAMPFIRES & MEMORIES

Jack Boudreau

MOUNTAINS, CAMPFIRES & MEMORIES

CAITLIN PRESS INC. 2002

Caitlin Press
8100 Alderwood Road,
Halfmoon Bay, BC
V0N 1Y1

www. caitlin-press.com

We acknowledge the financial support of the Canada Council for the Arts and BC Arts Council in publishing this book.

Cover design by Terra Firma Graphics
Layout and Design by Warren Clark Graphic Design
Index by K. Plett
Map by Rich Rawlings

The photos in this books have been gathered by the author from many sources. Where the source is known, it is acknowledged in the caption.

National Library of Canada Cataloguing in Publication Data

Boudreau, Jack, 1933-
    Mountains, campfires & memories

    Includes index.
    ISBN 0-920576-95-8

    1. Frontier and pioneer life—British Columbia. 2. Pioneers—British Columbia.
3. Outdoor life—British Columbia. I. Title.
FC3805.B68 2002   971.1009'9   C2002-910722-9   F1086.8.B68 2002

Contents

Dedication

This book is dedicated to all the courageous people who pioneered in British Columbia. To the countless number who went missing in their search for wealth and new lands to explore. To the engineers, surveyors and guides, I tip my hat. Also, to the Native peoples who assisted the early settlers in so many ways and taught them how to survive in a harsh and unforgiving wilderness, much credit is due.

For the trappers and prospectors who endured extreme privation and unbearable loneliness—many of whom lost their lives in the wild water along the raging rivers—I have a special wish: may some universal justice decree that all of you spend eternity in a beautiful wilderness country that is loaded with the best fur imaginable; where every rock-strewn stream is loaded with large gold nuggets.

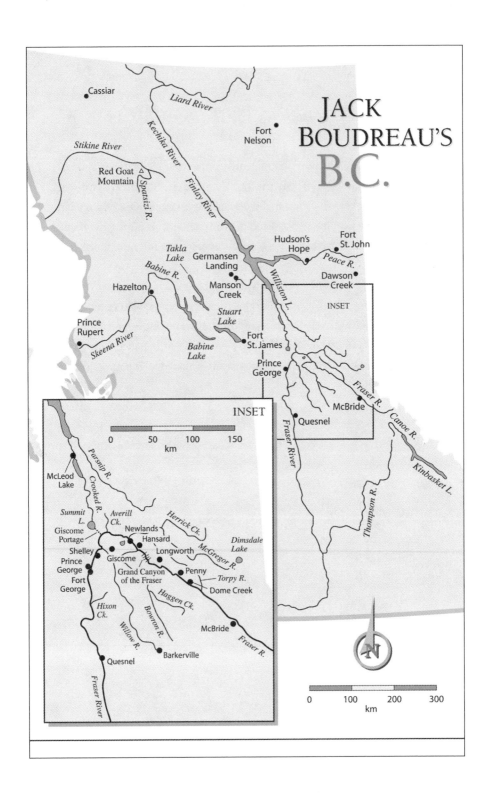

JACK
BOUDREAU'S
B.C.

Acknowledgments

FIRST, I MUST THANK ALL THE ELDERLY FOLKS WHO HELPED ME BOTH DIRECTLY and indirectly; often they pointed me in the direction of information or referred me to other people without whose assistance this book would have been impossible.

To the Boone And Crockett Club of Missoula, Montana, thanks for permission to use the original photographs from their book, *From The Peace To The Fraser*, www.boone-crockett.org.

Once again I thank the *Prince George Citizen* for permission to reprint; as well I wish to thank all the other newspapers which I have so frequently quoted.

To the Prince George Public Library—your endless assistance has been far above and beyond the call of duty; just saying thanks seems totally inadequate.

To Clarence, Olga and Larry Boudreau—once again your assistance has been much appreciated.

To the people that assisted in one way or another, I wish to thank Melanie Cummins, Sandy Phillips, Maxine Koppe, Helen Weaver, Mae and Maurice Fredette, Ted and Olive Williams for assistance both past and present. Also, many thanks to Steve and Helen Wlasitz, Ellary Evasin, Tim Cushman, Doug Gillette, Mike Nash and Rick Roos.

To Dean Scarrow of Vancouver Island Helicopters, Doug Beaumont of Harbour Air, and especially Mike Murtha of BC Parks, for the many leads and sources of information he pointed in my direction, I say a special thank you. Regrettably, Mike is leaving us for the greener fields of Banff Park; our loss is definitely Alberta's gain.

Finally, a million thanks to Eric Klaubauf and Steve Buba without whose assistance I most certainly would have murdered my computer. I recall the day I got them to come to my home because my old printer would only print modern art-type pictures (they didn't look too bad but you couldn't tell what they represented.) When the two experts arrived, they examined my printer and gave me the impression that it was not top-of-the-line. The reason I drew that conclusion was because I heard one of them describe it as "a piece of shit."

I took the hint and purchased a new printer, then put an ad in a newspaper offering the Stone Age printer for $50; I never got a call. Not discouraged, though, I renewed the ad, offering it for $20, and then lowered it to $10, but still never got a call. Finally, in desperation, I offered it free to anyone who would take it away. At last I got a call, but when I told the caller what the make and model was, he hung up. Perhaps the two gentlemen were right.

Foreword

In picking a title for this book, I agonized for a time and finally settled on the three words that best summarize life in the wilderness, both today as well as years ago. I decided that Mountains, Campfires and Memories covers it quite well.

Mountains—because they presented such tough obstacles to all the woodsmen who traveled this country, also because they are the epitome of beauty and grandeur—a world of their own.

Campfires—because they were a home away from home for the many people who spent years in the forests and mountains. Because of my many experiences, I simply have to close my eyes to find myself a young man again, sitting by a campfire in the subalpine in the evenings, watching grizzlies frolic about or listening to blue grouse hooting in the surrounding forest. I recall large pack of wolves setting up a chorus that echoed through the mountains and made the campfire feel so very welcome.

Memories—because this book is above all else a collection of memories of so many interesting and courageous people who walked this land before us. There are memories of great deeds of courage; memories of loneliness so overwhelming that it twisted the souls of some people and drove them to suicide or madness.

People often reacted in strange ways to long bouts of solitude—such as one elderly gentleman who stayed alone too long and when he finally got a visitor he responded in a rather weird way. A Catholic priest stopped by to see how he was doing and during the visit they decided to play a game of crib. During the game the loner sank to an all-time low when he stacked the deck and cheated the priest.

Also, there are memories of silence and the effects it had on people.

It was a constant companion of the pioneers who tamed a mighty wilderness. Many people found silence to be their worst enemy. There are also memories of humorous incidents—such as the endless nicknames people came up with to put a specific tag on each other. If a man was exceptionally tall, chances are he was called Shorty. If he was short and squat, he may well have been called Slim. Some were called names that would now be cause for a court case, yet were readily accepted—sometimes with pride—by the bearers. There were names such as Bull-nosed Pete or Big Ugly Jake. One of the most ridiculous nicknames I ever heard was Puzzleguts. When I inquired what it meant I was told, "Puzzleguts is when your face looks so much like your bum that your bowels don't know which way to move—they're puzzled."

Just how much effect being a loner can have on a person's mind is illustrated in the next story, which occurred during the 1950s. This man decided he had experienced enough misery and was going to end it all. For the grand finale, he tied a package of dynamite on his dog and then led him to the outdoor biffy, where he closed the door and lit the fuse. As the fuse burnt away, he suddenly experienced a change of heart. Out the door he came, with man's best friend running along right at his heel. Desperately he shouted to the dog to get away from him, but to no avail. Just at the last minute the loner climbed a tree and then watched as his dog was blown to smithereens.

Another elderly gentleman reminisced about how he had worked in a logging camp where he witnessed the following: they had a Chinese cook in the camp and for a time the men used to enjoy laughing at the cook because of the strange way he pronounced their names. Well it turned out that this cook was nobody's fool, because he quickly realized that when he said good morning to Steve, no one laughed because he pronounced it right. After that he greeted everyone coming into the cookhouse with, "Good morning Steve; good morning Steve."

Far from being just a collection of humorous stories, though, there are also stories of incredible hardship and suffering. One chapter in this book deals with trappers, while another deals with prospectors. Some stories tell of people who went mad in the forest and became a threat to everyone around them.

Some of the searches and rescues made by police and game wardens demanded far more than what should have been expected of any human, yet they were often described as "incidentals in enforcement work" by these officers.

There are stories of incredible tenacity and resolve—such as the Indians who carried one of their own dead through the mountains for almost 200 miles so that he could have a proper funeral in his own village.

Life was tough and often of short duration. The average life-span of the early prospectors, for example, was 30 to 40 years in some areas, with many succumbing in their 20s. Trappers generally lived longer, but many of these were found dead in their cabins or along their trails. In many cases their bodies were never found.

As I personally knew some of the people in this book, I would be bragging if I tried to put myself in their league. For instance, I cannot imagine spending six months alone in the forest; yet this was a common occurrence for many of these people. I feel certain that if I ever spent six months alone in the woods that there would be no point in my coming out to civilization again, and woe to anyone that came near my abode. I'm sure I would be so nutty that I would be eating with the squirrels.

My dad once told me a story about a trapper that spent an entire winter living on nothing but biscuits and moose meat. When he finished the story I suggested that I could never do that. Dad waved his finger and shut me up by saying, "Look here! You don't know what you can do until you have to do it."

It is my wish that people will appreciate the endless hours I spent researching old newspapers, books and microfilm, and the many interviews I had with people involved in this book. Many times these people helped me enormously by pointing me in the direction of information and I thank them for that. Often I tried to find confirmation for the stories, but this was often impossible. Where I was unable to do so, I always tried to take the information from the person or source that was closest to the incident, and ultimately, that is about the best one can do.

While discussing these stories with others, I found one of the stories was being rejected because it was too far-fetched. I don't blame people for disbelieving it, as I had the same feeling when I first stumbled on to it. This was an event that took place many times over the years between

1907 and 1911. As there was no way to move goods from the East along
the Fraser River from Tête Jaune prior to railroad construction, all of the
supplies needed for the surveyors had to be taken upriver by scows.
These trips against the river current were near-impossible tasks, especially through the canyons and rapids. The enclosed photograph taken
by George Williams attests to the fact that they really did it.

In an effort to allay fears that I have manufactured many of these
stories, I have named the sources, so that people can go to their library
and check the information for themselves.

Sometimes during my interviews, interesting points were made
almost as afterthoughts. For instance, Stan Hale—who packed with dogs
and later with horses in the mountains and wilderness areas of the
province—mentioned an important point. He stated that one must use
great care when swimming dogs with packs, for if their packs are not
perfectly balanced they will pull the dog over on to the heavier side and
drown it. Such are the lessons learned from many years spent in the
wilds. Sadly, Stan passed away July 2, 2002 at the age of 87.

Surveyors taking loaded scow up through the Grand Canyon, 1909.

Stan Hale, January 2, 1915 – July 2, 2002.

Another point I must deal with is the constant reference to First Nations' people as Indians. I found no alternative as I am dealing with history and continually using quotes. There is absolutely no intent to put anyone down, and I must make it plain that because of my research I have developed a great deal of respect for the Native people—a respect that should be apparent to the reader. I marvel that they were able to survive in such a harsh and unforgiving land. Certainly they saved the lives of many Europeans who had no idea how to live off the land or how to deal with scurvy. Without question, they were the best rivermen that ever graced this land, having spent countless centuries gaining that experience and knowledge.

In response to the woman who asked what my most satisfying experience has been as a result of my writing, the answer is easy: it occurred one day at a book-signing event. A young lady approached me and informed me that she was the granddaughter of one of the pioneers I had written about in a previous book. After introducing herself, she added, "I never knew my grampa; he died before I was born; but since I read your book, I'm just so proud of my grampa!" Somehow, I just imagine it ever getting any better than that.

I ask the reader to forgive my rambling writing style. I found it difficult to avoid, since I am dealing with such a wide range of subjects and time periods, including right up to the present.

Finally, I must make the point that this book is not intended for wimps or the faint-of-heart. It is only for those who appreciate the often-overwhelming obstacles faced by our forefathers. To water it down would be a sacrilege against those who endured so many hardships.

Jack Boudreau.

1 Dangerous Water

The dangers inherent in navigating unknown rivers have claimed many lives in this mountainous land of British Columbia. This danger becomes even more pronounced when the parties are traveling downstream. Throughout the years several tragedies have occurred on these Interior rivers. Some examples follow.

One such river is the Bowron, originally known as the Bear River, which flows into the Fraser River eighty-one miles upstream from Prince George. In *Stories of Early British Columbia*, author W. Walkem presents an outstanding anthology of life during the Cariboo Gold Rush. During an interview with Ned Stout of Stout's Gulch fame, Mr. Walkem was told:

"I mined every year in Cariboo, until 1870. In 1862 Rose and Johnson were lost in a prospecting trip to Bear River, from which they never returned. I was the last person to see them as they passed out into the wilds. For two years Dick Watters and I searched the country for them, doing a little prospecting at the same time, but we never came across any traces of them."

For a time it was suspected that the two men died of starvation, but Peter Ogden, the man in charge of the Hudson's Bay Company Post at Fort St. James, had a different view. He claimed that the two men were murdered by members of the Bear Lake Indians, who buried their remains beneath a campfire.

Since his statement was never proven, there is also a chance that they may have drowned and that their bodies may lie at the bottom of that river they used to call The Bear.

After the disappearance of the two prospectors, many stories emerged; such as the one that told how they had struck great wealth and that the Indians had killed them in order to prevent another gold rush. It was stories such as this that inspired men such as George Williams (described in a later chapter) to search for a fabled mine along the Bear River. These searches always proved futile to the best of my knowledge.

In late fall 1909, two trappers—Emmet "Shorty" Haines and Jack Dawson—left Bear Lake and made their way down this same river, then known as The Bear, where they intended to spend the winter trapping. Just a few days later Jack and the canoe disappeared, probably under one of the many logjams or sweepers along the river. After a brief search, Shorty walked all the way to Fort George where he reported the incident. A search party returned to the river, but it was frozen over by the time they arrived so the search was aborted. Jack's body was never found.

Another story concerning this same river has been taken from C. Galloway's book, *The Call of the West*. It describes his trip down this same river about a century ago, and gives us a better understanding of the perils our ancestors faced.

During late summer 1912, Mr. Galloway arrived in Fort George where he was supposed to meet some surveyors bound for Bear Lake. Upon arriving he learned that they were already at Bear Lake, in the process of building boats for their trip. He caught a ride on the stern-wheeler *BX* to Quesnel, where he took the stage to Barkerville. Upon arriving, he met one of the surveyors and the next morning they walked the 20 miles to Bear Lake.

After being introduced to the survey party, which consisted of five whites and four Indians, Mr. Galloway set to work with the others as they gathered resin from the trees with which to caulk the seams of the three boats. Meanwhile the four Indians were busy whip-sawing lumber, which was used to construct the boats.

A week earlier a large survey party had headed down river and suddenly their leader, Mr. Pearson, appeared back at the lake along with another man. They were bearing bad news: one of their boats had capsized in the rapids 40 miles downstream and a man had been drowned. This was not very encouraging news, but when the boats were completed the crew set off as planned. They made 30 miles and then camped for the night, after an enjoyable day.

Mr. Galloway wrote:

"On the morning of the second day we reach the first rapids, and here our boatsmen's skill shows itself. These Indians from Fort George have been born and bred on these rivers and know all there is to be known about handling a boat or canoe. In the calm places the paddles are used, but wherever the water is shallow and rapid, the poles are in requisition; it is wonderful how they will bring the boat to a standstill and hold it in the midst of rushing water, the captain at the stern and the mate at the bow. The passenger in the middle of the boat also gives what help he can with his pole. Then, when the passage has been decided upon the boat is perhaps poled back against the stream for some distance, and diverted into the required channel.

"Now and then they get out and wade, guiding the boat in the way it should go in shallow places among the rocks; it is a masterful piece of work, this handling of a fragile boat among the turbulent waters. At one place the passengers are landed on a long island, and walk down half a mile while the boats are skillfully guided down the shallow rock-strewn channel.

"At the rapids the water is boiling over the rocks; it needs a skilled boatman to see the channel and follow it. If the boat were to swing around and dash its side against a rock it would be all up with in a moment. If she commences to swing around, and cannot be held by the poles, there is only one thing to do, and that is to jump out and hold her. There is no time for thought; action must be instinctive or it will be too late. That is where a novice is so utterly useless; while he wastes a second in thinking what to do, the damage is done and the boat is lost. That is undoubtedly what happened in the case of Pearson's party; most of them were men entirely unacquainted with river-craft, and it is not surprising that they had several mishaps, fortunately without loss of life except in that one case.

"But, thanks to our expert boatmen, we get through with no mishap, and presently we find ourselves in a deep, dark canyon where the water is black and deep. And just below the other party is encamped, for in this pool lies that poor fellow's body."

After three days on the river, they reached the area where they were to begin work, some 80 miles from Bear Lake. They finished setting up the tents, and then Dan, the foreman, got in a dispute with the headman of the Natives. After supper the Natives got into one of the boats and left camp on the pretext of hunting beaver; as the evening wore on the surveyors realized they had left and were returning to Fort George 150 miles down river.

This held serious implications for the crew, because now they only had two boats and would have to do their own axe-work; this meant that the job could take six weeks instead of the intended three. As this was already late September, freeze-up was not far off.

One problem they encountered was returning to their camp in the dark. Sometimes shots had to be fired by the first men to return to camp, in order to guide the other men back to camp. Another hazard they had to face lay in the fact that their surveys forced them to wade back and forth across the river; often they had to cut poles to assist and balance themselves while wading waist deep in icy water. At night fires had to be kept burning to keep off the chill and these fires were built by placing four or five green logs piled on top of each other in order to reflect the heat back to the tents.

The crew worked very hard, so after a couple weeks they had completed their work in that area and moved to a second camp. It was then that the other survey party, under Pearson, passed by on their way downstream where they were to survey more pre-emptions in the area of Greater Bear Lake (Purden Lake).

The men continued with their work until one morning they awoke to find heavy ice sheets running in the river, and the ice frozen out six feet from the banks. Still they went on with the work, hoping for warmer weather so the river would not close up and prevent their travel. A few days later their prayers were answered when they awoke to find snow falling and a rise in temperature. Just as the work was being completed the cold weather returned, and though they managed to get the loaded boats into the river by ten o'clock, trouble lay ahead. As they attempted to pole the boats the poles had to be pushed almost their entire length into the water. Each time they were lifted up the water froze and the poles became heavy, large and slippery. Soon their gloves became wet and slippery and they were unable to hold on to the poles.

Time after time the boats became jammed in the ice, while more drift ice came and added to the mass. In one place they had to chop and break their way though an ice jam for a distance of 50 meters before they broke free. That evening, totally exhausted, they made camp just six miles from their previous camp, realizing that they still had 140 miles to go.

The next morning they pushed off into the river and after a brutal four-hour run, made camp only half a mile downstream. They held a meeting and accepted the fact that they had to walk to Fort George, about 48 miles in a straight line. After storing their boats and supplies they started off through the foot of snow that had fallen; they each carried a blanket and a six-day supply of food. Many times throughout their hike they had to stop and attend to frostbite as the temperature stood at 24 below zero. Even though he froze his big toe so severely that he had to cut his boot open, Dan plodded merrily on, running the compass and singing as he went.

Twelve weary miles the men covered on the first day and when they camped they made a huge fire ten feet long by four feet wide; it didn't take long to get warmth back into their bones. This fire they kept going all night, in a desperate attempt to keep warm.

By the following evening their spirits were lifted when they reached the Willow River and found it frozen over solid enough that they could walk across. But it was a grueling, often frustrating trek that they made, as time and again the writer complained about his heavy pack and the misery of continually having to climb over windfalls (downtrees).

The third night was spent in a cabin where the stovepipe would not draw properly. This resulted in the men having to open the door repeatedly to allow the smoke to exit. The entire night was spent lying on the floor, because the air above was thick with smoke. In spite of it all, though, at dawn these poor chaps awoke refreshed and happy.

Back on the trail, the men hoped to make it to Pinker's farm before nightfall, a distance of 15 miles. By afternoon they came upon Nine-Mile Lake (Tabor Lake) and realized their goal was near. A few hours later they arrived at the farm, where Mr. Pinker treated them to a steaming stew and a good night's sleep. The next day Mr. Pinker kindly gave them a ride to Fort George with his team of horses and sleigh.

And so another adventure was over and with it another story to pass on to the younger generation, so that they may know what it was like in the "good old days."

The East Fork of the McGregor River is another deadly stretch of water that has a series of rapids several miles in length. Situated about 75 miles (120 km) northeast of Prince George, Eight-mile Canyon had already claimed a trapper and his boat back in the 1920s, neither of which was ever recovered. The possibility also exists that there were many other trappers and prospectors that were lost throughout the years in these terrible rapids. In my search I only managed to find a few cases. One took place in July 1939, when a prospector named Matthew Houston lost his life. He was attempting to take his horses across the river above the canyon when a packhorse crowded his horse, causing it to buck him off into the river. His partner, Cecil Leslie who witnessed the incident, said the body never resurfaced. The police were notified and a search was conducted. Inspector J. Johnson, who attended the scene, quickly determined that the body would never be recovered.

What made these rapids so deadly was the fact that at the bottom end of the Canyon the river came down a narrow chute and then boiled under a huge logjam that completely blocked the river. There was no possibility of escape.

In early September 1965, three men launched a boat into the McGregor River near where the bridge now crosses about five miles northeast of Pass Lake. This bridge is just a short distance upstream of Eight-mile Canyon. While Clarence Mcdonald watched from the shore, Peter Van Dongen and Dave West took a 12-foot aluminum boat out into the river and headed downstream, unaware of what the river held in store for them. They had covered just a short distance when they struck a rock, which sheared the pin in the propeller. Helpless, the men tried to paddle the boat but it quickly filled with water and sank. Dave began swimming and noticed that Peter was also swimming, but they were almost helpless against the overwhelming power of the river. After swimming downstream for about a mile, Dave, a former BC Lions football player, finally found a spot where he was able to climb the steep bank to safety. At that time Peter was still swimming and drifting into even rougher water.

After realizing that his friends were in the water, Clarence drove to Prince George and reported the incident; this resulted in an intensive search that started the next morning. A helicopter and two fixed-wing aircraft flew the river while a 12-man search party followed the river

Eight-mile Canyon, above the falls.

wherever possible. This included near-impossible maneuvering through treacherous terrain, with the result that Dave was not found until the following day. When he was found, he was less than a mile from where he had climbed out of the water, and was in surprisingly good condition considering what he had been through.

For two days the police, aided by a helicopter and three search parties, combed the area. One search party worked along each bank, and another party used a boat along the lower river. That evening police issued a statement:

"As far as we can figure this is now a case of a man drowned and not one of a man missing in bush-land."

A few days later the police issued a statement to the effect that they believed Peter Van Dongen was under the logjam at the base of the Canyon. The search was aborted and nothing was ever found of the man or the boat.

The number of people drowned throughout the years in the Fraser River is nothing short of stunning. Some sources have estimated that at least 200 people perished in the Grand Canyon 100 miles upstream of Prince George. And it is entirely possible that this is a conservative estimate. Certainly the Grand Canyon is a book unto itself—one that will be published by BC Parks, hopefully in the near future. For this reason I will not deal with it at any length except to mention that I had the pleasure of working as a riverboat operator for the movie, *The Overlanders*.

Two rafts, The Knox and Golden Fleece, used during the filming of the Overlanders.

The Overlanders, for those unfamiliar with the name, were a group of people that came from England and various points across Canada and the Northeastern United States to join a stream of gold-seekers heading to Barkerville and the lower Fraser River area of BC. The year was 1862, and their trek was one of starvation, hardships and loss of life in the Grand Canyon.

During the summer of 1973, producer/director Don Eccleston made the movie, *The Overlanders,* based in part on the incredible journey these people made over a century earlier. The portion of the movie that I worked with started where two large rafts had been constructed about 70 miles upriver from the Grand Canyon. Hired as boat operators were Ray and Wayne Mueller of Sinclair Mills, about eight miles downstream of the Grand Canyon. Also hired as boat operators were Ken and Glen Hooker, and Ed Hale of Dome Creek, which is a small community fifty miles upriver of the Canyon.

The riverboats were needed to move the cast to various locations along the river and to keep the rafts off the bars and out of the eddies. I must state that I was impressed with the amount of effort that sometimes went into getting just a few feet of film.

When we finally arrived at the Grand Canyon, we set up a marshaling point near Kenneth Creek (so named because a Dr. Kenneth delivered a

Producer/director/writer Don Eccleston near the Grand Canyon on the Fraser River.

baby there during railway construction). Then we began moving people and their gear through to the bottom of the canyon where several scenes were to be filmed. I took two of the movie people along with a supply of their equipment and started downstream toward the canyon. Almost at once my outboard motor quit running and we began drifting toward the canyon. I shouted to Glen Hooker who was standing on shore at the marshaling point above the canyon. He saw that I was in trouble, so he ran to his boat and started out to my rescue. I tried several times to restart the motor but it refused and I knew that if we drifted into the canyon with my narrow style of riverboat that it would surely capsize. I was not concerned for

Wayne Mueller in upper Canyon, 1973.

our lives, as we all wore floatation devices, but the probability of losing the equipment, which included two large light reflectors, was my main concern.

Just as my boat was dropping into the rapids, Glen pulled in alongside with his riverboat and threw me a rope; I quickly secured it to the front of my boat and he towed us back to shore. It seemed weird to say the least that after working along the river for almost a week that a fitting on my engine had to pick that exact moment to give out.

The portion of the movie that I worked on was completed at the canyon, and then the cast moved on toward Quesnel and Barkerville where the remainder of the movie was finished. I have to say that I thoroughly enjoyed the time I spent with the movie; it made me realize that there is much more to making a movie than I had ever imagined.

Moving on from the Grand Canyon, I want to relate a few other streams where people erred terribly in their judgment and paid the ultimate price. To start with, I want to point out another dangerous river near Prince George, the Willow River with its deadly canyon.

On May 13, 1974, the *Prince George Citizen* carried a shocking headline that eight students had disappeared along the Willow River just east

Surveyor lining dugout canoe up over a set of falls in the upper portion of the Grand Canyon in 1910.

Four Canyon cats narrowly miss a rock as they move a loaded scow through the Grand Canyon of the Fraser River, circa 1912.

of Prince George. The City of Prince George and surrounding area was stunned. Eight teen-aged boys—Paul Trudeau, 17; Robert Haney, 18; Dwight McFarland, 18; Brian Weaver, 18; Ian Rice, 17; David Walker, 18 and Murray Sales, 18, all of Prince George, along with Jeff Pick, 16, of the Queen Charlotte Islands, were overdue. They had set out on what was to be a fun-filled canoe trip down the Willow River from the Highway #16 bridge to the Fraser River, and then back to Prince George.

The date of their departure was May 10, when they were let off at the Willow River Bridge. The following day, Saturday, they were expected back home. When Saturday evening arrived and they had not returned, fear mounted and a search was organized for the next day.

A large group of people, as well as vehicles and aircraft hit the search area on Sunday, and it didn't take the searchers long to realize that disaster had struck. Sheer canyon walls and a river in flood stage that roared and boiled around huge boulders told the searchers that it would be a miracle if anyone had survived.

What the searchers found was heartbreaking: pieces of fiberglass were all that was left of the three canoes and one kayak. These pieces were spread for miles along the flood-swollen river with its abundant logjams that precluded the use of boats. In another spot, a packsack was found at the bottom of a cliff. In total, two packsacks, a parka, and a sleeping bag and some groceries were recovered during the first day.

Hoping against hope, the search went on for several days. Members of the Provincial Emergency Program, the RCMP, a helicopter and an assortment of volunteers from pulp mills and the general public all did their best to cover the near-impassable cliffs and rough terrain in the area below the canyon. As well, several riverboats were used where possible to assist along the lower river.

The father of one of the boys, overwhelmed by the outpouring of sympathy and help, said that he found it hard to believe that other people would risk their lives by climbing around the canyon as they did. He felt that he could never repay them for all they did.

Just what chance of survival the canoeists had was expressed by a search leader who said:

"I don't want to sensationalize but there are many similarities to Hell's Gate; there's fast water and it's a big river at this time of year. When it comes down that canyon and hits those rocks it turns on edge."

Another searcher, obviously overwhelmed at the power of the canyon, summed up his feelings by saying:

"Out of eight strong, young men, not one of them survived; that tells us just how bad the canyon really is!"

As the days went by, all the bodies were recovered with the exception of Paul Trudeau. His father, Maurice, told me how he kept searching after all the others had given up. Every chance he got he would go out and follow the river, hoping that by some miracle his son had made it to shore and was lying in the woods somewhere. His search finally came to an end one day while he was searching when he walked right into a bear beside the river. This inspired Maurice to say:

"I thought someone was trying to tell me something, so I decided it was time to give up."

A few weeks after the tragedy, I flew over the canyon in a fixed-wing aircraft and was stunned by what I saw. Even though the water had receded, it still presented an awesome spectacle: a small tree lay across the top of a near-vertical drop; this meant that the canoes had no chance to avoid capsizing. Below the tree the water poured into a pile of huge boulders.

Willow River Canyon.

Eventually a memorial was placed above the canyon bearing the names of the victims. As well, a warning sign was placed above the canyon, just downstream of the Highway Bridge.

Probably the most astounding part of the tragedy was the fact that the young men planned their trip and talked it over with others. This begs the question of how so many people were unaware of the existence of this canyon; myself among them.

Another tragedy that gripped the Interior happened along Haggen Creek which flows into the Bowron river southeast of Prince George. Named after Barkerville prospector Rupert Haggen, this stream held a terrible surprise in store for three adventurers. This tragedy began in the middle of May 1981, when three men from Wells, BC, flew into the upper Haggen Creek by helicopter.

On June 4th, I was driving my Forest Service pickup truck along the Bowron Road, heading for Prince George after a day's work. As I was running late, it was probably about 6:00 p.m. when I drove down the hill into Haggen Creek. Suddenly a heavily bearded man came charging out of the woods with a shotgun in his arms and a dog running at his heels. He frantically waved for me to stop, and as I noticed the gun, I did just that. Breathing heavily, he asked if I could take him to the police and I agreed. As soon as he got into the vehicle he told me that he was a prospector working out of Edmonton and that he had been prospecting the upper creek for over three weeks. Just the previous day he had been following the creek when he came upon a man's body drifting with the

Memorial to eight young men lost in the Willow River Canyon.

current. He secured it to the bank and then returned to his camp as it quite late in the day. He then informed me that he had been hiking since daylight, following the stream which was in high-water stage. This meant he had been forced to ford the stream many times because of cliffs, logjams or deep water. Obviously exhausted from his ordeal, which must have been at least a 14-hour hike, this chap told me that he had experienced enough of the woods for a while and that he intended to return to Edmonton for a rest.

The police took action the following day and by late afternoon had found and flown the body to the Haggen Creek Bridge, where I was waiting. At that point they did not know who the individual was because he carried no identification and no report of a missing person had been filed. By the next day, the police had received word that three men from Wells were overdue. They pursued the search and a few days later found a second body in the stream, and just a short distance below the falls, a piece of a raft about twelve by twelve feet square.

On June 23rd, the Quesnel newspaper *Cariboo Observer* carried this item:

"Two Wells men drowned and a third became lost during a recent prospecting expedition 20 miles north of Wells. Dead are Yvon Rozan, believed to be in his late 40s, and John Miller. Still missing is Alex Fahr.

"'A prospector discovered on June 4 the body of Rozan. Prince George Search and Rescue sent a crew and helicopter into the remote area Friday

(June 5) and an aerial search was made,' said George Hartley of Provincial Emergency Plan (PEP). The search was called off the following day, said one of the local searchers who wished not to be identified.

"Cariboo MLA Alex Fraser was contacted on the night of June 6 (Saturday), and Sunday morning Search and Rescue from Prince George was again on the scene. 'A ground search was initiated June 8 when the body of John Miller was found. The search was called off once more,' said the searcher.

"Cpl. E. McGinnis, of the Wells RCMP detachment, said: 'It is believed their raft went over a waterfall at the junction of the Haggen and Dominion creeks approximately 15-20 miles north of Bowron Lake.'

"'The prospectors had been flown into the headwaters of Haggen Creek prepared to stay three weeks and were due back June 4 or 5. They had planned to hike or raft out of the remote area to the Bowron Lake Road. No trace of the third man has been found at this time but there is still hope that he is alive.' McGinnis said.

"'A bag containing the skulls and claws of a mother grizzly bear and cub were found, as well as the body of the sow, according to a searcher on the scene. Searchers speculate the bears may have been involved in the tragedy in some way.' He said. 'A search party from the Wells area continued until Friday (June 12) when it was called off,' he said.

"Some of the searchers had camped out all week and others flew out each day. The search was strictly a community effort, although one Prince George Search and Rescue member did return after the search had been called off. Men left jobs at mines or in the bush to aid in the search."

There is something wrong with the newspaper article. Since I stayed at the bridge at the junction of Haggen and the Bowron River all day of June 5th, I must state that the only people I saw were RCMP officers. I was present when the body of Rozon was brought to the bridge and again only RCMP officers were involved. I waited at the bridge because I had a chainsaw and emergency gear in my vehicle and had offered my assistance to build a helipad if one were needed.

In talking with the police and later with members of the search party, it became apparent that a great deal of liquor was involved in the tragedy, as over a case of empty liquor bottles was found at their last camp just a short distance above the falls. There was also abundant

Haggen Falls at low water level.
Two lethal drops.

signaround the last camp that showed where the men had constructed a raft. At some point they had pushed off and drifted right into the falls, which they could not see as the falls are right in a tight bend of the creek. These falls are composed of two drops: the first drop is about 20 feet and it ends on a slab of the rock face that juts out of the cliff; the second drop is about the same distance.

An interesting foot-note must be added to this story: apparently just a short distance below the falls the searchers found signs of a campfire with several empty cartridges around it. Some wondered if perhaps the other man had survived. My personal view is that no one could have survived the falls. I suggest that the prospector who found the body had been camping in that spot.

In the final analysis, there are two lessons to be learned from this tragedy: first, is the danger involved in traveling downstream when one does not know what lies ahead. If one is in fast-flowing water and suddenly finds sheer cliffs on both sides of the stream it may be too late and there may be no possibility of escape. The second lesson to be taken from this is that booze and wild water form a deadly relationship.

2 Trappers and Game Wardens

IN AN EFFORT TO SHOW THAT LIFE WAS NOT ALL DOOM AND GLOOM FOR THE early-day game wardens, I will start with a humorous story, involving a warden, that was carried in the *Fort George Herald* of December 3, 1910:

"W. E. Roberts, the game warden, won the mammoth cake raffled by Gordon Dyke at Blair's store last week with a throw of 34. In consequence of this stroke of fortune Mr. Roberts has been regaling with cake all those who have abstained from eating moose meat out of season. Judging from the number who have availed themselves of the generosity, there appears to have been no violation of the Game Act by patriotic and law-abiding Georgians."

Now that I have that out of the way, I want to get serious and deal with the disappearance of trappers in the forests and mountains of British Columbia. Throughout the first half of the twentieth century these numbers reached staggering proportions, and there can be no doubt that many of these men were murdered. The tasks faced by the police and game wardens of the time were overwhelming, as sometimes they did not receive reports of missing persons until many months had elapsed. This often meant that winter snows hid the scene of any crime or accident until the following summer and left no trail to follow. I have selected many stories from old newspapers that depict the insurmountable problems faced by officers of the law. Some cases were impossible to solve, such as the following mentioned in the *Prince George Citizen* dated April 2, 1920:

"The provincial police entertain grave fears for the fate of an old trapper named McKechran, who has a line of traps on the Little Salmon River [Herrick Creek]. He was last seen leaving Hansard for his trapline about Christmas time, and no trace has been found of him since that time. His

cabin was recently found locked and untenanted. Owing to the deep snow in the woods, it is not possible to make a search for him with any assurance of success until later in the spring, as if he had perished his body would be buried in the snow.

"A provincial constable left here on receipt of the report and is now searching in the country between Hansard and his cabin. McKechran is 65 years of age, and the chances of his being alive, in view of the circumstances, are considered remote."

Another case was noted in the Prince George newspaper *The Leader* dated June 17, 1921:

FIND BODY OF MAN WHO DISAPPEARED SOME YEARS AGO.

"This week's arrivals from the Big Salmon [McGregor] River country east of here state, that the body of a man supposed to be a trapper who disappeared a couple years ago, had been discovered by Forest Branch officials. Articles of clothing, a ring and trinkets found in the dead man's pockets will probably furnish conclusive proof of his identity. The provincial police are investigating."

If foul play had been involved in a case of this nature, it would have been miraculous if the case were ever solved. There is a possibility, however, that this was the body of the previous trapper who went missing a year and a half earlier. Odds are that it was just the wilderness that beat him down, but that was not the case in the following article reported in the newspaper *Leader* of September 30, 1921:

TRAPPER FOUND MURDERED IN NORTHERN BC

"Word has reached here that Shorty Bolton, a well-known trapper in this district, has been murdered in his shack by someone, 40 miles from Harcourt. Bolton left here last September with a full equipment of supplies for a four months' stay in his usual trapping territory. He was accompanied by a half-breed partner. It was Bolton's intention to return during September last. It happens, however, that the half-breed returned with some horses and a quantity of furs some time in November, but would give no information regarding Bolton's whereabouts.

"As Bolton did not return by the first of the year his friends became alarmed and communicated with the BC Police. The latter instituted a search that resulted in their finding Bolton's body in his shack with a bullet hole in the head. The door of the shack was locked on the outside. The half-breed is suspected of the crime, but his present whereabouts is unknown, although a diligent search is proceeding."

Regrettably, I was unable to find any resolution to this case.

Some stories of these wilderness wanderers were so touching and tragic that the editors of the papers must have had trouble holding back a tear when they first read them. Such as this one that appeared in the *Fort George Leader* on April 21, 1922:

"Lying flat upon his back in his bunk with the blankets covering his head and his dog nestled under his arm, the body of James Holden, a Stewart trapper, was found on March 23. Godfrey Anderson, another trap-

per, found him in a lonely cabin in the Bowser Lake trapping grounds in the wilderness northeast of Stewart. Both bodies were frozen solid and death had occurred some time between February 10 and March 20."

Elmer Micks displays an Alaskan mosquito trap (bear trap). Cabin belonged to deceased trapper, Paul Schulte. Building was restored and placed in Heritage Park, Terrace.

During the winter of 1924, a trapper named Andrew Rhonda was reported overdue while trapping along the PGE railway near Red Rock, about 20 miles south of Prince George. As he had been due back home on December 15th and failed to return, his partner, a fellow Finlander named Herman Suykho, started out to search for him. The following afternoon he found Andrew dead in the snow, only 30 feet (9 metres) from his cabin. He had obviously reached the end of his endurance because the evidence in the snow plainly showed that he had crawled the last 400 feet (120 metres) before succumbing to exhaustion.

Sometimes trappers got bad media coverage because of a few bad apples. One such person trapped the upper Willow River during the winter of 1920-21. While out on a timber cruise in late fall, a forest service employee named George Forbes and a partner made an unusual discovery. They found poisoned animals, trapped bears (the trapping of bears was not prohibited until 1926), and an even more startling discovery when they came upon a piece of moose-meat hanging in a tree. As Forbes moved to take it down, his partner screamed out a warning. The meat was connected to the trigger of a gun trained in a line under the bait. If Forbes had pulled on the meat he would have shot himself.

It was finally decided that the same person who had used the poison, and put up this spring-gun set was a newcomer to the area. The resident trappers were in unison that this was not acceptable practice. Game Warden Thomas Van Dyke searched for the alleged law-breaker, who had probably moved on to greener pastures, and as was so often the case, the search proved futile.

This same game warden—Thomas Van Dyke—started out his career with great enthusiasm. On the 16th of January 1916, he applied for the position of game warden for the Fort George area. He was accepted and immediately set forth to enforce the Game Act with great vigour. Within two months he had already prosecuted Ben Sykes of Penny, 70 miles east of Prince George, for shooting two cow moose out of season, selling 100 pounds of the meat and leaving 400 pounds of meat to rot in the forest. Van Dyke also charged Sykes for trapping without a licence by proving that he had sold $250 worth of furs to a fur buyer. Unable to pay the fine, Mr. Sykes spent 90 days in jail at hard labour. As if the penalty wasn't stiff enough, Van Dyke implored Provincial Game Warden Bryan

Williams to lift Syke's licence so he could not hunt at all.

In his response, Williams chastised Van Dyke for being too hard on people, stressing that it would be cruel to stop a man from providing what could be essential food in such a remote area, especially for a first offence.

Obviously the reprimand wasn't sufficient to get through to Van Dyke, so on April 19, Mr. Williams sent the following letter:

"Sir—I wrote to you yesterday with regard to using discretion in handling tourists who come in here for the purpose of hunting. Since then I have heard one or two things which I think makes it advisable for me to write to you again. I believe you are working hard and trying to do your best, but I am now inclined to think that it is possible you may be inclined to override it a little. Or it may be that you have not yet quite got into the way of handling the people in the way that it is advisable to do.

"You must use a great deal of discretion and tact. You have a hard lot of people to handle and if you don't hit it off just right with them, you will find that you will get no backing at all from them. I want you of course to do your duty but at the same time be as friendly and nice as you possibly can be with everybody. Even if you have to prosecute a man, do it in as pleasant a way as you can possibly manage it, and try and let the man understand that it is not a personal matter but just a matter of duty.

"You will find that most of the trappers and guides are first rate men and you can rely on their backing if you handle them right. But there is another class of men that it is pretty hard to handle, in fact I quite realize that some of them are impossible, but whatever you do use the greatest discretion. I cannot advise you too strongly to take advice from Constable Taylor as he knows the district and the people in it and knows how to handle them. He is very willing to give you all the advice you want but you have to go to him and ask him as he is not the sort of man to interfere with anybody's business unless he is requested to.

"You will please understand that I am not making any complaint as I believe that you have been doing very well for a start, and I want you to succeed."

I couldn't help but laugh when I read the above letter; if Mr. Williams wasn't making any complaint, then what was the letter all about?

Thomas Van Dyke didn't change his ways, though; he kept right on getting one conviction after another. Eventually the Provincial Game Warden had to commend him. In fact, Thomas was so successful at his job that he was elevated to the rank of Inspector in 1933.

Quite often the wardens got their man just by stumbling into a situation rather than by someone reporting a law-breaker. Such an occurrence was reported in the *Citizen* on the third of November 1922:

"Thomas Van Dyke, provincial game warden, made a haul at Summit Lake last Friday night, while on patrol. He was awakened late in the night by the sound of an approaching boat and was down at the landing when it came in. The craft was in charge of E. A. Seebach of the trading firm of Seebach and Huble, and the cargo consisted of 50 beaver skins and a quantity of rats, mink, weasels and marten. The skins were promptly seized and Seebach was charged with being unlawfully in possession of them, as the season has not yet opened. He appeared before Magistrate Herne on Tuesday and was fined $200 and costs. The skins, valued at from $600 to $700, were confiscated."

I have no intention of denigrating Edward Seebach by this story. He was an outstanding individual—one of many that were needed to develop the Interior. He not only ran the Trading Post at Giscome Portage from 1906 until 1914, but he was also one of the most successful fur traders in the north. For at least 15 years he traded along the upper Finlay River, into the Ingenika area, as well as into the Peace where he earned the reputation of being a "fair man."

Just as the majority of trappers were honest, so were the fur traders. Perhaps they were only being human when they were willing to take a chance if it would net them a few extra dollars. And when one considers the dangers inherent in their work, it is hard to be critical of them.

Seebach and Huble again made headlines when they were prosecuted for bootlegging. This little business deal turned out to be a profit-sharing venture when they were fined $300, a considerable sum at that time.

Mr. Seebach again made the news in April 1931, when he suffered a terrible fall at McLeod Lake. He was attempting to put out a fire on the roof of his store when he fell about 16 feet to the ground. The injured man was transported by dog team as far as Summit Lake and from there to Prince George Hospital by vehicle. An examination showed that he had suffered a compound fracture of such magnitude that his leg had to be amputated. This magnificent pioneer passed away the following March, his death caused in part by the terrible injury he had received in the fall. His pallbearers were a who's who of early-day notables, such as Herbert Porter, Alex Moffat, L. C. Gunn, George Kennedy, Jack McGaughran and E. H. Burden.

After his promotion, Game Inspector Thomas Van Dyke took a prolonged trip to familiarize himself with the district under his supervision. The first part of his journey took him to Fort Nelson, a 1200-mile trip by water. Accompanied by Warden Robinson and W. Dulley of Prince George, Van Dyke pushed off from Summit Lake on June 2, 1933. One of his objectives was to take a motor boat to Warden J. Clark at Fort Nelson. From Summit Lake the party dropped down the Crooked River and gained the Peace River Canyon, where resident teamster Jack Pennington took them through the 15-mile portage for the price of $15. At Hudson's Hope the party transferred to a 38-foot boat and the run was made to Taylor's Landing. From there, trips were made to Pouce Coupe and Fort St. John where inspections were made of the offices. From Taylor, they dropped down the Peace to Vermillion Chutes where 14 miles of rapids forced another long portage. The next portage came at Fort Fitzgerald with its 18 miles of rapids.

Fort Smith and Fort Resolution were reached in due course. From there to the Hudson's Bay Post at Hay River, they had to cross Great Slave Lake, which they attempted on June 25. Part way across a storm came up which hurled the loose ice about, forcing them to take refuge in a bay for a day. After getting on course again, stops were made at Hay River, Fort Providence and Fort Simpson. Then the long ascent of the Liard River was begun. The engine held up, and five weeks and a day from their start at Summit Lake, they reached Fort Nelson. It required a little more than seven weeks for the completion of the trip, but this could have taken another 20 days if he had not caught a few rides in aircraft on his return journey.

Such was the stuff the pioneer wardens were made of, and in some cases much more was demanded. Such as that faced by Warden Albert Farey of Lillooet in October 1932. Mr. Farey had previously prosecuted a guide and trapper named Francis Gott for an infringement of the Game Act, and this led to a showdown. The warden was in the process of inspecting a doe deer that had been illegally shot, when Mr. Gott, who had been hiding in ambush, shot him dead. A Vancouver man named Dalton witnessed the shooting and disarmed Mr. Gott, who then disappeared into the forest. A posse was immediately formed to pursue him, and they caught up with him the following day. As they attempted to arrest him, Gott came at them with a knife. Forced to defend himself, Constable Robertson of Kamloops shot him in both legs and then took him into custody.

During the month of March 1923, a fur trader-trapper disappeared in the Finlay area. On June 28, 1923, the *Citizen* printed:

"The provincial police have a problem on their hands to determine what has happened to G. Weston, one of the men who have been trapping during the past winter on the branches of the Finlay, above the forks. The missing man is well known to those engaged in the fur trade, having been in the district for a number of years. He was a Pole by birth, and was about 35 years old. He was constantly trying to improve himself, and while out on the trapline made a special study of engineering.

"Last fall Weston went north to the Finlay in company with H. Krebbs. Krebbs set out a trapline on a stream about 20 miles above the forks, and Weston established himself 10 miles north on a stream known locally as Scott Creek. [H. M. Scott had been trapping on the creek during the winter of 1920 and may have believed that he owned the area].

"During the months of December, January and February, Weston and Krebbs met from time to time, but after a visit to the Krebbs cabin in February Weston dropped out of sight and has not been seen since. Krebbs tried to look his friend up during the month of March but failed to find him. When he got to the Weston cabin he found a notice posted upon it which was from Scott, telling Weston to get off the creek if he did not want to get into trouble. By the side of the Scott notice was a note in Weston's handwriting to the effect that he was going to see Scott, to get three marten skins, and if he did not return it would be because something had happened to him. As no trace could be found of Weston the matter was reported to police at Pouce Coupe, and forwarded to the police at Prince George.

"Constable Van Dyke [not to be confused with Warden Van Dyke]

started on his trip of investigation on May 21. He reached the Krebbs cabin by May 24, and in company with the trapper went over the Weston trapline, but failed to find any trace of the missing man or his dog. They then followed the direction Weston would have taken in the wintertime on a visit to the Scott cabin. There were axe marks on the trees, but that was all they found. A couple of the Scott cabins were visited without result. An interview was held with Scott, who admitted having posted the notice in the Weston cabin, but his statement was that he had not seen Weston at the time or since. He stated the last time he had met Weston was in 1922, when the two had started out on a trapping trip.

"The theory of the police is that Weston is dead and that the body if ever recovered will be found in one of the rivers in the section during the low water stage."

After a prolonged search by police and especially by Game Warden Van Dyke, Weston was given up for dead. Finally in December 1930, Justice D. A. McDonald had Weston pronounced dead, thus allowing his life insurance to be claimed by his heirs, after a one-year period during which the claim could be contested.

This is another example of the police being frustrated—without a body they had no chance of getting a conviction—even though their gut feelings often told them the identity of the perpetrators.

One of the strangest stories I ever heard revolved around a trapper that had grown tired of people using his cabin and supplies. Determined to stop them, he went to work and set a small charge of dynamite inside the cabin door. One evening he came off his line and had no sooner entered the cabin when he was greeted by an explosion that blew him back out the cabin door. I suppose it is safe to say that he left the dynamite alone after that.

There is another story about a trapper that lived on the shore of a lake known for its good fishing. This fellow also had a problem with people continually using his food and cabin, as well as burning up his wood supply. He finally solved the problem by leaving the following note attached to the cabin door while he was away:

"Harry—I'll be back in a few days; I've gone to town to get something for the lice because they're unbearable."

Sometimes trappers and other woodsmen would appear perfectly

Trapper Charlie Hartsell. He went mad and the police took him away, circa 1935.

normal, and then suddenly they would do the unexpected. Such as a man named James Edwards, who came into Prince George and offered to take on the entire town. So belligerent was this trapper that he was quickly dubbed "the new white hope."

He arrived in town from his trapline on the upper Willow River, after spending the entire winter trapping, and then he began wandering the streets looking for people to fight with. Some suspected his mean attitude was caused by a diet of too much raw meat. Whatever the cause, James made a point of mussing up the hairdo of many of the town's leading figures. After he had treed nearly half the population, someone was sent up for Constable McCauley who took the bloodthirsty one to jail. James was charged with assault, but perhaps Magistrate Herne understood the rigors of bush life, because he was only fined $10 and costs.

The effects of long periods of solitude were again emphasized in November 1924. *The Citizen* noted that trapper "Hank" Munro, one of the best known trappers in the district, had gone mad and had been taken to the Westminster asylum.

In a similar vein, I remember an elderly trapper named Charlie Hartsell who lived just a short distance from our home. One day he went mad and shot at a passerby. The police had to come and take him away.

While trappers and prospectors certainly had their problems in the wilderness, fur traders took their lumps as well. The oft-touted idea that fur traders were making a fortune off the backs of the trappers was blown to bits in September 1923 when visitors to Ernest Livingstone's fur store in Prince George were surprised to find a notice in the window:

FUR TRADER'S BURDENS

"For the following reasons we are about to throw up the sponge—city fur trader's licence, provincial fur trader's licence, provincial trader's licence, hunter's licence, trapper's licence, auto licence, and to forget our troubles, a liquor licence.

"We are stamp taxed, receipt taxed, draft taxed, overdraft taxed, loan taxed, federal income taxed, provincial property and income taxed, light taxed, water taxed, royalty fur taxed, and our memory taxed to keep track of the taxes, and this letter is taxed.

"The game law's so changed, and our business so governed and misgoverned that we don't know it and probably never will. Our books are examined, re-examined and we have been informed, reformed and requested for all information respecting our business and now the Trappers' Cooperative Society is organizing to eliminate us.

"We have been inspected, suspected, but never respected and because we refuse to scab on the banks we have been cussed, discussed and boycotted until we are disgusted; called up, called down and held up. Talked about until our reputation is nearly ruined and now our only reason for hanging on is to see what in hell is coming next."

Mr. Livingstone wasn't just joking; he threw in the towel and moved to Vancouver. It seems that here was one fur trader that didn't get rich off the fur trade.

Another fur trader named W. Mennie attempted to save a few dollars by not purchasing a fur trader's licence. In April 1923 he was caught selling furs and the penalty was a $200 fine plus the confiscation of $800 worth of furs.

Many times it was fur traders who died of exposure or foul play, as several went missing throughout the years; but this should not seem strange when we realize that they carried large sums of money and travelled far into the wilderness to collect furs. But the assumption that they actually died of exposure could not always be proven. This next story is probably a legitimate case of exposure. It was carried in the *Leader* of March 17, 1922:

TRAPPER FOUND FROZEN TO DEATH
Overtaken by cold weather and perished in the snow
—deceased well known here.

"The body of Matt Hilton, a trapper, missing since last fall, has been found four miles south of Aleza Lake by Ed Lamee. Deceased was an old-timer and widely known. He was in poor health when last seen, and it is thought that after returning to his cabin he became delirious, and wandering out was overtaken by extreme cold weather and perished. The provincial police are investigating for Coroner Guest."

The dangers faced by fur traders became apparent in January 1934, when two of them arrived in Prince George after a harrowing journey. Enice Powers and Rupert Conlon had started out from Fort Grahame on November 26, with a party of other men. On their arrival at Finlay Forks, the rest of the group headed down the Peace River, while Powers and Conlon opted for the trip up through the Summit Lake route. The other party reached Dawson Creek on December 23, but no trace of Conlon and Powers was reported. The problems for the latter two men really began when they started up the Finlay River. It had frozen over once, but then a thaw came and covered the ice with a layer of water, which in turn backed up into the sloughs. The top of the water froze, then receded and left a thin shell of ice that would not support their weight.

When they continued on with their journey, they had to leave the river and walk along the low land where they continually broke through the light crust of ice. With the short days of winter upon them the best they could do was to cover the 80 miles to the Pack River in 10 days. Such was the tiring nature of their trip that they were forced to lay over at Fort Mcleod for three weeks. When the weather moderated a bit, the men took off for Summit Lake, and had just arrived and were preparing to spend the night when they picked up a radio message. At this time they learned that because of fear for their well being, a plane was to be dispatched the following day to search for them. As they did not wish to be the cause of a fruitless search, the boys slipped back into their snowshoes and walked all night, arriving in Prince George just in time to cancel the flight.

There are many examples of heroic travels by policemen and game wardens such as Thomas Van Dyke and Provincial Constable Muirhead.

For instance, in October 1925, Muirhead left Prince George and walked to Fort Grahame on the Finlay River and then returned to the city. The return trip was made on snowshoes and took over two weeks. The reason for this long and time-consuming walk was to deliver a summons to people who were required to testify against Hugh Muir, who was charged with stealing $3 000 from the Hudson's Bay Post at Fort Grahame. Since someone had seen Muir flashing the money around, a conviction seemed assured, but after Muir was finally caught and arrested in Alberta, the jury took only three hours to decide and Muir walked away a free man.

Sometimes trappers and prospectors would clash over their different views of what was best for a given area. A memorable case of this occurred in late 1925, when two men with opposing views could not come to terms.

For many years an elderly trapper named Alex Ducharme trapped the area of Chilco Lake. During that time, rumors had spread of small gold recoveries in the many feeder streams of that big lake. So inaccessible was this region that prospectors only dreamt about finding its great riches. It was these tales of wealth that led Fred Cyr to the area, where he began testing Ducharme and Gold Creeks for their values. On one of his trips to the lake, Fred encountered Alex and found the old man to be extremely upset about his prospecting in the area, as he felt that any significant find would herald a gold rush which would destroy his business as well as the solitude.

So determined was Ducharme to stop this prospecting that he offered to share his trapline with Cyr if he would refrain from prospecting and keep secret any gold he had found.

Ducharme then made it plain that Cyr only had two choices: Share the trapline or else leave the district. Cyr ignored the warning and returned to Gold Creek about 20 miles away, where he continued prospecting. This creek was on Ducharme's trapline. Several bitter arguments erupted between the two men with Cyr demanding he be allowed to work the area. Finally these fights led to a duel that ended in death.

Armed with an 80.40 US army rifle, Ducharme supposedly attacked Cyr who was armed with a 25.50 rifle. When the gunfire subsided, Ducharme was dead. Mr. Cyr then buried the body and took the eight-day walk out to civilization to report the death to the police.

Cyr was immediately charged with murder pending a trial; but first he was ordered to lead police and a coroner to the scene of the shoot-out. This was an eight-day walk through incredibly tough bush, with insects that nearly drove the men crazy. Included in the party was Coroner Hubert Campbell of Williams Lake, Sergeant Bowen of Ashcroft, Dr. Charters of Alexis Creek and several members of a coroner's jury. The body was exhumed, and then the investigation took place. Cyr went into great detail about how he had gone out of his way to avoid a showdown with Ducharme, but in the end he had to defend himself.

After the investigation was concluded, the party returned to Hanceville, where Coroner Campbell gave Cyr a preliminary hearing and committed him to stand trial for murder. Cyr was taken to Oakalla prison to await trial.

The Cyr murder case went to court in January 1926, and after a short trial, he was acquitted. Obviously his having turned himself in by reporting the incident stood him in good stead; for it must have been apparent to the court that the killing would not have been known about had he remained silent.

On October 13, 1929, the *Citizen* carried this story:

"Provincial Constable T. Van Dyke returned to the city on Saturday evening after attending to the burial of John Stack, the trapper who died in his cabin on the Missinchinka, one of the tributaries of the Parsnip River. Three years ago Stack was missing, in that he did not return for the renewal of his trapper's licence which was issued to him in 1920. But as he was reported to have been seen at Hudson's Hope and Pouce Coupe, it was thought he might have left the country. This ended the public interest in Stack until this spring when C. Muirhead and E. Caus, while trapping beaver along the Missinchinka, came upon the Stack cabin in which the body of the missing man was discovered; so they came out and reported their find to the authorities. As there did not appear to be any suspicious circumstances attending the death the police postponed the burial arrangements until they could get around to them. On August 28 last, Constables Van Dyke and Muirhead set out from this city to bury the body. The cabin is quite a distance above the canyons on the Missinchinka and to reach it the burial party had to make a trip over the mountain, and it was not until September 9 that the remains were committed to the earth.

"Con. Van Dyke says the body was quite mummified and the facial features were recognizable. He secured two photographs of the corpse and brought them out for identification purposes. From the appearance of the cabin it seems that Stack froze his feet in the first instance and that following this mishap and being unable to get out, he slowly starved and froze to death. There was absolutely nothing to eat in the cabin and everything in the way of fuel had been consumed, down to an axe handle. The only effects of the deceased recovered by the police were a canoe, and a gun which has remained in the shack for three years and is considerably damaged by rust."

The efforts put in by police in order to determine the cause of death is illustrated very well in this story taken from the *Citizen* dated September 19, 1929:

"The body of Ivor Smaaslet, the Prince George trapper missing since January, has been buried by the provincial police in the vicinity of Deserter's Peak on the Finlay River, a short distance above the mouth of the Ingenika. With the news of the finding of the body about a month ago the police sent Constable Joe Howe, along with Coroner Dr. H. Trefry to investigate the cause of death. It meant a round trip of more than one thousand miles, but in matters of violent deaths in remote sections, trips of this nature are but an incident in police work.

"Coroner Trefry found upon inquiry that Smaaslet had been caught and buried in a landslide at an approximate depth of 80 feet. The body was buried near the scene of the slide in the district in which Smaaslet had been operating his trapline."

In many cases where trappers disappeared, their furs had also gone missing. In other cases where trappers' bodies were found, their furs were never recovered. One suspicious example follows. I quote from the *Citizen* of June 3, 1926:

POLICE FAIL TO FIND ANY TRACE OF MISSING TRAPPER
Nothing Known of Charles Olson
since He Advised He Was Coming to Town
Number of Beaver Skins Missing From Cabin
May Have Been Stolen Since He Left.

"The disappearance of Charles Olson from his trapline on the headwaters of the Parsnip River remain as much of a mystery as it was a month ago, when information first came to the police that the Prince George man

had dropped out of sight. Uneasiness as to the fate of Olson came when a visitor to his main cabin found a note written by the missing man to the effect that he was about to make a trip to Prince George. This was dated January 27 and constituted the last trace of Olson. He did not make the promised trip, and nothing has been heard from him since. As Olson had a number of cabins on his trapline there was always a possibility that he might have met with some form of accident and was housed up in one of them. The police have investigated this and found no reason for belief that Olson had been along his trapline after he wrote the note advising of his intention to make a trip to this city.

"Returning from their long journey to Deserter's Canyon on the Finlay River, Police Constable Clark and Coroner Guest turned off at McLeod Lake and made their way to the headwaters of the Parsnip. They went over the entire length of Olson's trapline, searched his cabins, made inquiries of everyone they met, but added nothing to the information they already had concerning his disappearance. The note written on January 27 stands as the last record of the trapper's movements. Whether he met with an accident or was the victim of foul play, is something that may never be determined. The country covered by his trapline, and which he would have to travel through to reach Prince George, is one of the roughest sections of the province, and even if he met with a fatal accident the finding of his body would be very largely a matter of chance.

"One suspicious circumstance in connection with his disappearance is the suggestion that the bulk of Olson's furs is missing. He was known to have had something over 25 beaver skins before Christmas. With the trappers, these are known as the heavy skins, and as a rule are not brought out until trapping season is over. If Olson ever started on his promised trip to Prince George in January it is considered unlikely he would have attempted to bring out his beaver skins at that time. When the police visited his trapline, instead of finding twenty-five or more beaver there was but four or five. This does not throw any light upon Olson's disappearance. He may have started out with a part of his beaver, or the skins left behind by him may have been stolen in his absence. Tracing them, however, is almost out of the question, as all skins look alike."

One week later, the *Citizen* carried the following story which is just one of many where trappers committed suicide:

"Sergeant Walker of the provincial police, brought word from Fort St. James yesterday of the probable suicide of Clarence W. Lindblad, a man who had been prospecting and trapping in that section for the past five years. On Sunday, persons crossing the bridge south of the Fort were attracted by a handkerchief tied to the superstructure. Secured within the handkerchief was the sum of $17 and a note addressed by Lindblad to a brother residing in the state of Washington. It recited that Lindblad had got in wrong with the provincial authorities and that he proposed to finish things. Continuing, Lindblad proceeded to make a disposition of his estate, which he asked should be divided between his father and brothers.

"The trouble referred to in the letter apparently had to do with Lindblad's trapping without a licence. He made his appearance at Fort St. James about ten days ago with 60 beaver skins, for which he endeavored to find sale. As he could not produce his licence the buyers would not take a chance with them. Lindblad was last seen passing the Fort about 11:30 on Saturday night, and in view of the note the police believe he committed suicide by drowning. Constable W. H. Mansell is dragging a couple of potholes in the river in the hope of recovering the body.

"From the note left by Lindblad it is evident he has another cache of skins near the point where he was trapping, as he made mention of a couple of silver fox which he desired to go to one of his relatives.

"In the opinion of the police, the fact that Lindblad took his life because he could not dispose of his skins indicates he was far from normal, as a man who would systematically trap skins without a licence would have little difficulty in disposing of his catch to Indians.

"Lindblad was a man of 38 years and was visited in the Fort St. James district by one of his brothers from Washington."

Lindblad was just one of many trapper suicides. In fact, I found two different cases where trappers filled their pockets with rocks and jumped or waded into the Fraser River to their deaths, and both of these took place within a mile of Prince George.

The readers will draw their own conclusions from this next story taken from the *Citizen* of November 27, 1924:

"Victor Gluske, a trapper in the Middle River section north of Stuart Lake, had a close call for his life a few days ago. He threw his gun down upon the cabin floor, causing it to explode and the bullet entered his face.

The injured man was brought to Prince George and Dr. Ewert extracted the bullet that had lodged in one of the bones of the head. Gluske will be able to get back on his trapline in a short time."

If this wasn't an attempted suicide then what else could it possibly be? I don't know anyone that would throw their rifle down on the floor on purpose. Somehow it seems the sights would be knocked out of line.

The next story appears to have been a more obvious case of suicide, but there is no way to be certain. This story began when a trapper named Burke went to visit another trapper named Ben Olson during the month of February 1935. When he arrived at his cabin along the Beaver River near the Yukon boundary, he found Olson lying dead on the floor of his cabin. A 30-30 rifle lay by his side, and there were no tracks in the snow to indicate that anyone else had been around. In response to the information, J. Clarke, the game warden at Fort Nelson, set off on a 600-mile round trip by dog team to investigate the death. When he returned from his journey a month later, he advised his boss that the trapper had died by his own hand. When questioned by the media, Inspector Van Dyke of Prince George noted that this trip was but an incidental in the life of a provincial policeman or game warden.

The outstanding efforts often put into determining the cause of death was again illustrated in April 1938, after a trapper named Chris Holmberg was found dead in his cabin by another trapper. Upon receipt of word of the death, Coroner D. W. Hays of McBride ordered the body to be brought out to Valemount to see if "any auspicious circumstances surrounded the death." Constable W. Service of Kamloops and Constable Catis of Red Pass were sent on this mission. This entailed a 90-mile trip up Canoe River by dog team when the river ice was due to break up at any time. Once again, I'm sure that Constable Service would have commented that this was just an incidental in police work.

Constable W. Service mentioned above was a famous policeman who worked the Interior of the Province for many years. My parents frequently mentioned his name and often told us stories of the many searches and arrests made by this officer. He was first stationed in Prince George (Fort George) in 1914; then served in the war. He again served in Prince George in 1925. As well, he was also stationed at Kamloops for many years. Later he was transferred to Prince Rupert where he was promoted to the rank of Inspector in June 1938. At his promotion it was noted that he was "an efficient and fearless officer."

Just a month after his promotion, William John Service was shot in the head in the Prince Rupert Court House. Killed along with him was Sergeant Robert Gibson, also shot in the head. The murderer was a taxi driver named Mike Gurvich, and immediately after the slayings he made his way to a beer parlor where he was shot dead by another police officer.

Such were the dangers facing these officers of the law, but it never dampened their spirits nor detracted from their work.

Something that singled out many of the pioneers was their ability to get out of jams that would certainly have been the end of people with less fortitude. This next story taken from the *Citizen* of February 8, 1945, is an example:

"*Fort Nelson—Immersing a poisoned left hand in hot water each night and suffering intense pain which affected his eyesight so much that he put his faith in his dog team, Charles Brandt made an epic 80-mile trip here from his trapline west of the Alcan highway.*

"*He managed to build campfires in sub-zero weather to treat the blood poisoning in his hand, but on the last lap lost the trail in a bad storm. His faith in his dog team was justified as the animals found the trail and he reached here safely, to be operated on by a US army doctor.*"

A rescue trip that almost claimed the lives of members of the search party occurred in May 1951, when a Quesnel trapper named James Skokan went missing. During the search, five men almost lost their lives in a futile 300-mile trip. They became lost and one member of the party was buried in an avalanche. The others dug him out with their hands. Another member of the party broke through the ice of a wilderness lake in -10f temperature. After an exhaustive search Skokan's son, Adolph, found the body.

Another story that documents the frustrating and often futile searches launched by the authorities was carried in the *Citizen* of June 25, 1951:

SEARCH FOR TRAPPER ENDS, PRESUMED DEAD

"Summit Lake—No trace has been found of Gunnar Loving, trapper presumed dead either from an unexpected stroke or a fall through the ice. Last evidence of his presence was a calendar marked off at April 10. A Game Department representative and RCMP officer assisted in the search for the man. The trapper's partner, Frank Buchanon, has returned after spending a week on his trapline near Finlay Forks."

Often the skeletal remains of woodsmen left nothing to identify; this situation led to many arduous and frustrating searches by police. An example of this was carried in the *Citizen* dated November 22, 1954:

LONG RIVER VOYAGE BY RCMP
LEAVES BUSH DEATH UNSOLVED

Following a 300-mile round trip by riverboat into wilderness country 30 miles upstream from the mouth of the rain-swollen McGregor River by three RCMP constables ten days ago, mystery still surrounds the finding of a human skull and portions of a skeleton in that remote region more than a year ago.

"A party of moose hunters guided by Mack Henry, operator of the isolated Canyon Cliff hunting lodge, stumbled across the gruesome remains on October 1, 1953.

"Scene of the bush-land death was in extremely rough country eight miles upstream from the lodge, and circumstances made it impossible to carry out an earlier investigation.

"With Mr. Henry acting as guide, the four-man investigation party left Prince George on Remembrance Day, traveling by car to Hansard where they boarded a riverboat powered by an outboard motor for the long trip down the Fraser and up the McGregor Rivers. Included in the party were Constables Martin Kilcoyne, Max Harte and Sandy Saundry.

"At McGregor River Forks they questioned 'Caribou John' a well-known trapper and riverman of that region, but he was unable to throw any light on the mystery.

"Following an examination of the skull and an inspection of the surrounding terrain, the party returned to Mr. Henry's lodge where they found a party of four Vancouver hunters who had been stranded by failure of their

boat motor. Mr. Henry loaned them a boat and motor to go to Hansard where they secured another outboard engine from Ole Hansen, trapper and guide. The police party then returned to Prince George by boat, covering the 152 miles in five hours.

"A guest at Canyon Cliff lodge last year, Dr. H. Wiebe of Salinas, Cal., examined the skull and expressed the opinion that it was of a white man between 30 and 40 years of age who had been dead four of five years. Police will make further attempts to establish the identity of hunters or trappers who were in the vicinity about the time the death is presumed to have occurred."

On May 6, 1926, the *Prince George Citizen* carried the following story:

SUICIDE FOLLOWS CONFESSION OF DOUBLE MURDER
William Innis found dead in his camp at Deserter's Cabin on Finlay River
Said to have confessed the murder of Holtmeyer and Christianson in 1920

"Sergeant Walker received word on Monday of the finding of the body of William Innis in his cabin at Deserter's Canyon on the Finlay River. Innis was a fur buyer and was known to a number of Prince George residents. The body was found by Ole Johnson, who made his way out via the Peace River, and reported the death to the police officer at Hudson's Hope. Constable H. L. McKinney will be sent in to investigate the circumstances connected with the death and will be accompanied by H. B. Guest, the coroner for the district.

"While the local police officers were unwilling to discuss matters connected with the death of Innis, other than to state the circumstances pointed to a case of suicide. Reports which come from the north are to the effect Innis took his own life in a fit of remorse over the murder by him of two trappers on January 4th, 1920.

"Shortly after this date the body of a trapper named Holtmeyer was discovered by a trapper known as Shorty Webber, while making a trip out of the district to Hudson's Hope. And by a remarkable coincidence it was the same man who six years later secured the first clue to the manner in which Holtmeyer met his death. During the years that intervened, Webber had continued to work the same trapline. He took a lot of fur, had plenty of money, but as the years went by he came to be regarded as queer by the other

trappers, and had little intercourse with them. The confession of the double killing, Webber says, was made to him a short time ago while he was visiting Innis at his cabin. It came in a tragic manner. The old man was showing some snapshots, and came across a photo of Christianson. When his eyes fell upon the photo, Webber says Innis broke down and told a detailed story of the double murder. The motive for the crime was not disclosed. It may have been robbery, as the victims were known to have considerable money with them, or it may have been that Innis did not wish them to remain in his neighborhood. Webber asserts Innis told him he made a visit to the cabin of his victims on the morning of January 4th, 1920; that he met Christianson a short distance away from the cabin and killed him. He then made for the cabin where he found Holtmeyer preparing breakfast, and picking up Holtmeyer's rifle pumped a number of shots into him. Innis says he buried the body of Christianson in a root-house, and having taken what money there was upon each of them, returned to his trapline.

"Webber says he immediately went to the camp of Frey and Gregory when he heard the Innis confession and informed them. In company with Frey and another trapper he returned to the Innis cabin but was ordered away. The story of the confession was then told to Ole Johnson, another trapper, who visited the cabin ostensibly to purchase fur. He found the door barricaded but through the window he could see the body of Innis on the floor. On breaking down the door it was found Innis had been killed with a shot through the chest from his 30/40 rifle.

"This is the tangled skein through which Coroner Guest and Provincial Constable McKinney will have to straighten out when they reach the end of their long journey to Deserter's Cabin on the Finlay River. They may find enough to substantiate the confession of Innis, or they may come to the conclusion he was off his mental balance when he confessed to the double killing before taking his own life,"

This same story was continued in the *Citizen* of June 3, 192:

DOUBLE MURDER STORY REPUDIATED BY POLICE
Coroner Guest Decides Inquest Unnecessary on Death of Trapper William Innis. Nothing to Substantiate Report That Innis Confessed to Murder of Two Trappers

"Provincial Constable George Clark and Coroner Harry Guest

returned on Saturday evening from their long trip into the Peace River section of the province. They were just 25 days on the trip, during which they covered 960 miles by boat, with innumerable side excursions on foot. The police officer and coroner went first to Deserter's Canyon on the Finlay River; to investigate the circumstances connected with the death of William Innis, a trapper and storekeeper. Four weeks ago a story was circulated that Innis had confessed to Shorty Webber that he had murdered a couple of trappers named Holtmeyer and Christianson in the vicinity of their cabin on January 4, 1920. And that in remorse over the double murder Innis had taken his life. There appears to be nothing in the murder confession. Constable Clark says Webber disclaims that Innis made a confession of the murders to him and from such investigation as it was possible to make, the police officer is of the opinion the confession story was manufactured out of whole cloth.

"After viewing the body and surroundings the constable and coroner were satisfied that Innis committed suicide, but this appears to be the only true part in the circumstantial story credited to Webber. In the cabin where the body was found there was a short note in the handwriting of Innis, in which he directed that his personal property be given to some friends in the neighborhood. The deceased is known to have a number of living relatives but he did not mention them in the short note, which he described as his will, but which was not witnessed. The theory of the police is that Innis' mind became unbalanced and that in this condition he took his life by shooting. It was decided an inquest was not necessary, and the body was buried by Gust Dolstrom, who accompanied the police officer and coroner in the capacity of guide.

"Just what personal property Innis possessed is not known. In the cabin in which he killed himself was a quantity of stores as well as some fur. Constable Clark disposed of this by tender for $2500. Innis is believed to have had fur in other cabins, and police officers in the north have been instructed to secure and dispose of the same. The police also have reason to believe that about $2000 worth of Innis' fur has disappeared and an effort will be made to locate it . . . "

I find this story to be quite intriguing. It appears to me that there was definitely foul play involved. I'm not making an effort to disparage the police and coroner, as God knows they were faced with an impossible situation. But I firmly believe that they knew there had been foul play, and surely the finger must have pointed to Shorty Webber, who seemed to show up at other trappers' cabins at appropriate moments, even though they were 60 miles distant from his own trapline. I'm prepared to bet that the case was closed because the officer and coroner could have spent endless months pursuing it to no avail. Surely it would have been impossible to prove anything after years had passed. Innis was just one of many who mysteriously committed suicide and apparently went to great lengths to hide fur or money.

The fact that Webber was a strange bird was confirmed a few years later when he got into a feud over a dog in the Ingenika district. A feud that got underway after a man named Gust Trapp shot a husky dog owned by fellow trapper Webber. This event took place in December 1929, when Trapp supposedly mistook the dog for a coyote. The feud grew, as feuds are known to do, until a number of Webber's cabins were broke into and a rifle, pistol, snowshoes and a quantity of food was supposedly destroyed.

As the case was about to go to court, the presiding judge had to excuse himself from the case because it was learned that he had mining properties in the North with Webber. When the case went to court, Trapp pleaded not guilty. When Webber took the stand, his case was shot to pieces. He virtually admitted the commission of the several acts of malicious damage to the property of Trapp, but contended he was justified in that Trapp had shot his valuable dog. The court found Webber guilty and imposed a fine of $200 and also required him to pay Trapp $50 to cover the damage done to his property.

As if he hadn't got into enough trouble, within six months Webber was arrested along with Fred Anderson and R. (Bob) Wylie in June 1929. The charges were that they had stolen provisions from caches belonging to Martin "Deafy" Dayton on the headwaters of the McGregor River. One trapper hinted to me that "to have Bob Wylie go through your cache was comparable to leaving a cannibal in charge of a funeral home—there wouldn't be much left when they departed."

When the case went to court, the theory of the prosecution was that Anderson and Wylie went through the cache while on a trapping trip which took them from the headwaters of the McGregor and on through the Sherman (Gray) Pass into Alberta. In addition to the charges, Wylie was charged with having taken a large quantity of fur-bearing animals out of season.

The results of the court case were carried in the *Citizen* dated October 10, 1929:

ROBERT MALCOLM WYLIE WAS ACQUITTED
ON CHARGE OF THEFT OF MARTIN DAYTON'S REVOLVER.

"Mr. Justice McDonald completed the sitting of the assize court on Friday. In the case of Robert Malcolm Wylie, charged with the publication of obscene pictures in a trapper's cabin, many miles from anything in the nature of a settlement, the jury disagreed. The case was formally traversed to the next assize, but the probability is the last has been heard of it.

"Wylie was also charged with the theft of a revolver from one of the caches of Martin Dayton, on his trapline in the vicinity of Porcupine Creek. There was no doubt but that Wylie and his companion Fred Anderson rifled the caches, but Wylie was not charged with the theft of anything except the revolver and the jurors had difficulty in deciding whether it was stolen by Wylie or by Anderson.

"Anderson, who was charged jointly with Wylie, elected speedy trial and before the case against Wylie came to trial at the assize court, he had been acquitted by Judge Robertson. The testimony of Anderson and Wylie was directly contradictory as to who took the revolver, the accused protest-ing he had never seen it."

It is interesting to note that this problem between Wylie and Dayton never amounted to much, as these two men spent a great deal of time wandering the wilderness together. The above mentioned charge against Wylie of printing obscenities in cabins was well documented by others. He was not really a mean person; he was as one trapper put it, "Crazier than a cut cat."

Other pioneer trappers that knew him described him as a "crazy bugger" or "a loony son of a bitch." He was the type of harmless chap who would use your cabin and then rewrite any messages on the door or walls. For instance, if the owner had written, "Wash the dishes before you leave," Bob would stroke it out and write, "Piss on the dishes before you leave." If the note said, "Sweep the floor before you leave," Bob would stroke it out and write, "Crap on the floor before you leave" and so on. He was the epitome of a guy that had spent far too many months alone in the forest.

When I mentioned Bob Wiley's name to retired trappers and guides—Ken and Glen Hooker of Dome Creek—they both burst out laughing, and I think that speaks volumes. Ken told me about a fellow trapper that went to visit old Bob at his cabin one evening. As he approached the cabin he knew Bob was at home because there was a light in the window. Suddenly he saw a great deal of motion through the window, so he peeked in and there was Bob shadow-boxing in the nude. The trapper related this story to Ken and then added, "that's the most ridiculous thing I've ever seen."

Glen had a strange story to tell about this same trapper. During the winter of 1950, Glen's folks were visiting in the USA, and since the men were working away, they got Bob to look after the house for them. What they didn't know was that Bob hated to go outside to "take a leak" when the weather was very cold. Consequently he relieved himself in a large tub in one of the upstairs rooms. When spring arrived, the tub was full and too heavy to carry out, so Bob just left it in the upstairs room.

The crowning jewel, though, was the time a fellow trapper dropped in to visit Bob just as he finished eating a meal. Rather than wash his plate, Bob just put it down on the floor for the dog, which licked it clean. When the dog was finished, Bob put the plate back with the other dishes. After relating this story the fellow trapper added, "I never ate at old Bob's."

This Martin "Deafy" Dayton mentioned above was an exceptional individual. The more I peruse old newspapers, the more intrigued I become. First off, I must clear up something that has puzzled several people: I have previously stated that "Deafy" got his nickname because he was hard of hearing. Since his name is pronounced Deefee, this begs explaining. Back about 90 years ago it was common for folks to describe a deaf person as being "deef"; this is the reason his name was pronounced Deefee.

Another example that shows just how much "Deafy" made it a point to keep in touch with the media is shown by this article that appeared in the *Citizen* dated March 6, 1924:

"Deafy" Dayton and his partner Pete Pierre Roi, arrived in the city from their trapline on the headwaters of the North Fork of the McGregor, in the vicinity of Sheep Creek Pass in the Rocky Mountains. They were seven days making the trip and brought out furs valued at something in excess of $1500."

The $1500 mentioned above may not seem like a great amount of money; but at that time my father was only earning $0.40 an hour. Again I must point out that $1500 in 1924 was comparable to at least $40 000 in today's currency.

It is also worth mentioning that the seven-day walk out to civilization carried significant implications, because if he were to become sick or get injured, his chances of ever getting out alive were very poor. This was the reason many trappers always kept a good supply of firewood on

hand—to see them through any injury or prolonged sickness.

Some recent information I received about Deafy concerns the effect he had in the Big Salmon (McGregor) River during March April and May 1924. Deafy had arrived in Prince George in early March with a payload of furs, and after receiving his pay, went shopping. When he returned to his

Guide and trapper Walter Sande, circa 1940. Pass Lake/McGregor area.

cabin at Eight-Mile Canyon, he had in his possession a new radio, which was about to transform the snowshoe trails in that country. It didn't take long for word to get around via the moccasin telegraph, and soon he had a constant stream of trappers at his door. Some came to view this new-fangled contraption, while others wanted to find out what was going on in the outside world. In one of his endless number of interviews with the media, "Deafy" stated that among his visitors were such area trappers as Ole Hansen, Charlie Johnson, "Caribou" John Bergstrom, Frank Horn, Charles Olson, Jack Miller, Fred Berg and One-Finger Gus.

Also worth noting was that on his arrival in Prince George, "Deafy" had delivered a message from Ernie Burden who was surveying timber along the McGregor River that "the wolf packs were playing havoc with the moose in the area."

During the 1920s, 'Deafy" was noted for his abundant and tasty strawberries; in the fall of 1921 the *Citizen* noted that he had brought into Prince George the best strawberries to date.

One more story that deserves telling concerns "Deafy" giving a horse to a five-year-old boy. The boy was Gordon Solmonson, who said he would never forget that kindness. A young boy getting a horse in those days was truly manna from heaven.

It should be noted by the above stories that "Deafy" trapped in two areas about 70 miles apart during the same winter. This shows that prior to the registration of traplines on Crown Lands in 1926, that trappers moved about at will and frequently found themselves at odds with other trappers as to who had priority in a given area. This led to feuds, and, I firmly believe, the disappearance of trappers in some of the cases that were never solved.

During the month of January 1924, the Indian chief at Shelley laid an information (complaint) against a trapper named Charles Hagland, charging him with pointing a rifle at him and trapping within one mile of another trapper's line. This was just one of many similar cases, and as usual, Sergeant McNeil managed to bring the parties to agreement without resorting to the courts.

The above story of Bob Wiley robbing "Deafy" Dayton's cache brings up a subject that received a great deal of attention during the early years. Sometimes using another person's cache or cabin saved a life, and the law made allowance for these situations. I found an article regarding caches; it was in *The Semi-Weekly Standard,* a Kamloops newspaper dated October 31, 1898:

THE UNWRITTEN LAW OF CACHE

"A curious account from an eastern point of view, is given by Mr. Grose, who has just returned from a tour of exploration in the Canadian Northwest, concerning the law of 'cache.' A man going along wishes to leave, say, his coat behind, for reasons of personal comfort. He hangs it on a tree, and it will be there for him if he does not return for a week. Similarly, the ownership of a suspended gun or rifle is respected. Mr. Grose says that a man would be safe in hanging his gold watch and chain on a tree, with the assurance that it would be there when he returned to claim it.

"A cache of provisions is subject to a slight modification in respect to the rule of inviolability. A hungry Indian, discovering such, will make a fire in front of it, to make it apparent that there is no secrecy intended in connection with his visit. He will then take from the cache sufficient food for his immediate needs and pass on, without touching anything more. — Montreal News.*"*

The foregoing story may have been the rule, but definitely there were many exceptions, and this led to exhaustive chases by police and game wardens. Often the hazardous trips taken by police and game wardens seemed to be above and beyond the call of duty. A Provincial policeman named Frank Cook who was stationed in Prince George during the 1930s took one such trip that impressed me no end. On the trail of two fur thieves, Frank walked 125 miles through the forest in three and a half days. The thieves were caught and sentenced to five years in the pen.

The dangers faced by officers of the law during the early years were caused by all types of criminals that took refuge in the forests and dared the law to come after them. When the owner of a registered trapline north of Newlands reported poachers on his trapline, Game Warden Alf Janke left Prince George and broke snowshoe trail to Averil Creek and then back to Kelley's cabin off the upper Newlands Road. This area lies east of Prince George about 40 miles and in total constituted a walk of about 100 miles on snowshoes.

Janke finally caught up with them in an old deserted settlement seven miles north of Newlands. After taking the two men into custody, Janke brought them into jail, along with a supply of furs and 3000 rounds of ammunition. The two men appeared before Magistrate George Milburn who fined them $250 each, and when they defaulted, sentenced them to three months in Oakalla.

Obviously Mr. Janke caught them by surprise; if he hadn't, then there could have been one less game warden, because these men had enough ammunition to start a war. It must also be mentioned that Alf Janke was an exceptional individual. He not only did his job, but he did it in an outstanding manner. He was greatly respected by friend and foe alike, but was not the kind of man you wanted on your trail. It was generally agreed that he was the kind of man that would arrest his own mother if she broke the law.

Mr. Janke went through a trying time during the month of March 1937. He was discharging his duties in the north when he took a bad fall on the ice and fractured his arm. Several times he attempted to get someone to set the bones, but no one would attempt it. As a consequence, he had to walk many painful miles through the forest before he reached a spot where he was taken out by airplane. The injury took place on March 11, and he arrived in Prince George on the 24th. To make matters even worse, the muscles in his arm had contracted and he was forced to continue on to Vancouver before he got treatment.

There was a story that made the rounds back in the 50s, about how Janke had approached a man who had just shot a deer. He asked the man for his licence and when the hunter could not find it, Janke arrested him. As the deer was needed for evidence, Janke asked the man to carry it out to the road almost a mile distant. The hunter assured Janke that he was unable to carry the deer because of back trouble. Left with no alternative, Janke packed the deer out to the road himself, and had no sooner put it down when the hunter produced the missing licence. Whether the story was true or not is anyone's guess, but there is no doubt that these wardens had a few tricks played on them now and then.

Harry Weaver of Prince George, who was also a trapper for many years, told a story of a similar nature. He said that back in the 30s a man reported his neighbor for shooting a moose out of season. When the game warden called to investigate, the accused did some quick thinking and said, "I've been expecting you; I knew I was reported."

The game warden asked where the moose carcass was and the man answered, "It's hanging right there in the shed." The warden didn't believe him, of course, and knew that he had hidden it. As the accused left for work, the warden grabbed a broom that was sitting in the porch and began systematically pushing it into the snowbank all along the sides of the road, searching for the buried moose. When the man returned home that evening he found that the warden had punched holes in the snow for almost a quarter of a mile before he gave up and left. The moose carcass was hanging in the shed, just as the man had said.

Humour aside, many times woodsmen met their end by pushing their luck, such as in the following example taken from the *Citizen* of October 25, 1945:

LOST TRAPPER SHOT GRIZZLIES AS HIS HOBBY

"*Friends of Frank Johnson, 65, Manson Creek prospector and trapper, have continued without success the search given up by BC Police, after a trek into the desolate Cariboo Range, where a two-weeks old trail of Johnson was blotted out above timberline by a blizzard.*

"*Some people find release in a World Series or stamp collection, but Mr. Johnson had his antidote for the humdrum life of a placer miner–shooting grizzly bears. He once shot a 1000-pound grizzly named 'Omenica Ben' and was famed by Indians who had come to fear the animal. In all he killed 37 grizzlies.*

"*In a letter to relatives in Vancouver, he mused on July 2nd of when, 'Bingo, my dog, is going to run back and forth and sniff at my face and wonder if I'm ever going to get up again.'*

"*Although almost crippled with faulty circulation, he told a close friend, Jack Thomson, on September 6th, that he was again going hunting.*"

No Trails Blazed

"Over a month after, fears for his safety led to reports filtering out to Sgt. George Clark, in charge of Fort George Subdivision. He instructed that a patrol be undertaken by Constable Munkley of Fort St. James.

"Johnson had never blazed trails to his line cabins, so the searchers spent days in country 'infested with grizzly bears' to determine that he was not in one of his trapline cabins. They were accompanied by Vic Ostlund, a trapper from the Germansen area.

"While traveling over a pass the trio came face to face with an extremely large grizzly 40 feet away and withheld fire, knowing the awesome vitality of the fiercest of big game, known to charge 150 feet although shot dead. It ambled away after ten anxious seconds.

"As they reached the headwaters of Manson Creek, they noticed a blizzard had swept away all sign, but they managed to locate their goal. A barking dog, emaciated and dying, feebly guarded the door of the last of a series of scattered cabins. The animal had chewed on moose and caribou hides used for bed covering, then had encountered a porcupine and was riddled with quills.

"The searchers, Munkley of Fort St. James, Game Warden Phil Brown of Vanderhoof, assisted by the trapper, mercifully dispatched the animal before determining no humans had been in the cabin for at least two weeks. A pack-board and axe were located 50 feet from the cabin; snow covered the ground.

"Jack Thomson, close friend of Johnson, advised police that Johnson had left a placer lease cabin September 6th, to go hunting; fears for his safety leading to a report to police on October 3. This led to an immediate search being undertaken by a 150-mile trek out of Fort St. James, ending in the cabin beyond the headwaters of Manson Creek . . . "

During the month of January 1954, a search was launched for a missing trapper named Bendickson, north of Germansen Landing. Included in the search team was a former trapping partner of Bendickson who flew up from Vancouver to help in the search. This man told police that he felt Bendickson might be the victim of a long-standing feud with another trapper. As the police aircraft reached the trapper's cabin, 71-year-old John Bendickson was finally sighted alive and well, so it appeared that the trip was a complete waste. But on its way back to Vanderhoof, the plane flew over another trapper's cabin, only to find a message scrawled in the snow, "Sick, no legs." The aircraft was unable to land in the area so after returning to base, a snowmobile party was sent to the rescue. When they arrived at the cabin, they found trapper Chris Larsen, age 53, sick and suffering from a malady which prevented him walking out to civilization. He was also short of food. The patrol brought him out to Fort St. James where it was determined that he would have starved to death if his message had not been sighted.

What initiated the search was the report that Bendickson had said he would call at Germansen Landing before Christmas; investigation later proved that he had not made such a statement. Chris Larsen's survival had depended on a chance rumor.

During the months of November-December 1963, two trappers got lost near Fort St. James. I personally recall the search that followed. The two men involved were 20-year-old Paul Antoine and 43-year-old Frank Dennis. These men were dropped off by an aircraft near Phillips Lake, with the agreement that the plane would pick them up on December 1, but when the plane arrived on that date, no one was there.

On November 27, the pair had decided to hike to the Germansen Highway, which they figured was a two- or three-day hike. Their supplies consisted of two beavers, four packages of soup, a package of instant potatoes, part of a bag of flour, some coffee and a large bag of tea.

During their hike, snow continued to fall and made the trail difficult to find. After hiking the wilderness for three days, Antoine climbed a tree and saw what he thought was Baldy Mountain, so they continued on. On the fifth day, with their food running low, they considered turning back. Meanwhile, an air-ground search was underway because the men had not kept their rendezvous.

By the seventh day, the two men decided to try returning to their cabin, as they knew they were lost and in deep trouble. They had two guns with them, but they found no game of any kind to supplement their food supply. They made an unsuccessful attempt to find a trapper's cabin in the area on the eighth day and were thoroughly discouraged when they failed to do so; but their spirits were finally lifted when they spotted a search plane. Their hopes were again dashed, though, when the plane failed to notice their camp. At this point the two men began to wonder if they would survive.

The last of their food, some beaver meat, was consumed on the ninth day, at which time the men recognized some land marks about six miles from their cabin. The next morning, on empty stomachs, they walked the last miles to their cabin where they had a limited amount of food. Shortly before midnight two rescuers stumbled in through the door with a small amount of food and word that they would soon be rescued. The two rescuers made soup and helped the men in every way possible, but the rescue was delayed. When the plane finally landed, it was found to be fully loaded, so the pilot left with the promise that he would return as soon as possible. By the following evening, the food was gone and because of poor weather the plane could not return. This left rescuers and rescued wondering if they would ever get out alive. Finally, 13 days after their ordeal began, the plane returned and lifted the four men back to Fort St. James, after another three days without food.

As if trappers didn't have enough troubles facing the wilderness, there was another problem that sometimes beset them. The Indians knew this as the snowshoe evil; while to the French it was called *mal de raquette.* This problem was created by overexertion of the tendons in the heel and could be terribly painful and at times long-lasting. Trappers who have suffered from this malady told me that it would most likely occur when the snowshoes would load up with snow and therefore become much heavier than normal. If it was a serious attack, it could confine them to their cabins for days at a time.

Something that begs mentioning was the dependence of woodsmen on their suppliers. Several times I heard trappers mention that they couldn't say enough about some of the merchants that shipped supplies to them, and how dependent they were on getting those supplies. More than once I heard them mention Northern Hardware, a Prince George store that throughout the years had built up a reputation for dependability. Originally started by Alex Moffat, after three-quarters of a century this store is still owned by his descendants.

Some of the tricks learned by trappers were put to use in unusual ways, such as the following: As a child, I recall Dad coming home from work and saying to Mom, "I see Mrs. So and So was here for a visit."

Mom would question him about how he knew who had visited, but Dad would just laugh and let her wonder. One day I was walking with Dad along the path that led to our home when he told me that a certain woman was at our home. I queried him as to how he could possibly know that, so he confided in me. He pointed to tracks in the mud of the road and explained that he could tell by the size of the shoe and the way the toe was pointed. Since he had been doing this for years, he knew that some people walk with their toes at five minutes to twelve o'clock; while others walk with their toes at five to one or perhaps ten to two, and so on. How far they sank in the mud or snow told him about how heavy they were. Finally, he knew she was still at our home because there were no return tracks.

Another story accredited to a trapper was told to me by a man named Errol Widdis, who worked with me in the Forest Service for a time. Errol has a strange (at least to me) habit of eating the new buds off devil's club. Since some plant books declare devil's club is inedible, and as I had never heard of people eating them, I asked him what they taste like. He replied that they taste just like asparagus, and can be eaten cooked or raw. Somehow I was not surprised when he told me that this information originally came from an old trapper.

Charles Harold "Harry" Weaver was well known in the Prince George area. A trapper for a great portion of his life, he was called "Beaver Man" by many people because of the years he spent trapping them for different levels of government. About a year before his death, Harry gave me a manuscript detailing many adventures that took place during his lifetime. Several of these stories follow.

In one case Harry was tracking a pack of wolves when he found a place where they had been bedded down. A count of the beds showed there was 16 in the pack. He continued trailing the pack and came to a spot where they had found and attacked a herd of deer in their winter quarters. There was five feet of snow all around their winter yard, so the deer had no chance of escape. All 19 deer had been wantonly torn apart and destroyed. Nothing had been eaten; the wolves had simply moved on.

Harry was a man who strongly admired and respected wildlife, yet he picked no bones about his contempt for wolves.

Again, while trailing wolves near Ootsa Lake, Harry and a group of men came upon seven deer that had been killed by the wolves. Nearby they found four more deer that had been terribly injured and left to die.

Another observation told how Harry's brother-in-law, Bill Haws, counted 112 moose near Hansard Bridge back in the late 40s. They were bunched up waiting for the river to freeze so they could cross to their winter feeding area.

Not one to pretend he knew everything, Harry admitted that he had trouble separating animal sounds in the forest. Such as a moose calf talking to its mother, a bear cub talking to its mother or a couple porcupines talking to each other. Harry stated that on one occasion he had watched two porcupines walking together on their hind legs. He suspected that they were mating.

In one of his reminiscences, Harry related watching wildlife photographer Marty Stouffer on TV as he showed and explained that the penis of a pig is like a corkscrew, with a definite twist to it. Harry then considered a boar with a right-hand twist mating with a sow with a left-hand twist. This left him wondering if they would get cross-threaded.

One of Harry's challenges was for people to tell him where the green hair on a moose is. He would then enlighten them that it resides between the split of the hoof, and is a gland.

On the lighter side, there are many humorous events from his youth. In one story he describes the time he ran out of tobacco and in desperation, rolled a smoke out of horse droppings. His comment, "It burns hot and it ain't good."

In another remembrance, Harry describes a story he was told by veteran trapper and guide Jim Hooker of Dome Creek. Apparently when Jim was still a child back in the States, he and his brother were very interested in his father's 12-gauge shotgun. Their dad refused to let them fire it though, the reason being that it kicked like hell. One day while their folks were in town, the boys got brave and took the gun down to their hog pen and tied it up with a string to the trigger. Then they backed off some distance and fired the gun. According to Jim, "the hogs all dove squealing into the sty, and the gun jumped around in the corner of the pen for 15 minutes before it settled down."

Harry acknowledged that Jim could tell a mean story.

Left to right:
Trapper Harry
Weaver, his
mother and
brother Fleet,
killed in action,
Belgium, circa
1940.

Harry had another story about Jim: apparently he had four children and then stopped for a break. He thought it over and then said, "There's no use having good equipment and letting it rust." So he started another family.

Harry gave a rather strange rendition of an attempted suicide that supposedly took place on the Prince George Railway Bridge back in the 30s. The gentleman in question wanted to make certain the suicide was a success, so he took a pistol, some poison, a knife and a piece of rope out onto the bridge with him. First he drank the poison, then he tied the rope to the bridge as well as around his neck. As he attempted to shoot himself, the bullet missed his head and cut the rope instead. He lost his balance, dropped the knife and the gun as he fell into the river. While he was under the water, he drank so much water that he vomited out the poison. Harry noted that had he not been an excellent swimmer he would have drowned.

I recall the evening I was questioning Harry about his trapping days when I suggested that after all those years of experience he must be considered a qualified trapper. With the usual twinkle in his eye, he smiled broadly and then replied, "I thought I was a good trapper until I met my wife, then she showed me a few tricks I wasn't aware of." Harry winked and then added, "She had better bait than I did!"

Harry possessed one of the greatest gifts possible—a boundless sense of humour.

3 Hunting Tales

THERE IS SOMETHING ENCHANTING ABOUT A GOOD HUNTING STORY,
although some stories are only intended to fool the uninitiated. Such a
story was carried in the *Prince George Citizen* dated January 15, 1942:

BROTHER TRAPPERS SEE EPIC COUGAR FIGHT

"The biggest cougar ever known to have been shot in this district pro-
vided a savage and tragic ending to an epic of the forest at which Wilbert
and John Dyer of Red Rock, veteran trappers of this district, were interest-
ed spectators—and participants—last week.

"On Wednesday the Dyer brothers were inspecting their trapline across
the Fraser River from Red Rock and below West Lake, when they came upon
sign in the snow which showed that a large timber wolf had fallen into one
of their sets, but had later broken the chain and departed for the hills with
the trap still on its foot.

"They took up the trail, determined to retrieve their trap and, if possi-
ble, add the wolf's hide to their bag. But the brother trappers were not des-
tined to be the nemesis of the wolf.

"For 36 hours they followed the trail before they caught up to the quar-
ry a good 20 miles as the crow flies from where he had blundered into their
trap. And when they caught sight of him, it wasn't a thrilling tableau they
saw. The wolf, still holding the trap on his paw, and an enormous cougar
were circling each other in the snow.

"Round and round they went, sparring for an opening, until finally the
wolf, impeded by the trap, stumbled, and the cougar dashed in and crushed
its head with a single blow of its forepaw.

"The Dyer brothers then laid the cougar low with three well-directed
shots and recovered their trap and the hides of both the predators. The

cougar weighed over 400 pounds, and its hide is stated to be the largest ever brought to the city."

The above story proves that previous generations had their share of tall-story tellers and that this is not just a modern-day phenomenon. If, in fact, a single blow crushed the wolf's head, then it must have been a bear that did it. Further, I don't believe any cougar weighs over 400 pounds; in fact, I have been told by people that have hunted cougars with dogs for many years that it takes an exceptionally large one to weigh in at 250 pounds.

A writer named Thomas Blair contributed this next story. Flamboyant and verbose, it nonetheless carries an important message. It was carried in the *Prince George Citizen* of October 17, 1929:

TRADEGY IN HILLS OF BARKERVILLE

"For millions of years before history began, the jungles of BC were the rendezvous of prehistoric monsters, whose lives were survival of the fittest. Only one's imagination can picture the deadly combats that must have taken place between giants of the forest in those primeval days when predatory leviathans of the jungle with their greedy instincts fought in defence of their prey; or when giant males attempted to exterminate each other during the jealousies of the mating season.

"But no combat in unrecorded history surpasses in desperation a battle of the giants that took place a few days ago in the hills back of Barkerville. Norman Thompson, the well-known big game guide of Bowron Lake, and Stewart Button of Riverside, California, took part in the tragedy. When relating their experience two days later at Barkerville, they did so with a feeling of glee and high tension. Although Thompson Bros. of Bear Lake are old-time guides, and can relate many an interesting episode during years spent in the wilds of BC. Yet the experience of the younger brother with his big game hunter, which took place in the mountains about ten miles south of Barkerville, was the captivating event of his career.

"Ten days ago Thompson Bros. left Bowron Lake via Barkerville with two big game hunters, Dr. Montgomery of Los Angeles and Stewart Button. They took the old Proser Pine trail from town, then crossed Bald Mountain, the head of Gold Creek, and made camp in the sloping hills of Mount Meridian. Their object to secure a good caribou head, although they went

prepared for any kind of game they might encounter.

"The fourth day out Dr. Montgomery secured a handsome caribou head, one of the best seen at Barkerville this year. Having secured the object of their hunt, the doctor and Roy returned to Barkerville. Mr. Button, who was not so lucky, decided to continue the hunt for a few days with little hope of securing so valuable a trophy. Two days after Roy and the doctor pulled out, Norman and his hunter were traveling on a low unknown mountain, in reality one of the foothills of Mount Meridian about two o'clock in the afternoon.

"While plodding wearily through the brush, deadfalls, and through patches of green timber they stopped to catch their breath, while the wind was wailing through the trees. As they were about to move on, Mr. Button caught a peculiar sound. 'Only the wind' said Norman, who was accustomed to the apprehension of big game hunters, who, in the loneliness of the hills are given to hearing things that are not real and to seeing things that seem to move in the distance, which frequently prove to be optical illusions.

"But they had gone only a short distance when the sounds became more distinct. This time the guide caught the vibration. It sounded like something pounding to Norman. This put them on guard but with no thought of danger. Both thought it was a caribou rubbing his horns on a tree, fitting himself to hold his own among the other caribou during the mating season. They then worked their way quietly through until they found a caribou horn sticking up from a pile of loose dirt. He decided instantly that it was a grizzly cache, but he could not locate the bear. Getting down from the windfall they decided to work their way around to where they had a chance of getting a glimpse of bruin and size him up. The pounding sound they had heard was the grizzly hitting the earth with his huge paw and covering the caribou.

"They had got but a little closer when they heard a crash in the brush. The grizzly had caught their scent and was charging. The brush was so thick they were unable to see what was coming and had little chance of defending themselves, except at close quarters, but there was an open space on one side. Instantly about a 600-pound grizzly emerged with a roar that made the hair stand on their heads where there were no hair to stand. In the first part of the charge the grizzly, guided by scent, instead of coming at them direct, was coming at them at a tangent. He was traveling on high at a speed

downhill he could not stop. His course would pass the hunters about 30 feet to their right. Once he caught sight of them he put on all fours, and slid about ten feet in order to break his momentum. With a roar that sent cold chills up their backs, on getting his balance, he turned and made one spring in their direction. Another spring and he would have landed on his prey, and only the alertness and presence of mind of the hunters saved them. It was a question of seconds whether the grizzly landed the hunters or the hunters the bear. Both fired instantly. It was not a case for the guide to give the hunter first shot. One shot took effect in the shoulder, the other in the hindquarter. It threw the grizzly on his side but did not stop him; he made another lunge, though badly handicapped, but the hunters stood their ground and pumped lead. It took nine shots to stop him, when almost under their rifle barrels.

"Although a veteran guide, Thompson claims this is his largest grizzly and certainly the most ferocious. The hunters then proceeded to his cache where they found the partly covered caribou, dead about ten days.

"Lying within a few feet of the caribou, was approximately a 400-pound black bear, one of the largest of that species that either Thompson or the hunter had ever seen. The dead bear was quite warm, killed perhaps two hours previously. The ground around showed signs of a desperate struggle, every rib on one side of the black bear was broken. The flesh beneath the skin was pounded to a pulp. His skull was crushed in with part of the brain oozing out. Apparently the black bear found the caribou first. Whether the grizzly came upon him unawares, or whether the black bear, being a powerful and ugly character himself, attempted to defend his cache is history that cannot be recorded. There were a few marks on the grizzly, a number of teeth marks through its hide and scratched considerably about the neck. They were the only signs of the encounter. It was at a time when the grizzly's temper was at a high pitch, triumphant and confident from victory, and looking for other worlds to conquer that the hunters came upon him. But he knew little of high-powered guns, or of the cunning and skill of man. That meant his Waterloo . . . "

Something I like about the foregoing story is the description of this 600-pound grizzly being a large bear. Also the 400-pound black bear being an exceptionally large bear. It strikes me that this guide lived in the real world. I do wonder, though, how he competed with the tall-story tellers and their 1500- to 2000-pound bears.

During the 1920s The *Prince George Citizen* carried a number of articles called "Hunting and Trapping Tales." Usually the writer remained unidentified. Such was the case with the following story that made a timeless point. It was carried in the March 5, 1920 paper:

"It is funny how such narrowly averted tragedies are almost invariably, after the event is over, turned into humorous incidents. I have no doubt that the 'boys' in Mr. Burden's camp are having all kinds of fun in describing the incident [moose attack on a surveyor up Slim Creek] and joking the victim over his experience in being attacked by the moose . . . "

"On the other hand, I can't think of anything much funnier than the following true story. Being out on the trail of a bear, hunting with two others, one of whom was a fat, good-natured chap, never in a hurry and always saying, 'What you fellows in such a hurry for? Lots of time. Save your wind till we meet the bear; you'll need it then all right.'"

"Well it turned out that that this gentleman did need it all right, because a bear put the run on him and made him dance a pretty jig."

There is a great deal of truth in the foregoing; some of our most frightening experiences can be a cause for much laughter in later years. But for an all-time tall tale, the following one is hard to beat. It was written in response to an article carried in the *Prince George Citizen* of December 13, 1934:

"In your issue of the 22nd ins., you feature a prize bear story by the editor of the Prince Rupert Daily News. *I regret I cannot let this go unchallenged. A similar story was printed in the* Vancouver Daily Province *as one of my series of 'Driftwood Yarns' six years ago. In my version the bear fell from a high cliff into the canoe, got wedged, and swam ashore under the inverted canoe. After climbing the tree with the canoe, the bear eventually got out and left the canoe up in the tree.*

"The tree was ever afterwards known to the Indians as Canoe Tree. And my Indian informant assured me that parts of the canoe were still to be seen atop the tree fifteen years after the happening. I should be only too happy to be assured that a similar adventure had befallen Mr. Editor Fullen. But I trust he will not emulate the hunter who sought refuge from a storm in a hollow stump. The stump proved deeper than the refugee expected, and he could not get out of it. During the night a bear, apparently urged by some

great fright, jumped into the stump, right atop mister hunter, flattening him like a bannock. After much agony and effort the hunter drew his knife and jabbed his visitor's posterior, at the same time grabbing a firm hold of the tail. The scared bear, with a mighty yelp, jumped clean out of the hollow stump, dragging the hunter with him. The two were close friends afterwards, until the bear drank up his tillicum's home brew one night, then crawled into bed with him and slept with one paw around his neck. —Leo Bates."

In my book *Crazy Man's Creek*, I told a story about a man named John Norboe, who chased wounded grizzly bears through the forest, laughing as he did so. John was one of those rare individuals who seemed not to know the meaning of the word fear. Born in Texas, John and his brother Mack grew up as buffalo hunters, cowboys and Indian fighters. Eventually they made their way north until they ended up as guides in the East Kootenays during the first decade of the previous century. After leaving the Kootenays, the Norboe brothers made their way to Penny, where they guided for many years. They were among the original Salmon River (McGregor River) guides who earned a reputation for successful hunts and personal courage.

In his book *On The Headwaters Of Peace River*, author Paul Haworth describes a chance meeting in Prince George about 1916:

"While I was in Hood's store making a few last minute additions to our outfit, I happened to hear a man say that one of the Norboe brothers was in town. The name stirred old memories and I inquired, 'Is one of the Norboe brothers named Mack?'

"No one could answer, but a bit later I was passing a feed store when I looked in and saw a slender man of perhaps sixty whose face—or rather picture—I was sure I had seen before. I stepped within and said to him, 'Does your name happen to be Norboe?'

"He turned to me in mild surprise and said, 'Yes, it is.'

"Did you ever go out with a man named Hornaday and a man named Phillips and help photograph some mountain goats?'

'I surely did,' he answered, his eyes lighting up.

"In a word, I had happened upon Mack Norboe, who some years before had helped John Phillips to secure by all odds the most remarkable mountain goat pictures ever taken. These pictures were afterwards published in

Hornaday's Campfires In The Canadian Rockies, a book that I have enjoyed as much as any hunting book ever printed.

"He told me that he and his brother had left the Elk River country in Kootenay, where they guided Phillips and Hornaday. They were now located at Penny in the upper Fraser country, a hundred miles or so east of Prince George. They are still guiding hunters who have 'lost bears' and Mr. Mack Norboe told me that they had found a splendid country, high and open, with small lakes, a country into which horses could go and where there are plenty of moose and bears [possibly Caribou Meadows]. He also told me that Charlie Smith—whom every reader of Hornaday's book will remember—now has rheumatism so badly that he has been compelled to give up life in the open, and that, through the influence of Phillips, he is engaged in boy scout work in Pittsburgh. 'Grizzly Smith' he is called by the boys, and great is the success of his stories told round the campfires of the scouts.

"The Norboes are types of the kind of guides who see to it that their patrons have such a good time that the patrons ever afterward consider them as lifelong friends, and sometimes—it has happened to Mack two or three times—pay their expenses East so that they can show the guides a good time in the haunts of men. Beginning life in Texas, the Norboes gradually moved northward, working as cattlemen in the buffalo days and later as trappers, prospectors and guides, until at last they find themselves on the upper Fraser."

And so after a lifetime of roaming the mountains, the two brothers passed away. According to my father, Robert McLean (Mack) Norboe died a hero's death: he drowned while attempting to rescue a drowning child in Eaglet Lake. Regrettably, I was never able to confirm this story in the early newspapers, but that is easily explained because all the *Prince George Citizen* newspapers within a month of that date (August 18, 1917) are missing.

John Norboe passed away in the community of Penny, BC, during the winter of 1920—a victim of heart failure.

In memory of these famous woodsmen I want to relate a method of drying meat that was carried in *Campfires in the Canadian Rockies*, and much admired by author Hornaday. Where it appears to conflict a bit with other meat-drying methods I have found, I used an average. The proportions of ingredients are: Salt, three pounds; allspice, four tbsp., and black pepper, five tbsp., well mixed. Take a hindquarter and dissect it by following the muscles. Skin off all the membranes so that the curative powder will contact the wet flesh. Some sources state that each piece of meat should not exceed twelve inches in length, eight inches in width and four inches in thickness. One source stated that three inches in thickness was the maximum preferable to ensure penetration. After rubbing the mixture well into the meat, hang it by a string in the wind to allow drying. Avoid the hot direct sunlight hitting the meat, especially around midday.

The most important part of drying is to be certain that the meat does not get wet, or it will surely spoil. If one is preparing this meat on the trail and rainy weather persists, hang the meat where it will get a little heat from the campfire, but as little smoke as possible. In one month this meat is ready for eating and should not be cooked, as it is delicious the way it is, just sliced thin. If outdoors, some sources suggest covering it at night to prevent any moisture from forming on the meat. Several different writers stated that it is far superior to jerky or pemmican and much easier to prepare.

This next hunting story is one that backfired on me. It involves a retired mechanic that I had met just a short time before this event took place. One morning during hunting season I went to have coffee with the boys and this gentleman (if I may call him that) was seated at the table with them. I decided to test Walter's sense of humor by playing a joke on him, so I asked, "Are you busy today?"

Instantly suspicious, he asked, "Why, what's up?"

"I've shot a big bull moose about a mile and a half off the road and I want you to help me pack it out." I replied.

As Walter only weighs about 120 pounds soaking wet, perhaps the thought of packing 600 pounds of meat through the forest didn't appeal to him. Something definitely upset him, because he shouted those two famous words that everyone understands. I took that as a refusal.

What I didn't know at the time was that someone had gotten to Walter before I did. And that in the process of dragging a whole moose through the snow for one mile, they had almost done him in. This event took place when Prince George industrialist Ben Ginter shot a moose. Things got worse when the moose ran through the forest for a mile

Walter Betcher, second from left, dragging a whole moose for one mile through the snow. Ben Ginter is in the lead, 1952.

before it collapsed. When the five men succeeded in reaching the road Walter noted that, "They almost did me in."

I asked Walter if Ben, being the head honcho, did any pulling. He replied, "No, he just tightened the rope."

I finally forgave Walter for the terrible words he spoke to me. Let's just say that I caught him on a bad day and leave it at that.

Another hunting story I simply must tell adds new meaning to the old saying, "Pride goes before a fall." This story started one day when my brother Clarence and I set off to hunt moose. Just a short time into the hunt, I heard some shots, so I made way through the woods until I found Clarence dressing out a huge bull moose. When we finished quartering the animal, we went home and got Dad to bring his horses and stoneboat as near the moose as possible. This still meant a long, tough trip through the woods. Clarence and I each tied one front quarter of the moose on our pack boards while Dad stood beside us telling us to cut the quarters in half. With the ribcage attached, the quarters were about six feet long and far too heavy to carry over downtrees and brush. Clarence finally got his tied on the board and began staggering away into the trees, while Dad berated us with statements such as, "You fellows are crazy; you're going to fall and hurt yourselves."

Against his better judgment, Dad helped me get my load on my back and I staggered away, but not far. Soon I came to a small stream and as I attempted to cross it I took a loop and landed flat on my back in the water. Instantly Dad shouted, "Aha! Now you'll cut it in half, won't you?"

To his dismay I replied, "Not yet, if Clarence makes it out with his quarter and I don't, I'll never live it down."

With that I got Dad to help me up and once again I staggered off a few feet before I took another header and crashed down over a windfall right beside a large tree. With my ego thoroughly demolished I shouted to Clarence, afraid that he had already made it out with his load. Then to my surprise he answered and I found that he was down on his back on the other side of the same tree.

We finally managed to carry the quarters out to where the horses were, but throughout the entire trip Dad bad-mouthed us something terrible. He was not the least impressed that we had put our pride above our safety.

Having been a trapper for many years, my father took great care in the woods. On the trips I made with him into the forest, he always wore heavy, caulked boots. He felt that the sure footing more than compensated for the added weight.

Some of the early-day hunters were explorers as well, and they even went so far as to map the areas they past through. One such individual was a man named Prentiss Gray, who traveled a good portion of the globe and fortunately left a record of his exploits. The Boone and Crockett Club, Missoula, Montana published some of his journals and many of his pictures in a book—*From The Peace To The Fraser*. I have attempted to obtain this book through libraries, without any luck. Several people have managed to purchase a copy on-line, but at considerable expense. Now I have learned that a small number of these books are available from the Boone and Crockett Club in Missoula, Montana, for about $50. I consider this book to be an excellent read, especially for people who like wilderness adventures. As well, this is a collector's item that will only increase in value throughout the years.

Prentiss Nathaniel Gray was an adventurous soul. He traveled much of the world and made a name for himself in financial circles at a young age. The president of the J. Henry Shroeder Banking Corporation of New York, Prentiss was in the financial position to afford hiring pack trains and the like, and he certainly put them to good use.

During the month of August 1927, Prentiss made his way through Alberta for what was to be his second journey into the Rocky

Mountains, having previously toured the Banff/Jasper area of Alberta. On this trip, he met his pack train at Hudson's Hope. On August 27, they left Hudson's Hope and headed southeast through the Rocky Mountains into an area seldom frequented by humans. In his diary Prentiss describes the fourth day of their journey:

"This day was an endless drag of re-packing horses and pulling them out of muskeg, and was capped when two fell through a corduroy bridge that we had hastily constructed across a swampy little creek. My horse tore off one of my saddlebags, and profanity was running all over the place most of the day. The line of conversation would seem to indicate that every horse in the train was descended from a female dog and that their fathers were all bachelors."

Ten days into the trip, Prentiss wanted to take a side trip to beautiful Kinuoseo—meaning fish in Cree—Falls. This meant a side trip of a greater distance than they had expected. Along with Frank Dewing and Pete Callao—two guides—the three men set off with their horses on what was to be a short jaunt. This was tough trip, though, in that they got into areas of blowdown that were almost impenetrable. After attempting to cut a trail through the endless tangle of blowdown, the men gave up, tied the horses and continued on foot. They expected to be back at the horses by nightfall, so all they took in the way of sustenance was six sandwiches each, along with some tea and sugar. At one point Prent wrote:

"From the moment we left camp we were in windfalls and from there to the edge of the falls it was just plain hell. Nothing else can describe it. Windfalls with snags, windfalls piled higher than our heads, windfalls lurking in every bit of grass to entangle our feet. If a square foot of ground was not covered with downed timber, it was muskeg into which we sank above our ankles. Sometimes for 200 yards we never touched the ground, climbing over all sizes of downed timber that crisscrossed each other like jackstraws."

After a very difficult trip and another night in the open, Prent's group reached the falls, supposedly the second group of white men to see them. They took a good supply of moving pictures and stills, then had the long and difficult return trip to where they had left their horses.

This turned out to be a successful hunting trip during which Prent got his full compliment of game, including a grizzly. Then the men headed toward Jarvis Pass, where the group split up. Part of the group headed back for Hudson's Hope while Prent and three others headed generally south toward the Fraser River and the railroad.

As they made their way through the wilderness where few white men had trod, the roar of a gunshot astounded them. The guest turned out to be Mountain Jim Smith—a prospector out of Dome Creek who had wandered those mountains for many years. The many trappers that I interviewed in the Dome Creek area could add little information about this pioneer prospector; he was a man of few words who traveled alone in the summer and then spent the winters in Vancouver. "Mountain Jim" as he was known, was good enough to show the group a shortcut through the rugged mountains that brought them out to the railroad near Dome Creek.

Prent summed up their adventure quite nicely by writing:

"We had covered 108 miles by auto, 110 miles by boat, 344 miles on the trail on horses, and 6044 miles by rail, a long distance; but the 30 days in the woods, to say nothing of our trophies, made up for the many weary miles and compensated in part for the muskeg and downed timber."

Prent's main aim had been to study the range and numbers of bighorn sheep, and he was not disappointed, for they saw and photographed many sheep. At one sitting they photographed 26 sheep in a herd.

The year 1928 again found Prentiss Gray in the Canadian Rockies.

Fishing at Potts Falls, 1928.
COURTESY BOONE & CROCKETT CLUB.

Sherman Gray and Mike Murtha at Sherman (now Dimsdale Lake), July 2002.

That journey started near Rio Grande in Alberta and made its way through the Rockies to the same destination of Dome Creek, BC. On this second trip, Prent visited different areas and took along a survey-or named Dimsdale to generally map the area. As well, he kept an eye peeled for a railroad grade through the Rockies. This second trip was once again a story of perpetual excitement and adventure. On a side trip, they visited a stunning set of falls on the Red Deer River, probably being the first white men to see these falls. Prent named them Potts Falls after his assistant Bob Potts.

As they made their way through the spectacular Rocky Mountains, Prentiss was so impressed with the beautiful lakes they encountered that he named some of them. One lake he named Sherman, after his young son. Another lake he named Barbara, after his daughter. Unknown to him Barbara Lake had already been named Jarvis Lake after the famous railway surveyor. Dimsdale, who did the mapping, obviously knew Prent had named the other lake Sherman, after his son; yet he did the map work and named the lake after himself. A rather dirty trick to say the least. In due course another nearby lake was given the name Barbara, and for a time the Pass was named Sherman Pass, later renamed Gray Pass.

And so, rightfully, this great adventurer's name will live on in the Rocky Mountains and justly so, for the resulting information gathered during those two trips through the Rockies added much to the range and population information about the bighorn sheep. Adventurous to the end, Prentiss was killed in a tragic boating accident in 1935.

Sherman Gray at Kinuseo Falls, July 2002.

There is a surprise sequel to this story, and it came about because of the tenacity of a man named Mike Murtha. A former employee of BC Parks, Mike took a tremendous interest in the Gray expeditions and pursued it to a joyous conclusion. Through a great piece of detective work, he found out that Sherman Gray, the son of this adventurer was still alive in New Jersey, and so made contact with him. On July 19, 2002, Sherman, his 16-year-old grandson Matthew and Mike Murtha took a memorable flight: they flew by helicopter to Hudson's Hope and then followed the path that Sherman's father had taken 75 years earlier.

Greg Altoft was the lucky pilot chosen for the trip, and he was delighted to say the least. As for Sherman, he was almost at a loss for words while describing the flight. Many times he looked down from the chopper and wondered how the expeditions ever managed to get through some of the tough spots they faced along their journeys. Fate was kind to them on their flight, for they managed to see grizzly, moose, elk, caribou, mountain goats and bighorn sheep. Sherman rightfully described the area as a paradise.

Somehow it seemed so fitting that Sherman should follow and acknowledge his father's achievements, even though it was 75 years later. It struck me that he honored his father by doing so.

I suggested to Sherman that it would be nice if his grandson Matthew would duplicate their trip in about 60 or 70 years, and he agreed that such a trip would keep the memory of Prentiss Gray alive for future generations.

4 Manhunts

THROUGHOUT THE EARLY 20TH CENTURY, THERE WERE MANY EXTENSIVE manhunts in BC, the most famous by far being the hunt for Simon Gun-a-noot. Simon was an Indian who lived at Hazelton, and he went afoul of the law by allegedly shooting and killing two men. The alleged reason for the killings was that the two men had been bothering Simon's wife, and after being told to stay away, they had returned. When Simon came back from hunting, he found the two men had debauched his wife. According to newspaper reports of the time, he caught up with one of them at Two-Mile near Hazelton and shot him dead. The other man was caught and killed while fleeing up the Kispiox Valley. After allegedly killing the two men, Simon headed into the wilderness. This led to a chase that lasted for over 13 years, during which time the Pinkerton Detective Agency threw their weight into the chase. As well, the provincial police and bounty hunters were involved in the chase.

During the month of January 1913, Simon approached Reverend William Lee, who was business agent for the Indians. He asked for some money from the mill that was operated as a co-op. After the money question was settled with Simon, Lee asked him to surrender. Simon considered the proposal for a minute and then responded with, "But the white man would not take into consideration that I killed those two men because they attacked my wife."

Mr. Lee replied that if he surrendered it would sit well with the jury and he might only have to serve two years in the penitentiary at New Westminster. To this Simon answered, "But I don't want to go to New Westminster; I hear it rains a great deal there."

Later in the day Simon returned and told Mr. Lee that he had discussed it with friends who told him that a white man's jury would not pay enough attention to what led to the murder, because white men did not care what happened to Indian women. With that, Simon returned to the wilds.

While a great deal has been written about Simon, not as much is known about his brother-in-law, who was also charged with murder. Peter Himadan, also known as Peter Wales, actually spent more time in the forests than Simon. In fact, newspaper reports stated that not once throughout those 14 years did Peter come out to civilization. The price he paid can scarcely be imagined, as he lost his wife and a child during that time. It must also be mentioned that he was late for his surrender because he had to attend to his dying mother.

Only after Simon's acquittal did Peter surrender. This surrender took place in early March 1920 at Hazelton, after Peter had spent almost 14 years in the wilds.

Simon and Peter were not only dead shots; they were also knowledgeable woodsmen, which they had to be in order to elude their pursuers for so many years. On one occasion they were lying in wait and could easily have shot their pursuers, but wisely refrained. During Simon's trial, he told the pursuers the exact words they had spoken while he and Peter lay hidden only a few feet away. This stood them in good stead and showed clearly that they were not cold-blooded killers. Eventually both men were acquitted and rightfully so.

In an article carried in the *Citizen* of September 22, 1938, it was noted:

"*Finally a story filtered through to Hazelton that Simon had made a fabulously rich placer gold strike in the far north, and word was got to Stuart Henderson of Victoria, an old-time friend of Chief Gun-a-noot. It asked him to intercede with the authorities for the old Indian, so that he might cash in on his gold find and spend the rest of his declining years in comfort with his family at Hazelton.*"

Just how much truth there was in the gold story I do not know, but certainly something got the attention of those in power.

After all that he had been through, Simon's suffering was not over. He was attacked by the influenza epidemic and died alone in his trapline cabin during January 1934.

Another memorable manhunt began in April 1911, when two

Indians named Moses Paul and Paul Spintlam allegedly murdered a man named White. They were taken into custody and placed in the old log jail at Clinton. While awaiting trial, they made their escape and then murdered an Oriental man who was the only witness to their first murder. In an effort to escape the law, they took to the wilderness and the pursuit was on.

The posse following the two men suspected they had fled to the Big Bar Mountains near the Fraser River, where it was suspected they had a large cache of food. As the months went by and they eluded capture, a $1500 reward was offered. This was a considerable sum at that time, yet it failed to get results.

On May 3, 1912, word was brought into Clinton that the two outlaws were camped only five miles distant. Provincial Constable Alexander Kindness, along with a five-man posse followed the men through thick timber, found their horses and camp equipment, but there was no sign of the men. As Kindness attempted to capture one of the horses, a shot rang out from behind a log and he dropped, shot through the heart. A second shot wounded Constable Loring, who then fired several shots at the retreating gunmen. The remaining members of the posse followed the fugitives a short distance into the forest and then returned to Clinton to report the murder.

The next day another posse took up the chase and eventually caught up with the killers only to have two more men killed. Again the two fugitives made their escape. By mid-May, an Indian chief named Fernie was on their trail, but it is hard to know if he really wanted to catch them. To make matters even more difficult, it appeared that the two men had split up, but that was only a temporary diversion. A short time later an intensive search was made in the area of Pavilion Mountain after two horses were found there. Again the trail disappeared.

By June, the trail had shifted from Canoe Creek to the head of the Bonaparte, about 100 miles southeast of Canoe Creek near Fish Lake. Here the fugitives abandoned a horse they had stolen and stole another from a native woman at Fish Lake. At this point there were 60 officers on the trail, and it clearly points out that they were dealing with expert woodsmen, trained in the art of hiding their trail.

On June 14, two strange Indians were seen in the Blackwater area, west of Fort George, and both were reported to be carrying rifles. Then a report came to the police that two horses had been stolen in that area. Since no sign had been seen in the Chilcotin for several weeks, it now became apparent that they had moved north. Suddenly the authorities suspected that they may be moving north to join forces with Gun-a-noot, who had evaded police for three years and was still at large in the Hazelton area.

The June 29, 1912 edition of the *Fort George Herald* carried the following article:

WILL USE BLOODHOUNDS IN HUNT FOR OUTLAWS

"A large number of the special constables connected with the hunt of the outlaws, Moses Paul and Paul Spintlam, have been called in and paid off. Six of the Indian trackers, among who was the Indian who tracked Bill Miner after the holdup on the CPR at Ducks, have been sent back to Kamloops. Some 70 men were engaged in the hunt at one time and the indication appears that the police are cutting down expenses, and will resort to bloodhounds in future in tracing the men.

"The outlaws were tracked to the Big Slide on the Fraser River, but from there all signs were obliterated. Both outlaws carried boots with them, and it is believed that on arrival at the Big Slide they substituted these for their moccasins, which must have worn out. All the bridges crossing the Fraser River above and below Lillooet have been guarded night and day, and all the canoes in that vicinity have been taken possession of by the police, in order to confine the men to the southern side of the Fraser. The road from Lytton through to Clinton has been policed by automobiles, making runs on the slightest possible rumors of the appearance of the men in the neighborhood. The latest report has it that they were seen not far north of Bridge River, probably with the idea of crossing the Fraser at a convenient point. The Bridge is a very mountainous country, abounding in game, and a good many believe they are making their camping ground there. The Indians have many friends in that section; know the country like a book— where they have been on many a hunting expedition. If taken in that section it will be a stand for life, in which it will be hard to hazard a guess as to the number that will be toppled over by the fugitives. They are both good shots and appear to have ammunition to burn."

After being on the run for two years, the two hunted men finally surrendered, mainly because of the intervention of several chiefs. They were immediately charged with three murders. When the case came into court at Kamloops, several Indian witnesses testified that the accused were in the Potato Illahee, 17 miles from Spences Bridge at the time of the murders.

Charles Truman testified he had been with the first posse, saw the accused at their camp and went for the posse. According to Truman, when the posse returned, Constable Kindness was shot and killed. Another posse member, James Boyd, testified that he saw Spintlum fire the fatal bullet.

After a great deal of give and take, the two men were eventually arraigned at the Vernon assizes, but the jury disagreed on a verdict. Another change of venue was then asked for and the case was moved to New Westminster.

With horses, guns, saddles and all the equipment of a Wild West show among the exhibits, the trial got under way. The last witness to testify was James Boyd who swore he saw Spintlum fire the fatal bullet. From a distance of 23 paces he pointed out that he easily recognized the man he had known for many years. Others testified that they had seen the two men in the area just prior to the shooting.

The long but slow arm of the law finally ground to a halt on June 28, 1913, after four days of testimony. When the jury returned after an hour and a half's deliberation, the verdict was "Guilty".

When the court asked, "Paul Spintlum, have you anything to say why the sentence of the court should not be passed upon you?"

The prisoner maintained the stoical demeanor he had assumed all through the trial, then smiled slightly and mumbled, "No".

The judge then rendered, "The sentence of the court is that you be sent to prison from whence you came and therein on Friday, September 12, you be hanged by the neck until you are dead."

The trial of Paul Spintlum was followed closely by the news media and a typical response was carried in the *Herald* dated 5 July 1913:

"The sentencing to death of the Indian outlaw Paul Spintlum brings to a fitting close a typically western crime drama. It is not good to rejoice in the passing of the death sentence upon even the most abandoned of criminals.

Yet we feel that had Spintlum escaped the penalty of the murders of which he has been convicted, the result would have been demoralizing to the work of the provincial police amongst the Indians. Since the time when the Indian Gun-a-noot at Hazelton, killed a man and successfully escaped the vigilance of the law in the hinterlands, there has existed among the Indians at Hazelton certain insolence, which in their inflammable minds might at any time find violence and murder. The same spirit would have prevailed had Spintlum escaped the law. The days of the gun-fighter, the bad Indian and the posse are slowly drawing to a close. Development and the march of progress in the west leave such dramatic, but deplorable features of primitive days in the traditions of the country only. When on occasion, as in the Clinton outrage, a man harks back to the spirit of outlawry, and resists arrest by murder, the outraged justice of a civilized country demands retribution. And so a sordid tragedy comes to an end. Poor Kindness, the brave young constable who was murdered, lies in an honored grave, and his murderer stands in the shadow of the gallows."

I disagree with the editor's point comparing Spintlum with Gun-a noot, as I feel that the latter was put in a position where he had little choice. I wonder what any other man would have done in his place. Gun-a-noot was justified in his belief that he would not receive a fair trial, as there were other comparable situations that proved him right.

In her book, *The Color of Gold*, author Margaret McKirdy describes the justice an Indian woman received when a crazed white prospector murdered her husband. When the case came to court in Golden, BC, the lawyer for the accused humiliated her. The murderer walked away a free man. The shamed and terrified woman tried to return to her people but the winter snows had arrived, so along with her two children, she perished somewhere in the wilderness.

This was the same justice that may well have been in store for Gun-a-noot if he had surrendered at the time of the murders. During all the years he spent in the forest, there can be no doubt that a great many people were on his side. In fact, several elderly people have told me that their parents were secretly cheering for him and hoping that he would never be caught. Certainly Gun-a-noot stirred the imagination of a generation and won the respect of friends and foes alike.

During the month of October 1922, an 18-year-old English lad named John Bennett set out on a risky adventure; his intent—to walk from Pouce Coupe through the Pine Pass to Prince George. When several weeks passed without any word from their son, the Bennett family in England arranged with the Imperial Bank of Canada to offer a $500 reward for information that would lead to the rescue of their son. As a result, the Grande Prairie branch of the bank sent Kelly Sunderman and Ted Strand off to follow his trail, if possible. After a strenuous trip through the pass with only one day's rest, the two men eventually reached Prince George where they reported their findings. They found three notes left by Bennett that told of his difficulty in finding the trail. There was nothing alarming in the first note, but the second note was left at a point three or four miles below Tillicum Creek, which runs into the Missinchinka. This note indicated that Bennett had decided to turn back. As there was but one trail through the pass and no trace of the missing man was found, it was assumed he had started wandering— possibly along some little-used trail. The two searchers related that they had a trying time coming through the pass and that there was seven feet of snow in which they and their dogs floundered.

When they found the third note, the searchers learned that Bennett had left Frank Horne's cabin on the Missinchinka on November 8, but was back again on November 15. After taking a good supply of provisions from the cabin and promising to pay for them later, Bennett left a note stating:

"Your cabin and food have just about saved my life and I am deeply grateful; I am setting out today back across the Pine. My feet and fingertips have been frost-bitten and I have abandoned my horse, but I think I will make it."

Bennett then set off again and simply disappeared in that endless wilderness; just one of many that the wilderness beat down.

When the police were called upon to investigate an incident they often had little or no idea what may be waiting in store for them. Such was the case in May 1929, when Prince George Constables Walker and McClinton headed into the woods about 12 miles west of Prince George. Their mission was to search for a rifle, which had been reported stolen by a man named Nick Ureshka. With warrant in hand, the two officers intended to search Ureshka's cabin. But the accused, who was busy sawing wood at the time, saw the men coming and ran into his cabin. When the officers reached the cabin he threatened to shoot them.

This action resulted in a standoff for a time, until suddenly the accused came tearing out the door with an axe in his hands and a pistol swinging from his belt. A free-for-all erupted during which Sergeant Walker received an axe cut to his face; at the same time Ureshka sank his teeth into McClinton's wrist. When the battle was over, Ureshka was brought to town where Drs. Lyon and Trefry examined him and decided he was insane. A few days later he was taken to the asylum at Essondale.

Such was the dangers facing officers of the law. When they were called to duty, they had no idea if they would ever come home again.

In *Crazy Man's Creek*, I told the story of a trapper named Goodson who disappeared along the Torpy River after a fight with trapper Emmet "Shorty" Haines. This event occurred during the winter of 1925-26. Perhaps a year after my book was published I received information that cast a totally different light on this story. This new information came to me from Paul Paulson who grew up next door to "Shorty" at Decker Lake. He was a close friend to "Shorty" throughout the 30s and 40s, and was at his side when he died in the 50s.

The original information came to me from Chris Gleason, who also trapped the McGregor area from 1915 until 1924, and was living in Dome Creek when Goodson disappeared. In 1976, I visited Chris in White Rock, BC, and he told me that the reason "Shorty" had done away with Goodson was because after they had a wicked fight, Goodson had burned his cabin down. He also made it plain that "Shorty" was nobody to fool around with, and that he simply did what had to be done.

Perhaps a hint of what Goodson had been up against can be derived from this brief note in the *Citizen* of July 23, 1919:

"Shorty Haines arrived back from France and Germany Saturday night. He enlisted with the 102nd and served two years on "sniper duty" during the war. One of the first white men in this section, Shorty is sure glad to be back in God's country, and says he has seen enough of Europe to last him for the rest of his days. The reverse English applies to the cognomen of Shorty, as he stands something over six feet and is the type of soldier that made Canada famous."

The conflicting part of this story is that several other people from the Dome Creek area assured me that there had been no cabin burning, although they were elusive about the cause of the Haines-Goodson feud. This puzzled me, as everyone who knew the Gleason brothers agreed that they were totally honest; one individual even put it this way, "If they told you something—it was the truth."

So how was I to make sense out of all this?

Finally, Paul Paulson filled me in on a story that had been told to him by Carl Swanson, one of "Shorty's" friends at Decker Lake. Carl told Paul that he too had trapped the Dome Creek area at the time of William Goodson's disappearance; he further added that he had attended a trappers' meeting in Dome Creek where the topic of discussion was what they should do about a fur thief in the area. "Shorty" made it clear to all at the meeting that he would deal with the problem, and just a short time later he informed the other trappers that they didn't have to worry about Goodson anymore.

A thorough police investigation followed, but several months had passed since Goodson's disappearance; this meant that all sign had long since vanished. A diary was found in Goodson's cabin that detailed the long-standing battle he had been having with Shorty. In it, he described how Shorty had struck him with a hammer during an altercation. When I mentioned this to Chris Gleason, he replied, "If you seen the size of Shorty's fist, you would believe that it felt like a hammer."

After a prolonged search, a 30-30 rifle was found hanging in a tree in the area Goodson had trapped, but this rifle was not Goodson's property. Another area trapper had found the Goodson rifle hanging in the tree and since it was a new rifle, he exchanged it for his own much older 30-30, which was taken by police as evidence.

After a frustrating search, this article appeared in the *Citizen* of May 13, 1926:

"Provincial Constables Service and Martin returned on Sunday evening following a fruitless search for W. A. Goodson, the trapper who disappeared from his cabin 17 miles up the Fraser River from Dome Creek during the latter part of February. The disappearance of Goodson is one of the most remarkable which the local police have been called upon to deal with."

For a time I wondered why Chris told me the burnt cabin story, until I finally realized that he was attempting to protect the families of the other trappers that were involved in the trappers' meeting. Since Chris knew that Shorty was the guilty party, he thought it best to let him take all the blame.

After all these years have passed there is no way to know if in fact Goodson had been a fur thief. But if he was, then he surely had adopted a dangerous lifestyle, for there was no more certain way to die young than to be a fur thief in those days.

Perhaps the most surprising part of all was that their conspiracy of silence had held for over 50 years until after everyone involved had passed on. As for Goodson, no trace of his body was ever found; the wilderness often keeps its secrets.

Just recently I discovered that shortly after Goodson's death, Shorty left his trapline at Pass Lake and took over the line previously ran by Goodson. This is attested to in the book *From the Peace to the Fraser* in which author Prentiss Gray describes stopping at Haine's cabin on his way through the pass from the McGregor to the Torpy River in 1928.

And so the obvious question seems to be whether people held "Shorty" in contempt for his action. This was answered in the following article that appeared in the *Citizen* about five years later—on June 11, 1931:

"Corporal Stewart of the provincial police received word on Wednesday that "Shorty" Haines had returned safely to Dome Creek from his trapline on the Raging River [Torpy River]. Haines was about two weeks overdue, and some apprehension was caused his friends by the report he had met with foul play. Emmet B. Haines is one of the best known trappers in this section of the province and the news of his safe return was received with rejoicing in Prince George."

Perhaps it is worth mentioning that after Seabach and Huble gave up on moving freight through the Giscome Portage, that "Shorty" and a partner took a stab at it for few years. His name will live on in the area of the portage because nearby Emmet Creek was named after this tough and memorable woodsman.

At this point I want to change gears and relate a few stories involving helicopter accidents. One story I found quite interesting occurred in

1980, when Pat and Len Sexsmith journeyed to Norman Wells in the Northwest Territories. The purpose of their trip was to visit their son Lee, who was employed as a chopper pilot in that area. Shortly after their arrival, Lee was ordered to fly about 120 miles to the west to move some prospectors and their equipment back into the mountains. Since he was traveling empty to and from the rendezvous point, Lee decided to take his parents along on the trip.

After the 120-mile flight in a Jet-ranger helicopter, they landed near a small lake where they met the crew and then Lee proceeded to move them and their supplies back into the ridges as planned. Because of the long days at that latitude, he was able to fly during the night, which he did. About two hours after midnight he had completed the job so he returned to get his parents for the return flight to Norman Wells.

Once he arrived back at the rendezvous point, he pumped 30 gallons of jet fuel into the helicopter. This fuel was taken from three ten-gallon barrels that was part of a fuel cache stored in that area. Lee got his

Jet Ranger after Lee's crash.

parents aboard and took off uphill, away from the small lake he had parked beside. Only a moment later, Lee noticed he was losing rotor speed and at once the chopper descended and crashed, just a short distance from the lake.

The main rotors chopped off the tail section, and one rotor blade was torn off in the process; the other blade was bent at right angles, and the chopper was totaled. A sling that had been rolled up in the back seat had somehow been driven right through the door and by some miracle had just missed striking his mother. All three emerged from the machine without a scratch.

After they realized that they were all safe and without injuries, Lee realized just how close they had came to disaster: for if he had taken off out over the lake, they would surely all have perished, because the water was unbearably cold. About eight hours later another helicopter flew to their rescue after they were reported overdue. As they waited for rescue, Lee discovered what had caused the engine to fail. One of the ten-gallon drums had contained methyl alcohol—a substance that looked like jet fuel and easily passed through the filters in the fuel pump, filters that are designed to prevent water from entering the fuel tank.

Lee Sexsmith with steelhead at Tuaton Lake, 1980.

As I listened to Lee's story of this near-fatal accident, I had no problem sensing how thankful he was that his parents had emerged unharmed from a terrible crash. What could ever be more heartwarming than that?

Another helicopter accident with a surprise twist occurred in 1976. Prince George pilot Grant Paulson was flying a Bell 47 just a short distance from the Alaska Highway when he experienced motor trouble. A blade broke off the cooling fan and pierced the oil cooler, causing a massive loss of oil. As Grant was flying low over thick timber he had no place to set the chopper down, and so was forced to continue until the engine seized up. Then he auto-rotated down into a swampy area where his rotor hit some trees, ending in a crash-landing. He pulled himself out of the wreck and surprisingly found he was uninjured.

Just prior to his accident he had noticed a road a few miles distant, so he walked out and followed this road a short distance until it merged with the Alaska Highway. A short time later a pickup truck happened along and gave him a ride to Johnson's Crossing, where he called out to Northern Mountain Helicopters' base and reported the accident.

This was how Grant's day started out, but wait—it wasn't over yet.

After reporting the accident, Grant called to their base camp and a geologist drove to meet him at Johnson's Crossing. They drove back to the side-road and then walked back to the stricken chopper where Grant retrieved his camera and personal gear. On their return trip, they stopped at a place called Holsteads Café, where he found two young ladies employed.

Grant's employer in the area was a man named Cam Stevens, and it was his habit to throw a big party on August 28, every year. As fate would have it, the party was on for that very evening. Summoning up his courage, Grant invited the two young ladies to the party, never daring to believe that they would show up. But to his amazement, they did, and Grant fell hopelessly in love with one of the young ladies. Six months later he married Tara Holstead—the daughter of the owner of the café.

Tara was just sweet sixteen at the time, so they changed the date on her birth certificate so she could marry without her parents' permission. Six months after they met, they were married in a little church and found

Tara and Grant Paulson with Rieder, 1991.

out later that Grant's parents had been married in that same church many years earlier.

Three children and twenty-five years later Grant and Tara are still together. This forced me to ask if that was the luckiest or unluckiest day of his life. With an obvious grin of satisfaction on his face, Grant replied, "Ask me again in about ten years."

5 First Nations People

DURING THE YEARS AFTER THE FIRST EUROPEANS ARRIVED IN THIS COUNTRY, much valuable history was lost. But it pales into insignificance in comparison to the lost history of the Native Indians. We cannot begin to imagine the challenges they faced before rifles came into their possession. It seems apparent that they must have faced terrible confrontations with grizzly bears and other animals of the forests. Little wonder that they held the grizzly bear in such high regard.

While some confrontations between whites and Indians ended in disaster, there were other times when they were funny beyond words. One memorable meeting occurred at Rocky Mountain House when a group of Blackfoot Indians came to trade. On this occasion a chief complained that his pemmican and robes when placed on the balance scale did not warrant more than a bit of tea or sugar:

"What for you put on one side tea, and on the other a little bit of iron? [Metal weights used on balance beams] We don't know what that medicine is—but, look here, put on one side of that thing that swings, a bag of pemmican, and put on the other side blankets and the tea—that would be fair, for one side will be as big as the other."

The trader thought for a minute and then replied:

"We'll let it be as you say; we will make the balance swing level between the bag of pemmican and the blankets. But we will carry out the idea still further—you will put your marten skins and your otter and fisher skins on one side; I will put against them on the other my blankets and my gun and ball and powder. Then, when both sides are level, you will take the ball and powder and the blankets, and I will take the marten and the rest of the fine furs."

The chief thought about this proposition for a minute and then decided to go back to their original formula.

When it came to bargaining, many of the Natives showed that they could hold their own with anyone. Author and adventurer J. Turner Turner found this out for himself way back in 1887. He found that when he traded for a pile of furs, that he had better inspect the furs on the inside of the pile because the worst furs were always hidden from view.

Mr. Turner—while I enjoy reading of his adventures—was a pompous ass. Anyone that reads his work with an open mind surely must arrive at the same conclusion. His favorite pastime appeared to be throwing insults at the Natives, while at the same time asking for their help in learning how to set traps and otherwise survive in the wild.

The Natives were good enough to take him up the Fraser River, help him erect a cabin, show him where the furs were and how to get them; yet the following spring when they came upriver to trap, he belittled them for trapping his beaver. Small wonder that at times they considered the white man "strange in the head."

A story I found rather intriguing was carried in the *Fort George Herald* of September 13, 1913:

"Fearful of what the inventions of the white man may lead to, superstitious Indians of Skidegate have watched the operations of the new wireless station there with awe. A party of old Indians called on Dr. Spencer, the Methodist medical missionary, and told him they thought it was time to die. They had seen the new station working and were convinced that men hundreds of miles apart were talking together. "We hear but we cannot see them talk," said one Indian, "pretty soon white man can tell what we are thinking about."

I must add that it didn't take these Natives very long to adjust; in fact they were some of the first to have running water and other modern services in their community.

During the time that the Grand Trunk Pacific Railroad was attempting to purchase the Indian land for their station and yard area, Fort George had many a humorous moment. For not only the railroad was interested, but the Natural Resources Co. (NRC) as well. On behalf of the railroad, the government had offered $68 000. In an effort to get the jump on the railroad, the NRC assembled a meeting with about 50 members of the band. Through an interpreter, they went to work trying to convince the band to sell to them. The results of this meeting were carried in the *Fort George Herald* on January 14, 1911:

"*. . . After the assembled had done fitting justice to tea and a profusion of cake, the NRC employee, as conveyer of the gathering, mounted the rostrum. With the aid of an interpreter, he sought to interest and entertain the company with a discourse on, 'Forty Natural Reasons why the Fort George Indians Should Not Sell Their Reservation.'*

"*A diagram of the 1366-acre reservation was drawn on the blackboard with a deep circle around the cemetery. 'This, brothers, is the resting-place of many a lineal descendant and heroic warrior who has remained in tranquil peace ever since Alexander and Fraser overlooked the Nechako as a navigable stream. For 103 years has this strip of land 'around which I draw the magic circle' been the happy hunting ground of OUR fathers, and I say BROTHERS, are you going to part with it for a song? Are you going to allow a railroad company to desecrate the tombs of our ancestors, by allowing the erection thereon of a depot, a roundhouse and a turntable? All for $50 an acre?'*

"*At this point the Indians yelled out, 'Whappoo, Whappoo.'*

"*. . . Now, BROTHERS, I again advise you not to sell; but if you are inclined to part with the western portion of the reservation, you had better go into the real estate business yourselves. Just fancy the enormous amount of money we have been enabled to make out of our 'graveyard' townsite, and it is in the woods. Why we have sold 1000 lots to people 3000 miles away from here. We get one-fourth down and the balance is never paid by the buyer once he sees his property. It is nice clean money, too. We sell the same lot over and over again. A sort of endless chain proposition. Works with all the natural avidity of a hungry eel. Of course if you finally decide to take my advice and embark in a real estate business, it is necessary to have an experienced promoter—one with a record. It does not matter much if he is a jailbird, the blacker, the better judge of character. And further, it is necessary nowadays to buy up several papers and subsidize others. I would recommend you to the Saturday Sunset. It has done excellent and meritorious work for us in the past, and I really don't know what we should have done without its aid. All our lot holders are supplied with a copy of this journal weekly. Advertising comes high, but brothers without it, it is like Hamlet with the Dane overboard. Just a few words more before I close.*

Now, if you decide to dispose of the western half, don't give it to the Grand Trunk; they have lots of government money and don't understand the real estate business. Give it to the NRC. They will handle it on the equitable profit distribution plan, so successfully worked elsewhere, and you will all emerge rich.

"This was too much for Joseph Q. and the other braves, who had gone mad with enthusiasm, and amid the yell of 20 'Whappoos' they disappeared."

The next day, the speaker approached the interpreter and commented that he had never before heard such appreciative applause. The interpreter then explained to him that he had misunderstood and that "Whappoo" simply meant the equivalent of "bullshit."

During the month of June 1931, Game Warden Thomas Van Dyke arrested three Indians for trapping beavers during the closed season. When their case came up for trial, a tremendous gathering of Native people arrived at the courthouse. As the case proceeded, it became apparent that Magistrate Milburn was in for a bad-hair day. While he did his best, he was clearly out-foxed. First off, the court had trouble proving that the skins were green, as the Natives had cleverly proceeded to dry them as soon as they were caught. At length, two of the skins were proven to be green and so a fine of $125 was levied. Suddenly the court was surprised when one of the women present declared that she has caught one of the beavers. Then things got even more complicated when the court was advised that the accused had no money to pay fines. Placed in an awkward spot, the magistrate inquired of the woman, "How many children do you have?"

Although she only had three children, she replied that she had twelve, and then added that they were at Fort McLeod and she didn't know if anyone was taking care of them.

This put the court in the hopeless position of taking care of all the children if the woman was jailed; as well, the woman couldn't be allowed to go free if the men were sentenced to jail. At last His Honor solved the impasse by getting a promise of good behavior from all three; then he allowed them to be set free for the two days served since arrest, plus their good behavior. Five will get you ten that His Honor went home wondering if there wasn't another and perhaps easier profession.

For almost 40 years, I have known that animals pick up sound through the ground. I'm not taking credit for this, though, as I believe this was well known to the Native people in bygone days. There is an old story about a mountain man traveling along on his horse when he came upon an Apache Indian stretched out with his ear pressed to the ground. "Is something around?" he asked.

"Two white men, two horses and a wagon about one mile away heading east." Came the reply.

"That's incredible—do you mean you picked that up through the ground?" asked the mountain man.

"No!" groaned the Indian, "they ran over me about five minutes ago."

I couldn't resist retelling that old joke, but I'm serious about believing that they knew about animals picking up sound through the ground. And just look at the footwear they wore—isn't it a fact that moccasins were ideal for sneaking up on wildlife? On the other hand many modern-day hunters wear hard-soled boots that break everything they step on. In fact, it is not uncommon to hear modern-day hunters coming through the forest while they are still at a great distance.

I found several different sources that described the excellent physical condition of the Native people many years ago. For example, there is the testimony of J. Turner Turner who hiked into the mountains with them in 1887. Although he was an active individual who considered himself to be in good form, he found himself gasping for breath. As he rested, he noticed a young Native boy about 13 years of age, as he ran around aimlessly, putting in more miles than necessary. "Aren't you tired?" asked Mr. Turner.

"I don't know what it means to be tired," the boy replied.

There was also the testimony of Twelve-foot Davis, that his Native packers carried a minimum of 150-pound packs across the portages. We shouldn't be surprised, though, because many people that live close to nature are renowned for their strength.

The following story tells of a heroic effort by a group of Native Indians to return one of their own people for proper burial. It was taken from the *Citizen* dated May 24, 1923:

"Packing the body of Isaac Alexander from the far away Manson Creek

country, a big party of Indians were camped at Canyon Creek on Monday last en route to Moricetown where burial is to take place in Native fashion. The journey of 187 miles [300 km] was made almost entirely on foot and the party had been 22 days on the trail up to last Monday.

"Over three weeks ago two Indians dropped over the Babines and landed at Tyee Lake to report the death of Alexander at Manson Creek early in April, and a council meeting of Indians decided to bring the body to Moricetown for burial. For this task twenty Indians were employed to pack provisions and help bring out the body.

"The packers were divided in duty: some bearing the remains, other packing ice, while others carried a canoe which was utilized in the small patches on the lakes, cleared of ice. Owing to the deep snow it was impossible to come over the mountains with their burden and the trip was made by Burns Lake, a double box being provided which was kept well supplied with ice."

This next story was taken from the *Citizen* of December 31, 1930:

"Billy Seymour of South Fort George, who made a name for himself by reason of his ability and endurance on the rivers and in the bush, when the land boom was in full flower in Cariboo in 1909, has been given a place in Ripley's 'Believe it or not.' The incident in Seymour's career that has been singled out, is a trip he made from Quesnel to Fort George and return on snowshoes. This was a trip of 192 miles [300 km] in those days, and Seymour is credited with having made the trip without a stopover. Henry Johnson, formerly of this city, spotted Ripley's reference to the incident, and sent it on to the Citizen so that Seymour may get the full benefit of it."

This was but one of many references to the name Seymour that I have found in old newspaper articles which pointed out that several generations of Seymours were among the best of the early-day rivermen. During the 1880s, Twelve-foot Davis employed one of them who was considered the best white-water man on the Peace and Fraser Rivers combined.

One outstanding talent that many Natives possessed was the ability to track or trail any creature through the forest. Author Cecille Carroll of Queen Charlotte City told me a real keeper. It occurred in 1953, while she was living at Canyon Creek in the Yukon. One day she dressed her three-year-old son Pat and sent him outside to play. Within a couple minutes, she dressed her daughter and brought her outside. To her dismay, her son was nowhere to be seen. A small search party was formed, but there was no trail to follow in the dead grass of spring. Then someone suggested they get an Indian named Bill Jamieson to assist. Fortunately Bill was camped with his wife just a short distance from their community. As soon as Bill arrived on the scene he began showing the others a skill they had never seen before. With the rest following and watching in amazement, he tracked the boy for several miles, at times explaining to the others exactly what was happening. He told them that the cocker spaniel dog was repeatedly running ahead of the boy and coaxing him away from home. In due course Bill found the boy and returned him back home unharmed. Cecille cannot hide the admiration and respect she still holds for this man.

Cecille tells another story about this man. This event took place while he was guiding an American hunter for grizzly bear. Apparently the hunter shot from too great a distance and wounded the bear, which then took cover. Against Bill's advice the hunter followed the bear into a thicket and was attacked before he had time to shoot. In recounting the tragedy, Bill said that the grizzly slapped the hunter so hard that he sailed a good distance through the air before he hit the ground. Bill also said that he plainly heard bones breaking when the man was struck.

Instantly after slapping the hunter, the bear attacked Bill, who dropped it with his 30-30 rifle. Then Bill checked the hunter and realized that he was seriously injured. He sought help and with considerably difficulty finally got to Whitehorse. He was then flown out for medical assistance, and a prolonged recovery. Some time later the thankful hunter sent Bill a .300 magnum rifle which he suggested Bill carry with him in the future.

The resolve the Native people possessed is clearly shown in the following article taken from the *Citizen* dated April 19, 1934:

INDIAN WOMAN MAKING SOLO HIKE
TO HOME ON STIKINE RIVER

"Mary Johnny Bob, an Indian woman, has started from Burns Lake on a 500-mile [800-km] hike to her home on the Stikine River, according to the Interior News. *She doubtless owes her life to the airplane. Believed to be*

dying she was brought out from the Stikine last fall in G. McConachie's plane, but a winter in the Burns Lake Hospital restored her to health and strength and she started out cheerfully on her long trip to her home in the north."

Many people may be unaware of just how much the Indians wandered the backcountry many years ago. Only within the last few years have I been aware that they traveled to Grizzly Bear Mountain in bygone years.

When I was just a lad, trappers and prospectors frequently visited our home, where they would engage my dad in endless conversations about the wilderness. Several times during those years the subject of Caribou Basin, or as it was sometimes called—Caribou Meadows— came up. One of the stories that interested me was the fact that Fort George Indians frequently hunted the area for caribou up until about a century ago. Now part of the Sugarbowl Grizzly Park, this is a scenic and easily reached area with excellent trail access.

Trapper Oliver Prather, who guided and trapped that area for many years, told the story of how in 1922, his father Orv first visited the area. Along with a man named Lawrence Ward, they went to the meadows where they arrived in late evening. They made camp and the following morning as dawn broke they shot a caribou right in their camp. Caribou sign was everywhere. On this same trip, they found a large cooking pot or Dutch oven that had been packed into the area years earlier by the Indians. Oliver also saw this pot several times in later years.

I told Oliver about how trapper Einar Jensen had seen a great herd of caribou only a few miles from Caribou Basin back in the 30s. I further asked if he believed the story. Oliver made it plain that he did in fact believe the story because he had seen a great many caribou himself prior to the 1950s.

He was very emphatic when he said:

"I keep telling people that there were great numbers of caribou back then but they don't seem to believe me. It was the wolves that got them. You had to see the slaughter to believe it."

Surely the Indians must have had a paradise hunting in that area, although it meant an upriver trip of 120 miles by river, as well as a full day's hike from the river to the basin.

During the summer of 2001 I visited the meadows with Rick Roos

Norton Dowd and Dave King search for the elusive Dutch oven, July 2002.

of BC Parks. We spent a few hours looking for the elusive cast iron Dutch oven, but to no avail. Just this past month I again visited the area with two mountain-climbing enthusiasts named Dave King and Norton Dowd. Since Dave has frequented the area for the past 23 years he has become an authority on the area. He showed me traces of several old trails—one of them appearing to have came from the direction of the Grand Canyon. This is the path the Natives would have followed on their way to the meadows so many years ago. Dave has also found several old campsites throughout the area of the meadows, and with a great deal of good luck we may yet find the Dutch oven that has lain there in peace for perhaps a century or more.

And why did the Natives go to such extreme lengths, not to mention hard work, to get these caribou? One reason was because the Interior of the Province had a shortfall of big game prior to 1900; the hides of big-game animal hides were items of extreme value. Fortunately there were places in the mountains where big game existed in pockets, and Caribou Basin was most certainly one of these.

I was more than just a bit surprised to learn of the leather shipments to central BC in the 1820s from Saskatchewan. This shows more than anything else does just what a shortage there was of big game, especially around the area of Fort St. James. This leather was in great demand by the Indians who were willing to part with a substantial amount of furs in order to obtain it. For the first several years these furs were brought down the Fraser River, but this route was changed to a more northerly route in later years.

To give an example of the movement of hides from Saskatchewan to New Caledonia (Fort St. James), I want to cite their statement for 1836:

"500 large moose skins; 55 small moose skins; 25 buffalo skins; 25 moose parchment skins [for writing] and 30 pounds of sinews."

Also for interest sake, I will give the food supplies for 1836 for the Forts in New Caledonia:

"781 sturgeon; 67 510 salmon; 11 941 smaller fish; 346 trout; 2160 rabbits; 153 ducks; 10 lynx; 8 marmots; 3 porcupines; 1 swan; 14 dogs and some horses."

Perhaps it warrants mentioning to state that porcupine was often eaten by the early-day travelers. Many suggested it was delicious as long as all fat was removed. As well, the glands had to be removed from inside the forelegs to prevent contamination. But for delicacy of taste, they stated that porcupine liver is in a class by itself and far and away the sweetest of all wild animal livers—possibly because of the animal's diet. When fried with bacon it is a chef's delight.

Another story that caught my attention concerned a clever life-saving technique that was used by two Natives during the month of December 1937. While flying between Lower Post and Whitehorse, Pilot Ernie Kubicek and co-pilot Danny Trowsdell spotted something unusual. They circled and noticed two campfires just a short distance apart. Between the fires they noticed a message framed by spruce boughs. The two men landed the aircraft nearby and went to investigate. What they found was two Indians who were out of food and desperately in need of help. After delivering the message to the authorities, the pilot noted, "Just who figured out the idea of the sign, I don't know, but it was effective."

Nature lovers should be interested in this next story. It is just another example of the knowledge possessed by the Native people in the long ago.

In his book, *Wanderings of an Artist,* Paul Kane told a story about taming a wild animal. They were heading from the Prairies into BC and were concerned about finding enough animals to feed themselves. There was an abundance of animals where they were at the time, and they had just shot a cow buffalo. Since they were only able to carry a limited amount of the meat with them, they knew that shortly they would be out of food again. The buffalo they had shot had a calf with her, so they attempted to take it along and then butcher it later. The calf balked, though, and refused to follow them. At this point one of the Indians showed his knowledge of wildlife: He forced the calf's mouth open and then spit into it a couple times; almost at once the calf accepted and followed him.

Since the cover of this book shows a picture of Red Goat Mountain in Spatsizi Plateau Wilderness Park, perhaps a brief outline is in order.

The Tahltan Indians named this mystical land Spatsizi because the mountain goats sometimes rolled in the iron oxide-stained rock of Red Goat Mountain and consequently appeared red. This mountain is situated in an area several miles south of Mink Creek in what is now called the Spatsizi Plateau Wilderness Provincial Park. One must mention, though, that there are several mountains in the park with this reddish, pink-coloured rock.

Encompassing more than 675 000 hectares (1 667 000 acres) the park spreads across the Spatsizi Plateau and the Skeena Mountains. The Plateau ranges in elevation from 1600 to 2000 metres and is an undulating panorama of alpine tundra. Anyone hiking into the park should carry an excellent pair of binoculars with which to view caribou, mountain goats and sheep on the open mountainsides.

In June 2001, my brother Clarence and his wife Olga spent two weeks with me in this remote area and we came away with some lasting memories. Foremost among my memories is the fact that aside from the call of loons and the chatter of the other abundant bird life, there is only a timeless silence that drives home the fact that this is indeed a wilderness area.

Our adventure began after the long drive to Tatogga Lake at Iskut, on Highway 37, about 50 miles south of Dease Lake, BC. At this point we chartered a DeHaviland Beaver aircraft for the 50-mile flight into Cold Fish Lake in the park. Our pilot, Doug Beaumont who flies for Harbour Air, had just arrived back at base from a fishing trip with a 30-pound rainbow trout taken from a nearby lake.

Doug is a veteran flier with many years' experience flying float-

Author with 30-pound rainbow trout, June 2001.

equipped planes. This became apparent when we touched down at Cold Fish Lake, because aside from the change in sound, there was no bump when we touched the water, as is so often the case when one is flying with less-experienced pilots. Once on shore, a Park Ranger met us and introduced himself as a Tahltan Indian named Curtis. He pointed out that he was proud to work for Parks in the land of his forefathers, and I had no trouble believing that he belonged there. A few hours later, the park attendants left in the aircraft and except for a lone hiker named John Bartlett, a vacationing letter carrier from Terrace, we were on our own in this land of silence.

Just prior to this trip, Clarence and Olga had suffered through a long session of flu and cold, so they were in no condition to go hiking during our first few days in camp. Consequently, I found myself going on a hike with John during our second day at the lake. We climbed up through Danihue Pass into the Eaglenest Mountains, but because of heavy cloud and a light rain, we were forced to turn back at the highest point on the trail. This endless cycle of cloud and rain persisted throughout most of our 12-day stay.

I'm not complaining about the weather, though, because just as the mosquitoes were coming out in droves, a snowstorm dropped three inches of snow on the area and wiped them all out. This was a blessed relief to us but it sure puzzled the barn swallows that are so abundant in the area. They spent a great deal of time flying around without catching any feed for their young so anxiously waiting with open beaks for the food that never came.

An interesting phenomenon lies directly across Cold Fish Lake from the camp. It is called Airplane Valley, so named because it often fooled people into believing an aircraft was coming. This valley with its many streams is aimed like a giant speaker right at the camp, and it certainly came by its name honestly. This valley is an easy two-hour hike from the camp on an easy-to-follow trail.

On my third day at the lake, I came down with the flu and cold; weak as I was, though, I was determined to go hiking almost every day. I thought I might just as well be sick in the forest as in the cabin at Cold Fish Lake.

We tried our hand at fishing several times, but it appeared to be too early in the season, as the lake had just been ice-free for a few weeks. Not deterred, though, we spent several hours in an attempt to climb the Spatsizi Plateau, a broad plateau that stretches for miles just north of the camp at Cold Fish Lake. In our sick and weakened condition we had a

Author on Spatsizi Plateau with Cold Fish Lake and Eaglenest Mountains in the background.

tough hike up the plateau and finally settled for just a glimpse of the area and a rather prolonged look at the upper portion of Black Fox Creek. This area is an important wintering area for caribou, in that it is in the rain-shadow of the Eaglenest Mountains, and therefore relatively little snowpack develops.

In one area we walked through, I noticed an almost unbelievable amount of moose droppings in what was obviously their winter range; in fact, going by the amount of sign, I would put this up against any moose wintering area I have ever seen. It was also a common sight to see moose swimming Cold Fish Lake.

A few days before we left the area, Clarence and I decided to walk through the Gladys Lake Ecological Reserve. This was about an eight-mile round trip walk on brushed-in trails flooded with water from the endless rains. I was disappointed that we were unable to see the peak of Mount Will because it was socked in with cloud. This mountain towers 2500 metres and is the highest peak in the Eaglenest Mountains.

As we moved along through the willow thickets we were quite startled to see an animal close in front of us. Because of its large size, we both mistook it for a cub grizzly. It was sweet relief when we recognized it as a porcupine, because we were much too close for comfort if it had been a cub bear.

Cold Fish Lake Camp and the Eaglenest Mountains.

On our return trip from Gladys Lake, we took a wrong turn and ended up on a game trail that slowly petered out on us until we were left with no trail at all. Fortunately I had taken a compass shot on a mountain before we left on the hike, and working off that bearing we came out dead on target. It was a good feeling, to say the least, and it serves to show that no one should head into this remote area without a compass and adequate maps of the area they intend to hike through.

For hikers in good physical condition, there are two trails leading into the park. These trails are found by taking the Ealue Lake Road from Tatogga Lake for 22 km to where it crosses the Klappan River and intersects the old BC Rail Grade. Then one heads south to the 28-km trailhead sign. From that point the McEwan Trail heads east and involves about a two-day hike to Cold Fish Lake.

The other trail is reached by continuing along the BC Rail Grade to 50 km, where the Eaglenest Trail heads generally east until it reaches the southern end of Danihue Pass. At this point the trail splits: one branch goes through the Pass to Cold Fish Camp—this is an easy three-day hike (about 50 km). The other branch goes through the Ecological Reserve to Gladys Lake and then to Mink Creek which must be forded. From there the trail follows the lake back to the camp which is about a five-mile walk. This is considered a four-day trip for the average hiker. It must be remembered, though, that no fires or camping are allowed in the reserve, requiring additional planning, as the trip through the reserve is about 15 km.

But for those with less time or energy and more money, the aircraft is the way to go. There are excellent cabins for rent at Cold Fish Camp for $10 per day or $25 per day for a family. These cabins hold anywhere from five to nine people and are on a "first come, first serve" basis. There is a time limit—individuals can only stay at the camp for seven consecutive days or a total of fourteen days in any one-year period. A letter-of-authority must be obtained from the Parks' Office in Smithers, before anyone is allowed to enter the park by aircraft or with horses. In fact, all persons planning to enter the park should consult with BC Parks, as they may have information of washouts or of streams that are too high to ford due to heavy rains.

The hazards of flying this area have been demonstrated several

Clarence, Olga and author at Black Fox Creek.

times by crashed aircraft. A badly damaged airplane float was just recently dug out of the ground at Cold Fish Lake and flown back to base at Tatogga Lake by pilot Doug Beaumont.

There are numerous trails to hike and some time should be set aside for watching mountain goats and sheep on the surrounding mountains. Black and grizzly bears frequent the area, and although we didn't see any, I did see their tracks.

Another asset to staying at the camp is the availability of first class drinking water which is piped down to the camp. This is as good as any water I have ever tasted, and we always packed some with us on our hikes.

When our stay was over and the aircraft returned for us, I felt a tinge of sorrow; I took a long look around before leaving, well aware that I may never pass this way again. I had taken the book, *Spatsizi* by Tommy Walker, along to read and it helped me understand the area and appreciate the problems they had to deal with some fifty years earlier. Tommy and his wife Marion moved into the Spatsizi in 1948 where they began guiding; they spent the next two decades in this activity and were in large part responsible for the forming of the park and adjacent ecological reserve. A memorial in their honor stands near the lake's edge at the Cold Fish Camp.

But all things must come to an end, and as we winged our way back

The pontoon of an airplane that crashed at Cold Fish Lake.

through the mountains, our pilot Doug was nice enough to give us an extra bonus with a view of some of the rugged mountains in and near the park. As I gazed down on the precipitous peaks I remembered a story I had read about this area, and I think it is a very appropriate way to end the story of Spatsizi. It was carried in the *Prince George Citizen* long before the Walkers ever visited the Spatsizi area. The article was dated December 10, 1918:

TRAGEDY OF TRAPPER IS TOLD IN DIARY
Charlie Spencer dies in lonely cabin far from the haunts of men

"Records in the form of a diary now in the hands of Government Agent Hoskins' tell a story of the terrible suffering and lonely tragic death of Charlie Spencer in an isolated cabin between Groundhog Pass and Telegraph Creek, says the Interior News. *Spencer was a familiar figure around Hazelton, owning a pre-emption in the Upper Kispiox, and more recently being employed at the Hazelton Vie mine.*

"His decomposed body was found by a hunter lying on the floor of the cabin. Spencer had kept a diary and on one page stated that he had only three matches left. In one of his pockets was found two matches, and from this it is taken that he died shortly afterwards. According to the diary Spencer was taken down about the middle of March with muscular rheumatism. Early in May he improved and made an effort to come out.

The Walker cabin at Cold Fish Lake.

From his main cabin to the cabin where he died is a distance of 35 miles and it occupied five days. The diary further notes:

'I had to leave my sleigh about two miles from the cabin, just above the divide between the Skeena and Spatsizi rivers. My furs lashed on the sleigh consist of six silver fox, 22 cross fox, 14 marten, four lynx, two wolves, six ermine and one mink. Whoever finds this please take it to Hazelton and give it to C.V. Smith, who will see that my bills are paid.'

'I have now been here close on one month, and have not been able to leave the cabin. When I am lying down and warm, I seem to feel no pain, but oh, God, when I get up and try to cook something for myself the pain is unbearable. I have been able to cook but one hot cake a day for myself. If I only had someone to cook for me I might be all right. At times it seems the struggle to live is too hard. Now, whoever finds this try to find my furs. You can't miss them if you look close. Good Luck. C. A. Spencer'"

The hunter found the furs, most of which were spoiled; but the most heart-wrenching part of this story is the fact that even though he was dying, Spencer's last thought was to pay his debts to others.

6 Bears

DURING THE MONTH OF MAY 1929, EIGHT PEOPLE LEFT PRINCE GEORGE on an expedition. They drove to Summit Lake and then boated their way downstream to the Peace River where they split into two groups: four people headed down the Peace, and the other four went up the Finlay River past Fort Ware. Eventually one group arrived at the Fox River and followed it upstream, through Sifton Pass to the Liard River. Among this group was Mr. and Mrs. Davidson and two friends. After they reached the Liard, they rented some horses from Skook Davidson, a rancher, packer and wilderness guide. With the aid of the horses, they made their way to the beautiful Kechika Valley, where they spent the winter of 1929-30 trapping.

On March 7, 1930, a son was born to the Davidsons, and he was named Sifton, after the Pass. Shortly after his birth, his mother came down with milk fever, which put the family in a dangerous position. All they had for the baby was seven cans of condensed milk, which they carefully rationed. With the aid of dried fruit and mush, they managed to keep the child alive until his mother was able to nurse again.

Stories such as this were common about a century ago; they serve to show the important part women played in the development of this country. Often overlooked in history, they were every bit as tough as the men they traveled with; in cases of starvation, it was often the women that survived while the men perished.

The Davidsons were brought into the picture for another reason, and that has to do with grizzly bears. Mr. Davidson, who spent many years in the wilderness, knew of a situation that appears to confirm a story in *Grizzly Bear Mountain*. This story tells of a lone grizzly that teamed up with a lone wolf. The Davidsons' story was witnessed several times along an inlet near the BC coast. About every ten days this bear and wolf would make their rounds, and on one occasion the trapper watched as the wolf came out into an opening in the forest. It looked the area over to be certain there was no danger, and then the grizzly emerged into the open. When it came time to feed on the moose carcass, the grizzly fed first; when it was finished, the wolf moved in and ate its fill. The old trapper went one further by saying that this was not the only time this happened—that he had heard of it from other woodsmen as well.

I have previously mentioned that throughout the years I have found carcasses of moose and black bears that were buried by grizzlies, and that I was surprised in some cases when the bears never returned to feed again. Since that time I have had a woodsman suggest a possible reason for their actions. He suspects that a wolverine happened by and sprayed its scent on the carcasses; he suggested that the bears could have returned only to leave in disgust. I have to admit that his observation merits serious consideration.

I must correct an error in *Grizzly Bear Mountain.* In it I mentioned that the big grizzly taken by Herb Metzmeier had a twelve-inch hind foot, the largest I had ever measured. It should have been twelve and one-half inches, and make no mistake, this can make a considerable difference in the size of a bear.

Another subject I dealt with in my book was the ability of bears to pick up sound through the ground. I wish to expand on this a little more. Sometimes a group of people will walk right up to a bear without it paying notice. There are so many possibilities involved in these situations that one could belabor it all day and still not take everything into consideration. But a few points must be mentioned. If people are walking on soft ground such as deep humus, the sound doesn't travel as well. Alternately, if a bear is standing on soft ground it doesn't pick up the sound as well. Also among the possibilities is the chance that the bear has recently picked up the scent of other animals in the area, and it believes they are the cause of the vibrations. We must also remember that the continual movement of her young seriously hampers the detection ability of a grizzly with cubs or yearlings.

The one case that stands out in my memory was the time my brother Clarence and I walked across a mountain and then stopped to watch a grizzly with cubs feeding half a mile distant. When our hiking buddy followed us, the mother bear picked up the vibrations of his footsteps and left the area. It seems obvious that Clarence and I sent out more vibrations walking together than our partner did by walking alone, so this begs the question as to why the bears didn't leave at our approach. The obvious answer is that there were four feet hitting the ground when Clarence and I walked, but only two when our friend walked, and so a totally different rhythm. These bears know that only one creature walks on two legs, and that particular rhythm doesn't belong high in the mountains in their territory. The fact that bears more readily accept the vibrations sent out by animals, all of which have four feet, explains why it is easier to approach bears while on horseback.

But the most likely reason for a bear's lack of concern, in my experience, is that the bear knows there are other bears around. This is especially true with grizzlies high in the mountains. They simply cannot run every time they sense something near them, or else they'll spend a lot of time in flight. It is humorous, though, to see a grizzly go tearing away across a mountain because it has heard an echo of its own activity.

Another thing I want to address is bear-human conflict, and just how tough humans can be. This was especially true of the early pioneers, so I have chosen a few stories from early newspapers that emphasize this point.

On June 1, 1912, an article was carried in the *Fort George Herald* and Quesnel's *Cariboo Observer* stating that a man named Ben Murray had been attacked by a grizzly while out walking. And that he had been taken to Quesnel for treatment of head lacerations and the loss of an eye.

Three weeks later a letter was received by the *Observer* from a man named Alex Moffat (who later owned the Northern Hardware in Prince George). Alex resided at Stoney Creek, Nechako, at the time:

"Dear Sir—I noticed a statement in your paper some time ago where a man by the name of Ben Murray had been badly handled by a grizzly bear, and had lost one eye, while walking along a trail in this vicinity.

"I wish to state that Joe Murray, the man you must have meant, although badly torn about the face, did not lose his eye, and is now quite recovered from his awful experience.

"Mr. Murray, who walked 40 miles to the nearest pre-emptor

[homesteader] after he was attacked, presented a pitiable spectacle after his long journey over swamps, dead falls, and the rough country through which he had to come. He was quite exhausted, and would surely never have withstood the journey through to Quesnel. He fortunately fell into the hands of a trained nurse, Mrs. Lamont, and although he had over 50 wounds and scratches on his body—one on his head which required thirteen stitches, and another above the eye which required five—he does not seem to be any the worse today, and says he will get that bear yet."

The following year another article was carried in the *Herald* of August 25, 1912:

ATTACKED BY A GRIZZLY

"Duncan McIntosh, a prospector well known in South Fort George, nearly lost his life in a struggle with a grizzly bear at Hunter's Basin near Telkwa, recently. The bear forced his way into the cabin where McIntosh was sleeping. Mr. McIntosh awoke and fired at the intruder, but not before he was badly bitten and clawed. Exhausted and bleeding, he walked 17 miles to Telkwa. The body of the grizzly was found near the cabin."

Something that should be pointed out, especially to the inexperienced, is the danger involved in trailing wounded bears. As bears are hunters themselves, they know a few tricks about the woods. Steve Wlasitz, a veteran of the Second World War, described what can happen to people engaged in

Steve Wlasitz with black wolf at Lindup, circa 1950.

trailing wounded bears. During the month of May 1952, two hunters named Roland Gascon and Steve Gaal were driving the Pass Lake Road north of Sinclair Mills, BC, when they spotted a grizzly bear beside the road. It was feeding on the remains of a moose that had been taken the previous fall. Both men got out and fired at the bear, which, though hit, ran away into the forest. The men gave chase along the bear's trail, which was easy to follow in the remaining snow. After following its trail for about half a mile, the men decided to give up, as it was starting to get dark.

The following morning the two men returned to the scene with Steve, who was already an experienced bear hunter. They reached the spot where the men had quit the previous evening and then went just a short distance further where they made a chilling find. They found where the bear had made a circle the previous evening and doubled back beside its own trail. A pool of blood showed that the bear had waited for them for several hours before moving on. If the two men had gone just a short distance further the previous evening the bear would surely have attacked them from behind. As soon as the men got over their shock,

Steve Wlasitz with grizzly circa 1946

they proceeded to follow the bear again, making certain that they were spread out and prepared for any more tricks. After a short walk, they heard a loud roar, and then Steve, who was in front, dropped the bear with three shots. The bear had been bedded down and was much weakened from loss of blood.

Steve had another confrontation with a grizzly that he found camped on a deer carcass. This occurred in the mountains behind Lindup, a tiny ghost town just west of Penny. Although alone at the time he wounded it, Steve had the courage to follow it through the snow. He took great care to see that it had emerged from a thicket before he continued on past that thicket. Eventually he made out the shape of the bear and fired only to have the bear let out a roar and stand erect. At this point he dropped it.

Steve is in total agreement with my estimates of grizzly bear numbers. He states emphatically that there are far more grizzlies now than there was back in the 40s and 50s. It was common to spend days around timberline back then without seeing any bears.

Retired guide and trapper Glen Hooker of Dome Creek also agrees. He spent five years guiding with his father back in the 40s before he saw his first grizzly.

Several of these guides offered an important point that I totally agree with. Wounded bears will almost always circle downwind. This is by design rather than by accident, as the bear wants to get the scent of whatever is trailing it. Make no mistake about it—the wind is a bear's best friend.

Many people in the Prince George area may remember the story of Harvey Cardinal who fought a losing battle with a grizzly. The story was carried in the *Citizen* of January 16, 1970:

GRIZZLY EATS INDIAN GUIDE

"Fort St. John, BC.—RCMP Thursday night released the name of a big-game hunting guide who was killed and partly eaten earlier by the grizzly bear he was hunting in dense forest 35 miles north of this northern British Columbia community.

Harvey Cardinal, 40, of the nearby Doig River Indian Reserve, was found dead in 60 below weather, his mitts still on his hands and the safety catch on his rifle still engaged. Senior Conservation Officer John MacKill, who went to the scene with RCMP after Mr. Cardinal's body was found by friends, said it was the first time he knew of a grizzly eating a human instead of only mauling or killing."

Three days later the story continued:

SLAIN GRIZZLY HATED WORLD

"Fort St. John, BC—The grizzly bear which killed and partly devoured a man near here last week, probably hated the world—with good reason. It was old and fight-scarred, had broken teeth, a serious gum infection, a piece of its right paw torn off and it was hungry. These findings were made on Sunday by an autopsy on the bear after it had been tracked by helicopter, and shot last week in rugged wilderness about 40 miles north of here.

"The bear was shot in the Doig River area last Friday, 24 hours after the partially-eaten body of hunting guide Harvey Cardinal, 40, of Fort St. John was discovered in dense bush. Tracks in the snow where the body was discovered showed the bear had stalked his victim from behind and killed him without a struggle."

"Fred Harper, a regional wildlife biologist for the Peace River district, said about a dozen men went into the bush on snowmobiles Saturday to haul the bear to Fort St. John. 'It was a very old bear with badly worn teeth that were cracked and broken,' said Mr. Harper. 'It had a serious gum infection and a two-inch section of its right front paw was torn off.' Mr. Harper said the grizzly, an old male over 6-feet long, which weighed about 575 pounds, had several long and deep scars on its face. 'They were very bad wounds. The only thing that could have done that was another bear. He was a fighter, and in pretty bad shape.'

"Mr. Harper said the bear's stomach contained part of a shirt, human hair and bones. 'He was obviously hungry, but fat as a pig with two or three inches of fat on him. We don't know why he would have been out in the weather and not hibernating.' Mr. Harper said that the bear was first seen last week by two Indians who were cutting firewood near the Doig Reserve. 'They told Harvey Cardinal about it and since grizzly hides are valuable this time of year, Harvey went out Thursday to get the bear.' When the hunter failed to return, a search party went out Friday and found his partially eaten body.

"Beginning where the body was found, Mr. Harper and Gordon Gosling, chief conservation officer for the area, began following the bear's snow tracks by helicopter, flying almost at tree-top level. When they spotted the bear, the men felled it with shots from a heavy-caliber rifle and a slug-loaded shotgun. The hunt, however, almost claimed another human life. Conservation officer John MacKill suffered serious head injuries when struck by a rear rotor of the helicopter after getting out of the craft to inspect the dead bear. Mr. MacKill was in fair condition at Vancouver General Hospital after weekend surgery."

I discussed this case with Harry Chingee, former chief of the McLeod Lake Band—and he said he had trouble believing that Harvey had been attacked from behind. As Harvey was an experienced guide who had previously guided for him, Harry was willing to bet that his gun froze up and would not fire. Regardless of what happened in those final seconds, I think it is safe to say that the bear had everything in his favour. The -60f temperature guaranteed that Harvey had his ears covered thus causing his hearing to be impaired. The bear coming at him from behind in the soft snow may have made little or no noise. As for the reason the bear was out of its den, I believe it was because of the gum infection and other wounds. It would have been unable to sleep because of the pain.

Charlie Springer and Virgil Brandner with a golden-coloured black bear, easily mistaken for a grizzly bear.

Harvey was just one of many people that have been attacked by boar grizzlies and quickly killed. It only confirms what I have always believed: sow grizzlies maul people with the maulings sometimes resulting in death; boar grizzly attacks usually result in death, and often the death occurs within the first few seconds.

Another grizzly attack, also resulting in death, occurred in October 2000. Cy Ford, a guide out of Fort St. James, was the victim. With 35 years experience in the guiding business, one would think that he would be hard to fool, but somehow the grizzly got him. This event took place near Nutli Lake, about 240 km southwest of Prince George, after his American client wounded a large male grizzly that got away into the forest. Cy gave chase and then failed to return to camp that evening. Ground and air searches were launched, but failed to find any trace of the guide. The next day a search party found the body, as well as the carcass of the grizzly.

If we learn anything from this tragedy, it should clearly show us that there is no such thing as an expert where grizzlies are concerned. I don't believe the person ever lived who could truthfully say a grizzly couldn't get him. One reason I feel this way is because two of the best woodsmen I've ever known were killed by grizzlies. After a lifetime of wandering the forests, hunting and studying grizzlies, I humbly suggest that it is bad luck more than good management that decides who gets mauled and who doesn't.

In order to lighten things up a little, I want to move back in time and relate a different and rather humorous version of a grizzly hunt that was carried in the *Citizen* of November 18, 1937:

"J. Travis was hunting in the Dunster Mountains, accompanied by local settler Mr. Russell, when he shot a caribou. While trying to prepare the carcass for transport down the mountain, a grizzly appeared and put up an argument as to the ownership. Failing to scare the grizzly away with a shot, both hunters happened to remember that they never cared for caribou meat anyway and relinquished all ownership rights. Without much effort they arrived at the foot of the mountain in a surprisingly short time."

The report that a white bear had been shot at Rock Creek in southern BC elicited a response from a guide named A. E. Read of Longworth, BC. It was carried in the *Citizen* dated November 25, 1937:

"A pure white grizzly was shot at Longworth in mid-winter 1913-14. A trapper named Fred Berg found it feeding on a moose he had killed and had to shoot quickly as it came for him. This is exactly the same condition under which Meany was killed by a grizzly north of here about ten years ago.

"There is the possibility that another white grizzly may be found as some of the grizzlies on Toneko Mountain [Bearpaw Ridge] have large patches of pure white on them . . . "

Mr. Read also added that trapper Fred Berg referred to the animal as a polar bear.

Since many people were unaware of albinos in the early days, similar stories of albinos were treated as tall tales; the originators treated as people to be laughed at. As for the bears with patches of white on them, they were just normal grizzlies, many of which have silvery patches on them.

Many years ago a biologist named Al Oeming came out with a theory about the Swan Hills grizzly bears. The basis of this theory centered on an isolated pocket of grizzly bears that inhabited the Swan Hills area of Alberta. These bears supposedly were remnants of the Plains' grizzlies. The fact that these bears were larger than bears throughout the general area played a part in his theory. If this will ever become a proven fact, I will certainly sit down and eat humble pie, because I have never believed it for a second. First off, I have seen the places that grizzlies go in the mountains, and I don't believe there can be such a thing as an isolated area—unless it is an island a few hundred km offshore. I also believe that it is the food supply in an area and the length of the feeding season that determines the size of bears, especially over a long period of time.

There is another point I want to make about grizzlies. During all the years that we watched grizzlies around the area of Grizzly Bear Mountain one thing became apparent—though there may have been eight or ten yearling boars with their mothers in late fall, the next fall we were lucky to find one or two of these boars in the area as two-year-olds. I feel certain that these young boars are moved out of the area by older bears that constantly put the run on them, until they get the message and search for a new range somewhere else. In what may be credible support of this idea, a young boar grizzly tagged north of Prince George, was killed a few years later near Houston, about 200 km distant from where it was tagged.

Just recently I was thinking about two-year-old grizzlies leaving the areas where they were born, when I was struck with what may be an obvious answer to something that has puzzled me almost all of my life. Several times I have watched mid-sized grizzlies chase what appeared to be three-year-olds. In one case I knew it was a sow doing the chasing because when she returned from the chase, she had two cubs waiting for her. I now believe that the three-year-old may have been her previous cub and that it was attempting to return to the fold. If it is true that they do try to return to the fold, then maybe sometimes they are successful. Perhaps if they hang around long enough the mother will eventually accept them back into the family unit. This could explain the cases where people have seen, as I have, what appears to be a three-year-old and cubs in the same family unit. Since a mother grizzly will not allow another bear near her cubs, the previous cub concept is the only explanation I can think of to explain the three different age groups traveling together.

A point I must make about grizzlies concerns people going into the mountains and not seeing any grizzlies, even though it is prime habitat. I know from experience that many people scare the bears away by making their presence known one way or another. Another reason for not seeing them is because it is common for the grizzlies to be absent from the alpine area during August. This is when they are on the salmon streams and in the berry patches, often until almost mid-September weather permitting.

People who take a great interest in bears may be interested in the following story. It details the problems created when humans feed bears and they get habituated. While this is fairly well documented, especially in parks, the problems involved with landfill garbage sites are not so well known. A controversial study was conducted on such a site, the results of which are titled "*Landfill Closure to Garbage Habituated Grizzly Bears. The Mackenzie Experience*" by Andrew MacKay.

This study was conducted over a three-year period, in which an electric fence had been placed around the Mackenzie landfill dump in an attempt to force habituated bears away from the site and back to their natural food. The conservation officers (COs) were in for several surprises, though: first, they found many more habituated grizzlies feeding at the site than the 30 full-time residents that were compiled in a 1991 study. Secondly, an unexpectedly large number of migrating fall grizzlies had also become habituated. As well, they were also surprised to find the bears moving into the nearby town of Mackenzie after the landfill closure, where they were drawn to curbside garbage as well as fruit trees and other attractants such as grass on the golf course. This presented more risk of bear/human conflict than the original landfill site.

Although the Mackenzie dump had been in operation for almost 30 years, a few important changes had taken place. During the earlier years, black bears frequented the dump to a great extent, and they would usually flee at the approach of the grizzlies. My sister Margaret lived in Mackenzie during the early years of the landfill and relates how they often went to the dump in the evening to watch bears. The black bears would feed until evening when the grizzlies would arrive; then the blacks would scamper in all directions. There was one exception, though, a large black that had an injured leg would sometimes refuse to run away. On one occasion they saw it fight with a sub-adult grizzly. The black bear held its own and the grizzly ended up leaving it alone.

But toward the 90s, the black bears stopped coming to the landfill. It is my belief that the reason for this was because of an increase in grizzly bear populations in those years.

In response to the invasion of grizzlies into the town, COs had no choice but to start trapping, tranquilizing and relocating bears out of the area, with many bears being destroyed outright. This program required enormous effort and proved to be a failure. Between June 22 to 29, 1993, ten grizzlies were handled. While a total of fifteen bears were captured, five of them were returned bears that had been relocated by vehicle 60 km to the west. A single sow returned within 12 days, a sow with two yearlings took 17 days, and a sub-adult male took 57 days.

From 1992 to 1994, the COs in Mackenzie destroyed or relocated 25 grizzlies from the landfill and town-site and estimated that there were still up to a dozen feeding at the landfill in the fall of 1994. The electric fence was activated in April 1995, without any bear problems during the summer in the town-site. But in September, there were 120 complaints in 49 days. During this time 43 grizzlies were destroyed or relocated.

People storing curbside garbage the day before pickup brought on much of the townsite problem. As well, there were many dumpsters that were not bear-proofed.

From September 1 to October 18, 1995, a total of 43 grizzlies were captured in or near Mackenzie. Seven were flown 150 km north. A sow had to be destroyed when her two-year-old got caught in the trap. This bear weighed 350 pounds, a drop of 150 pounds since she had been relocated the previous year.

The 1994 bear relocation by helicopter to remote areas had been considered a success until two of the bears returned. The 1993 relocation by vehicle program had been a complete failure. Of the bears that did not return, little hope was held for their successful relocation and survival.

During September and continuing through October 1995, 120 complaints were received from the town residents. This resulted in 43 grizzlies being removed, all but 17 from the townsite. One humorous story emerged when a grizzly outsmarted COs by diving into traps while still leaving his feet out. When the trap was set off it would hit his feet, allowing him to remove the bait without getting caught. This 800-pound male was the largest encountered throughout the program and was believed responsible for taking a quarter of a moose from a shed. He also chased a resident returning home from work one night.

With this great influx of bears, it seems miraculous that there were no serious confrontations or maulings. In one instance children were seen chasing two yearlings along the street with sticks, unaware that mama was following along behind them. In another case, children were throwing rocks at a grizzly that was feeding on berries in a trailer court. When ordered to desist, they refused, and police had to be brought to the area to stop them. The situation was certainly ripe for disaster.

MacKay points out:

"Many residents spent sleepless nights as bears noisily roamed their yards at all hours. In total, six fences and several crab apple trees sustained extensive damage. A sundeck and a shed containing a moose were moderately damaged. Numerous complaints of grizzly bears in carports, on decks, and in back and front yards were received. Complaints of grizzly bears looking through house windows were common. As well, two residents reported

being followed by grizzly bears. Considering the unnaturally high number of habituated bears in such a small area, the townsite was fortunate not to have experienced human injuries or fatalities during this time."

It has generally been agreed upon that trans-locations of garbage habituated bears is unsuccessful. During the Mackenzie experiment one bear returned emaciated and in poor health; others lost a great deal of weight. Bear expert Stephen Herrero refers to trans-location as not much more than a holding action.

In summary, between 1992-95, sixty-seven grizzlies were removed from the townsite and landfill area. Of the 67 bears handled, 63 were confirmed dead. The largest boar grizzly reported weighed 800 pounds, and the largest sow reported weighed 500 pounds.

Many residents of Mackenzie were upset with the entire program. Some felt that the COs and biologists had forced the bears into town by the landfill closure. In view of the low incidence of human/bear conflict prior to the closure, one mauling reported before the closure, they may well have been right. One resident felt that a possibility that didn't receive consideration was moving the landfill several miles distant from the community.

As for bear-proofing the community, this will always be doomed to failure. Carried to its ultimate conclusion, this would not allow people to have gardens or fruit trees and would in effect make people prisoners in their own homes. The effort to get the townspeople to pick all the fruit off the mountain ash and crabapple trees seemed counterproductive. Since the bears were in the townsite anyway, wasn't it better that they ate berries rather than have entered into homes when they smelled food being prepared?

If we start telling people what they can and cannot do on their own property, are we not walking down a slippery slope? Is the day soon coming when farmers will not be allowed to plant clover to feed their stock, because it is a favorite food of bears? Will it soon be against the law to have a lawn because green grass is a favorite food of bears? Please don't force people to destroy or pick all the berries off their mountain ash trees; they add such beauty to the city in late fall!

A most interesting event took place near Houston BC on October 3, 2001. Two wildlife personnel managed to bag a huge grizzly that had been killing cattle in the area. They set a cable snare near one of the dead cows and caught the bear. When Kevin Nixon and Brad Lacey approached to check the snare, the huge bear broke free and attacked them—this provided the two men with some heart-stopping thrills. Fortunately both men were armed—Kevin with a 30.06 and Brad with a .338—and after several bullets were fired they brought the beast to earth. It didn't take very long for the men to realize that they had bagged an exceptionally large bear. The weight, not counting blood loss, was 1012 pounds (459 kg). The circumference of the neck was 44 inches.

Kevin informed me that the bear had six inches of fat over its hindquarters and fully four inches over the brisket area. He added that in September 1996, they had trapped a grizzly at the Hazelton dump that weighed 858 pounds, but that he had never seen anything to compare with this giant.

Roger Britton, the Smithers' taxidermist who is in the process of full-mounting the giant, told me that this was by far the largest bear they have ever came across. For several years Roger and his father, Roger Sr, have advertised that they would full-mount for free any grizzly that honestly squared over nine feet. They never dreamed that one day they

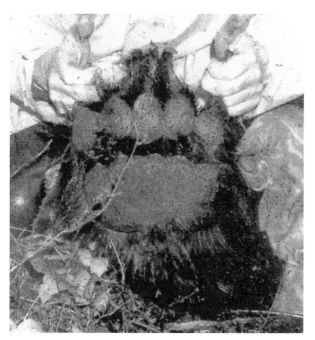

would be required to do just that. But that is now the case, because this grizzly squared out an inch and one-half over the nine foot mark. The span across the chest, front claw to front claw was ten feet, four inches.

Big grizzly front paw.

Roger explained that they purchased the largest Alaskan brown bear form available anywhere in the world and still they have to add eight inches to the girth of the form in order to make it large enough to accommodate this huge bear. The strangest thing about this bear is that its front pad width was only seven inches, and this really shocked me. I suspect an error. The hand measurement across the knuckles of the man holding the pad is—give or take a fraction—three and one-half inches. And since there is little difference in this measurement among men of average size, I have often used this formula to cut the bull out of exaggerated animal sizes. Yet when I use this in the photograph as a comparison, the bear's pad measures eight inches.

When my nephew, Larry Boudreau, first told me about this bear and how much it weighed, I told him two things: first, that the bear's front pad would be about eight inches straight across, and also, that it would be dark to black in colour. I was right about the colour—it was black with a beautiful orange collar around its neck—but I was well off on the size of the front pad if Roger's measurements are accurate. Roger admits he was shocked at the unusually small size of its front feet in comparison to its huge body. Surprisingly, the skull measurements are not in the top of the Boone and Crockett records. The exceptional size of the body may be explained by the diet that this bear enjoyed, probably for several years.

In an article written for *Beef in BC*, Sharon Kerr quoted Kevin Nixon as saying that the front pad was between eight to nine inches across, and that the measurement nose to tail was nine feet and one inch. This is an obvious error because the grizzly bear never lived that made that length. Roger gives that measurement as seven feet and eleven inches. Why is it so difficult to get conformity on the sizes of bear hides and tracks?

There is a side story to this tale. It seems that the Northwestern Guides and Outfitters Association gave Kevin a present which included a porta-potti, a pair of shorts and two rolls of toilet paper, along with a note that read. "For future hunts." I like these people—I admire their sense of humour.

And what is to become of this bear? Apparently this magnificent beast will be staring down from its lofty height and scaring travelers in the airport at Smithers.

I find it interesting that the method used to dispatch the cattle was

Cattle-killer, 459 kg.

the same technique often employed by lions to kill their prey. The big bear would pull his prey to the ground and then cover its nose and mouth with his, thus suffocating them. As well, this bear was a night killer, apparently killing under cover of darkness. It is possible that this bear had some previous bad experiences with humans, as this often leads to an educated bear that will feed and travel under cover of darkness. Had it not been for the snare this bear may never have been taken.

I want to make a point regarding the colour of large boar grizzlies. When I think back to all the exceptionally large Interior boar grizzlies I have seen, as well as the old photographs I have seen, one thing becomes apparent: almost without exception the true giant boar grizzlies have been dark to black. Although I have seen a few very large brown boars, they are not in the top ten, so to speak.

On August 30, 2001, another giant night-feeding bear was taken in Manitoba. This was a black bear, which must surely be the world's record. The bear was hit and disabled by a Mazda car while making its way to an area dump to feed. In what was a surprisingly honest observation, Conservation Officer Doug Shindler stated that the average male black bear weighs about 300 pounds, a statement I completely agree with. As for this giant, it weighed in at 886 pounds. In the pictures it

The huge bear broke the snare cable and attacked.

appears to be half as wide as it is long. There can be no doubt—this bear ate well.

Throughout the many years that I spent watching and studying grizzly bears, three young were the most I ever found in a family. Yet during the month of September 2000, several groups of fishermen along the Babine River reported seeing a grizzly with four yearlings. In one instance a Prince George fisherman named Dan Schlitt watched as they chased his nephew, Chris, away from the stream. I found these sightings to be surprising because of all the old woodsmen I talked with, not one reported seeing a grizzly with more than three young. In fact, several told me that they seldom seen a mother with more than two young. This fits in with what I observed in the mountains during the 1950s. Perhaps the large families that are so prevalent now are a direct result of the logged-off cut blocks that provide such an abundance of food for these creatures.

For some strange reason humans have an endless series of love affairs with carnivores. First there was the all-consuming affair with wolves—to the point where they could do no wrong. In fact, one pseudo-expert had the public and many in governments believing that wolves lived on mice and didn't bother the ungulates at all. Some other experts tried to convince us that they only preyed on the old and weak. Several different studies have shown these "experts" to be far off base.

Forgive me for saying that I have little time for "experts" and the reason may be because of what an "expert" is. Since x is an unknown quantity and a spurt is a drip under pressure, it is small wonder that "experts" repeatedly contradict each other.

The real experts—the trappers and guides that lived among the wild—always knew the truth of the matter.

Moving on from the wolf problem, a save-the-black-bear program got underway. This, when the forests were crawling with black bears. By their own statistics, wildlife officials state that they had to put down "almost twice as many bears this year [2001] in the Prince George area as they did the year before."

Now it is the grizzly that is the center of attention. Someday, perhaps, we will attempt to look at nature as a whole, and not put one animal above others, as we have been doing with grizzly bears, and it is being justified by pretending that bear populations are in trouble.

I realize that there are some biologists out there that are proclaiming the impending extinction of the grizzly. But this is not a new phenomenon in society.

My own experience tells me that only during the 1960s were their numbers even close to what they are today. I further believe that poisoning the wolves in the 1950s was a contributing factor in that increase. Prior to the poisoning campaign, the wolves and coyotes had cleaned up the majority of train-killed moose, as well as the moose that had drowned along the rivers, by the time the bears began eating carrion, in some cases as long as one month after they emerged from their dens. After the wolf-poisoning program these carcasses were left for the bears, especially the carcasses that were covered with snow on the shady side of the grade. But putting that aside, I mainly go by the sign they leave in the mountains because this allows for the fact that bears may be less nocturnal now than when they were being hunted to a great degree. There is no question in my mind—there is much more digging sign in the mountains now than there was years ago.

During the first ten years that I traveled the area of Grizzly Bear Mountain, I didn't see many bears. The amount of digging was minimal and to see two families of bears on a two- or three-day trip was something to brag about. The last few years it is common to see ten to twenty bears in a single day. To those who doubt, I must point out that during the month of September 2000, a filmmaker from the USA spent less than two days at Grizzly Bear Mountain and got pictures of 22 grizzlies. Local writer Mike Nash has a copy of the film in his possession. As well, Mike has seen my videos, one of which show 17 grizzlies on the side of Grizzly Bear Mountain at the same time.

But to those who still feel that grizzlies are endangered, may I suggest that if we protect the high-density nursery areas such as Grizzly Bear Mountain, we will have gone a long way toward ensuring the survival of this magnificent species.

Do I think the grizzly species will survive? The answer has to be "Yes, if they are given half a chance." There is really nothing new about the grizzly extinction scare, though, as the following article shows. In the *Citizen* dated August 17, 1981, a grizzly bear specialist—Rick Langshaw of Banff, Alberta—noted the impending demise of the grizzly bear, "The population levels are already at critical levels; I'm convinced that the population will be wiped out in one to two decades."

Well the two decades are up and the bears are still there.

Almost a century ago a man named William Hornaday wrote an excellent book, *Campfires in the Canadian Rockies.* It is interesting to note, though, that he too foresaw the extinction of the grizzly bear. These men were hunting in the East Kootenays at the time of the prediction, and although a century has passed since their observations, guides and residents state that there are more grizzlies in that area now than at any time during their lifetimes. It also becomes obvious from reading this book that there were fewer bears back then.

From the time of my childhood, I have always had the greatest respect for grizzlies. By comparison, I cannot say the same for other predators such as cougars. But after an experience I had in 1962 that opinion changed considerably.

It was in August that my brother Clarence and I decided to take our motorbikes for a drive along an old logging road. As it had poured rain for days, the road was wet and muddy. I had a Harley Davidson army bike, which was heavy and hard to handle; this meant that I ended up a considerable distance behind Clarence who had a small bike. Just a short distance into the trip, my bike started sliding around so I gave up and decided to return home. Right at the edge of the community I started down into a small valley and noticed a cougar standing in the middle of the road looking at me. When I got close to it, it jumped off the road and immediately disappeared from view. As I drove into the valley bottom, I stood up on the bike and attempted to peer into the spot where the cougar had jumped. Because I was not watching where I was driving, I drove into a deep rut and got stuck, at which point the bike tipped over. As I was attempting to push the bike out of the ruts, I glanced back to find the cougar standing in the road right behind me. I laid the bike down again and turned to face the cat, not the least bit worried. I was wearing a hard hat at the time, so I took it off and waved it as I took a few running steps forward; at the same time I shouted with all my might, expecting the cougar to take flight. But the cougar didn't budge, instead it glared at me with its ice-cold eyes and I felt shivers run up my spine as I realized that I had just made a terrible mistake. The fact that the cougar didn't run away when I charged it really shocked me; I was not at all prepared for that eventuality.

Then I started backing up around the bike and up the hill; during this time the cougar just stared at me with eyes that didn't appear to blink. The only movement I noticed was a slight turn of its head as it followed my movements. Once I was out of its sight, I turned and ran the hundred meters to the home of Victor Mellows, who accompanied me back to the spot with his rifle in his hands. When we reached the spot, not a trace of the cat could be found, although its tracks were plainly visible in the muddy road. Victor kept a diary throughout those years, and its entry for August 17th told the story of my encounter.

I had another interesting encounter with a cougar, although this one was more in my favor. It began when I set off to visit Roy and Betty Sinclair in the small community of Grasmere in the East Kootenays. At the time I had no idea that I would end up going on a cougar hunt; or that it would turn out to be one of the most humorous trips of my life.

Along with my wife Ann and my son Kelly, I drove to Grasmere, a few miles north of the Montana border. It was April 1967 when we drove to their farm for what I thought would be a few days of R & R.

Shortly after our arrival I learned that Roy had other plans. He confided that his cousin—Bob Totten—had some cougar hounds and that they intended to take me back into the mountains on a cougar hunt the following morning. This was much more than I had hoped for, so I could scarcely wait for the new dawn to arrive. If memory serves me right, I was so anxious that I only dozed off for a few hours during that long night.

The next morning Bob arrived with his hounds and so we drove for several miles in a pickup truck; then continued on with a snowmobile into the Wigwam River area. It didn't take long to find fresh tracks in the remaining snow, but Roy and Bob quickly realized that they were made by a wolverine instead of a cougar. We carried on and shortly came upon fresh cougar tracks, and that was when the show got underway. The tracks were hot and we went just a short distance with the dogs baying in the lead, before we caught up with the cat. It was about 50 feet up in a large pine tree, peering down at us—more puzzled than concerned.

Bob sized up the situation and told us that this wasn't even a work-out, and that he intended to give the cougar a fighting chance. He then added, "You guys wait here, I'm going back to the snowmobile for an axe."

Perhaps half-an-hour passed before Bob reappeared with an axe in his hand; he then went to work chopping down that big tree. I did my level best to deter him by saying, "Bob! If that tree comes down and lands on that cougar there won't be anything left of it." All I got in return, though, was a short burst of laughter.

At last Bob's effort produced the desired result, and the tree started toppling over with the cat on the underneath side. I had visions of that cat being smashed flat as a pancake and thought that Bob was surely a madman. Then to my amazement, the cat moved around to the top side of the tree and when it was about 15 feet from the ground, it leapt out and landed on all four feet; a second later it disappeared into the forest.

Since the dogs hadn't seen the cougar escape, Bob had to call them over and give them the new scent; then we were all on our own. One sight that I will never forget was the hounds crossing a slide area that the cougar had leapt across. It was a steep, wet slide area and as the dogs ran across it they went sliding downhill. Not once did they look around or hesitate; instead they kept on barking furiously as they galloped across the slide and disappeared into the forest. It was as if their very lives depended on their catching that cat. As I had never seen anything to compare with their performance, I found myself laughing to such a degree that I could barely run.

Bob seemed to have the stamina of a mountain goat—probably built up from years of chasing his hounds—because he quickly pulled away from us and left Roy and I in frantic pursuit. Then Roy faded from view and I found myself all alone on the mountain with only the baying of the hounds in the distance to tell me which way to go. I kept running along after them as fast as I could, though, which wasn't easy because I was thoroughly broke up with laughter. I had never seen anything to compare with the obsession these dogs had for the chase. I later learned that Bob fed them raw cougar meat.

After stumbling along for what seemed like a half-hour, I noticed that the baying sound of the hounds had changed, meaning that they had treed the cat again. A few minutes later I caught up with them and found the cougar in a broken-off and stunted tree, only about 12 feet above the ground. This was an amazing scene: the dogs were jumping up

My cougar after the long chase, 1968.

as high as they could, tearing pieces of bark off the tree in their desperate attempt to get the cat. Meanwhile, the cat was staring down at us with its eyes bulging out with what I thought was wonder—wondering what all the excitement was about. I walked right beneath it and began taking 8-mm movies, with the cat only a few feet above me. At this point, Bob said, "Do you realize that cougar could be on you in a second?"

I looked at the dogs leaping and tearing at the tree and replied, "I don't think it wants to come down here right now!"

It didn't. In fact we took the cat about 20 minutes later and the second it hit the ground, the dogs were on it. As soon as they realized it was dead, the dogs turned on each other, all wanting to claim the kill. This was not a mock fight; these dogs were deadly serious and would have torn each other apart if Bob had not intervened. He rushed in and tied the two youngest dogs to different trees, then left the oldest one to claim the kill, and a proud dog it was indeed.

Cougars have always endured a love-hate relationship with humans; at times this has led to calls for their complete destruction. The same holds true for wolves, which were hunted and poisoned to the point of near-extinction in many areas during the 1950s.

I have found a surefire method of getting a good argument going. To anyone that doubts, I suggest they bring up this subject next time they are camped out and looking for a subject of conversation. Simply ask folks whether they believe wolves have ever attacked a person and then watch the fur fly.

During the winter of 1922, a trapper named Ben Cochrane was reportedly killed and eaten by a pack of wolves on Lake Winnipeg. During the encounter he was said to have killed eleven of the pack before succumbing. When Ben Cochrane emerged from the forest alive and well, the entire incident was dismissed.

But this begs a question—just because Ben Cochrane was not killed, did someone else perish there? According to the report they found pieces of a body strewn about. If that were the case, how would anyone know whose body it was—Ben's body or that of someone else?

When we were still children, our parents used to tell us that during the early 1920s a reward had been offered in a Canadian newspaper (*The Family Herald* or *The Free Press,* I believe). A sum of money was offered to anyone who could prove that a human had been attacked by a wolf. Suddenly the reward offer was discontinued, although my parents never saw any explanation for its withdrawal. Is it possible that someone claimed the reward money at that time? Could the people who reported the Cochrane incident possibly have claimed the reward? I would be most interested in obtaining any information concerning this reward and the reason for its withdrawal from the newspapers.

There are so many reports of attacks in old newspapers as well as books, such as *The Great Lone Land* by Major Butler or *Travels and Adventures* by A. Henry. In one case a wolf came right into a tent while the man was sleeping; several other stories tell of wolves feeding on a human body. I find it difficult to believe that wolves would starve to death rather than attack a person.

I found another tidbit about wolves. It took place during the winter of 1922-23, when a trapper came in from his trapline with eight wolf pelts. First he claimed the bounty of $15 per pelt; then he sold the furs and averaged $25 per pelt. This resulted in a windfall of $320 or the equivalent of about $10 000 in today's money. When the authorities realized what had happened their eyes turned green; they quickly took action and passed a law which stated that in order to get the bounty money the trappers had to surrender the pelts. Well that was one law that was repealed in short order, because when the trappers became aware of it they raised pure hell. This resulted in the law being rescinded in July 1923.

Several of the trappers I interviewed during the 1960s and 1970s, related that they had noticed a great deal of disease among the caribou, and more so among the moose populations after the wolf poisoning programs of the early 1950s. If this were in fact the case, it tends to support evidence from other sources of the importance of predator/prey relationships. For instance, several studies in the United States proved that the decimation of coyotes from an area was followed by a substantial increase in mice and gophers, to the point where they seriously damaged crops. In one instance, this led to the erection of signs such as "Our Friend—The Coyote." In Canada the decimation of coyotes was followed by dramatic increases in rabbits, gophers and mice.

A similar lesson was learned by the United States Biological Survey staff. After a vigorous campaign that lasted until 1920, they succeeded in wiping out all predators from the Kaibab National Forest in Arizona. This was followed by a deer population explosion to the point where all the foliage was consumed and massive starvation followed.

Surely everyone remembers the results of the rabbit epidemic in Australia. Where they reached such high populations that it was literally declared a war. Again the cause was a lack of natural enemies.

New Zealand had its own experience with deer populations out of control, when Sir Heaton Rhodes brought in Austrian red deer during 1921. Within a short time the government was forced to put a bounty on them as their populations rose totally out of control. By 1937 this bounty was paid on over 23 000 deer. Once again the obvious conclusion was the lack of a predator.

There has been many articles written about coyotes, with some of the authors stating that these predators do not attack and kill deer. During the winter of 1951/52, I worked on a logging show along the Kootenay River in Southeastern BC. Every day during the winter we drove about eight miles each way to and from work, usually seeing between 30 and 60 deer during the drive. One evening I was returning home from work with my two companions, Roy Sinclair and Bill Oestrich of Grasmere, when we witnessed a takedown. Right in front of our vehicle, two coyotes exploded out of the forest onto the road; one had a deer by the throat while the other ran alongside the deer, tearing out its intestines on the fly. Suddenly the deer dropped and, in the same instant, the two coyotes spotted us and departed. Every day we passed by that carcass but the coyotes never returned to feed on it; probably because they were being poisoned at that time and so would not return to a kill once humans had been near it. Many times when we arrived at work, the area looked as if a stampede had been held there overnight. There was endless sign where coyotes had chased deer, and the sign plainly showed that they had been on the run the entire time.

Another item concerning wildlife that I found intriguing was told to me by a Prince George resident named Ron Abernathy. I know from personal experience that it can be a frustrating job to try to get horses near a moose or bear carcass as they will rear up and snort something terrible. Yet according to Ron there is a simple solution to this problem: just take some blood off the carcass and rub it on the noses of the horses; they will instantly calm down and can be led right to the dead animals.

Another gem provided by Ron concerns something he witnessed at Newstub Lake; now part of Ootsa Lake in North Central BC. Ron was at the lake when the guide, Mr. Ericson, arrived with four horses. As the men watched, Mr. Ericson loaded the four horses into his riverboat— each one's head tied over the rump of the one ahead—for transport to the other end of the lake. Ron asked the guide if he wasn't worried about the horses moving and tipping the boat, whereupon Ericson answered, "No way! Once they're in the boat they brace their feet and don't move a muscle until we get to the shore."

We have all read plenty of stories about bears and humans, but here is one with a different twist. It was taken from the *Prince George Citizen:*

"The best bear story in many years comes from the Burns Lake district. It is told by Arthur Gammon, who follows trapping for a living. According to Gammon his leg was broken while he was felling a tree several miles from his cabin. To get back to his cabin he had to crawl over the rough ground. It commenced to snow and he sought shelter in a hole in the ground. When Gammon got into the hole he found a young black bear domiciled therein. The bear did not resent the intrusion and Gammon, having little choice, decided to remain. He says he remained in the hole with the bear for several days, during which time the bear fended him against threatened attacks from marauding coyotes. When Gammon returned to camp and told his story, a number of doubting Thomases started out to verify his story. They found the den and traced bear tracks from it to a brush thicket where the tracks were lost."

I have no comment on this story; I think it best to let the readers decide for themselves whether it has any merit.

Finally, I must point out several items that I found in old newspapers, something I was unaware of until recently. In these articles are statements supporting the existence of buffalo in the Interior many years ago. The first indication of this came from Alexander Mackenzie's *Journal of a Voyage through the Northwest Continent of America,* published in 1801. In it he describes meeting with several herds of buffalo in their trip up the Parsnip River in June 1793.

This has been corroborated several times throughout the years. For instance, during July 1938, buffalo horns were found at a depth of 20 feet in a gravel pit near Prince George. J. F. Fletcher of the provincial museum, who was collecting small mammals for the museum at the time, confirmed they were buffalo horns.

Further evidence of their previous existence in this area is the fact that the Carrier, Stuart Lake and Sekani Indians all include names for buffalo in their languages.

7 Humour

EVER SINCE *GRIZZLY BEAR MOUNTAIN* WAS PUBLISHED, PEOPLE HAVE ASKED me to write more about early-day humour. I don't mind this a bit, as humour has always been my first love. As I am a person who always tries to see the funny side of life, I am always on the lookout for such situations. The following articles suggest the type of humour prevalent in the first half of the previous century.

Several of the early-day newspaper articles that caught my attention are included here, such as the new invention supposedly discovered by the French during the First World War. It may well have scared the hell out of any German that deemed it possible. This article was carried in the *Fort George Herald* dated October 24, 1914:

NEW GUNS USED BY FRENCH IN FIRING TURPINITE

"Remarkable tales of novel engines of war are appearing in all parts of Europe, but nothing has yet equaled the reports circulated concerning new guns used by the French in firing turpinite, a substance said to produce instantaneous and painless death for every living thing within its reach.

"Although it is so deadly in its work, turpinite cannot be objected to on the ground that it violates humane principles of war. In fact, it is so humane that it must not be confused with lyddite and other explosives, which have deadly fumes.

"English correspondents have reported that entire lines of German soldiers stood dead in their trenches as a result of the fumes from the mysterious turpinite discharged by the French in engagements along the Marne. The dead Germans are reported to have maintained a standing posture and retained their rifles in their hands, so sudden and unusual was the effect of the new weapon. Instantaneous paralysis is said to have been caused by turpinite.

"The French gun used is shrouded in mystery, as is turpinite itself."

Even the newspapers got into the act, when one of them decided they were not selling enough papers. Their story described what happened to a family too stingy to take the paper:

BETTER TAKE THE PAPER AT ONCE

"We once knew a man who was too stingy to take the newspaper in his hometown, and always went to borrow his neighbour's paper. One evening he sent his son over to borrow the paper. While the son was on the way he ran into a large stand of bees, and in a few minutes his face looked like a summer squash. Hearing the agonized cries of the son, the father ran to his assistance, and in doing so ran into a barbed wire fence, cutting a handful of flesh from his anatomy. And ruined a $4 (sale price) pair of trousers.

"The old cow took advantage of the hole in the fence, got into the corn field, and killed herself eating green corn. Hearing the racket, the stingy man's wife ran out of the house, upsetting a four-gallon churn full of cream into a basket full of kittens, drowning the whole flock. She slipped on the cream and fell downstairs, breaking her leg and a $19 set of false teeth. The baby left alone, crawled through the spilt cream into the parlor and ruined a $40 carpet. During the excitement the daughter eloped with the hired man, taking all the family savings with them."

The paper neglected to mention in later issues just what effect, if any, the article had on sales.

On December 24, 1918, the following advertisement appeared in the *Prince George Citizen*:

LONELY MAN ASKS BOARD OF TRADE TO FIND HIM A WIFE

"(Winnipeg Free Press) Cheer up, girls; why worry if Canadian boys are marrying English girls at the rate of 12 000 a month. Here's some encouraging news that came to the Board of Trade this morning, from a lonely rancher at South Fort George, BC:

'Dear sir Will you Please by Return mail, if in your city some War Widows or any other women which will like to communicate with some good party here, some Rancher and other trade. There are a few men here which will like some good women, and also some Returned Soldiers. I wish you will advise us how to get introduce with some those lady. Please let me

*no returned mail.' The Board of Trade officials are working on a transla-
tion."*

The imbalance in male-female populations was most evident in France after the First World War, as shown in this article taken from the *Citizen* of August 3, 1920:

*"Patriotic Frenchmen, headed by Dr. Carnot, are forming a big organ-
ization to bring 2 million husbands to 2 million girls and war widows of
France; otherwise condemned to celibacy as a result of France's losses of men
under 35 years of age during the war.*

*"France will welcome the surplus men of the United States, Western
Canada, Australia and South America. The new association plans to work
out some means of financing the importation of husbands on a large scale.*

*"The number of men and women in the world is believed to be about
equal, says Dr. Carnot, but their distribution bad. There is need of a read-
justment marital clearing-house. The dangerous decline in the French
birthrate is not due to the nature of the French race, which is prolific. The
largest families in the world are French-Canadians. Individual attempts to
solve the problem have been unsatisfactory. Marriages of many Canadian
and American soldiers have been failures, therefore this measure to put husbands on the French import list and bring the commodity into the country
in large quantities."*

The most ridiculous part of this scenario appears to be that at the exact same time there were countless numbers of Canadian men living in extreme loneliness, such as trappers, prospectors, homesteaders and the like. I discussed this situation with an elderly gentleman who sized it up this way:

"When I was about twenty, I was hornier than a four-balled tomcat, but I couldn't find a woman around anywhere. Now that I'm in my eighties and useless as teats on a boar, I'm staying in a place with over twenty women."

After shaking his head vigorously this gentleman concluded, "Nobody can tell me that God doesn't have a sense of humour."

Another retired trapper and guide summed up his concept of women by saying, "Women are strange creatures: If I have one in bed with me, I can just roll over and go to sleep; but if I haven't got one, I run all over town looking for one."

Even though he was approaching eighty, this man echoed the old saying:

"Women are like rain—you can't live with them and you can't live without them.

In the *Citizen* of January 21, 1919, an article appeared that was for the birds. It was titled—Some Chickens:

"*Saskatoon, Sask. Canada—A. Milhalko, the manager of a flouring mill here, raises chickens as a pleasure and only experiments with the best breeds of fowl. For some time he has been feeding them a mixture of sour milk and screenings, but noticing one day that they were partaking quite freely of some sawdust that he had accumulated when he built an addition to his coops, he resolved to offer the fowls a new mixture, consisting of sawdust and sour milk. The hens seemed to like it and he continued to feed it to them.*

"*Later on he set one of his Plymouth Rock hens on twelve eggs and got a startling surprise when the eggs hatched out. Eleven of the chicks had wooden legs and the twelfth one was half chicken and half woodpecker. Until it died it would climb trees and pick the hard bark with its long bill, evidently in search of bugs.*"

Another article carried in *The Leader* of September 30, 1921, speaks for itself:

"*The owner of the clothing and huge roll of bills found on the CPR track at Huntingdon last week was met walking out of the barn minus any dress whatever, and having no recollection of the whereabouts of his wardrobe. He was able to give his name as Rourke, a native of Newfoundland, and stated that he left Vancouver last week, walking on the advice of his brother, who told him he 'must walk naked 25 years on the earth or go to hell.' The constables were able to persuade him that he would be better resting at Essondale.*

Gambling got the attention of the media and they continually spoke out against taking needed money away from husbands who should have taken their paychecks home. One story that I found humorous told of a poker game in in Prince George during the 30s. With a large amount of money in the pot and several Chinese gentlemen at the table, the door was flung open and several police officers rushed into the room. The next day the *Citizen* read, "Police win biggest pot at poker game."

Another gambling story that must be told occurred during the month of June 1913, when the steamer BC Express was on its way to Tête Jaune. On board a poker game was in full swing. Just as the biggest pot was about to be won, a passenger suddenly identified himself as a policeman. He took the pot and headed back to his room to count his winnings. The steward, who had witnessed the proceedings, ran up on deck and notified the captain, who pondered the information for a few minutes and then told the steward to approach the policeman and offer to split the take with him. They hassled for a time and then the policeman agreed to split the money with the steward. Once the money was in the captain's hand, he informed the policeman that he had broken the law; that in fact he had no authority whatever on the vessel. As soon as they arrived back in Fort George, the captain informed the officer in charge and the policeman suddenly joined the ranks of the unemployed. He was on the next sternwheeler heading south.

An article that brought back memories from my childhood was carried in the *Edson Jasper Signal* dated August 14, 1930:

SIDEHILL GOUGERS ARE ONLY MYTHS

"The sidehill gouger, whose legs on the left side are worn shorter than those on his right through continual perambulations around the slope of a circular mountain, and the wampus which always goes backwards up a hill and yodels like a Swiss climber when it gets to the top, after all are only myths painted by glib-tongued guides upon the credulous imaginations of visitors to the mountains.

"This, at least, is the conclusion reached by Richard W. Westwood of Washington, DC, Secretary of the American Nature Association who, with a number of members of the association, has just finished an extended trail trip through the mountains of Jasper Park.

'At Maligne Lake,' said Mr. Westwood on his return to Jasper Park Lodge, 'we were told we would find the sidehill gouger and the wampus on their home grounds. We found however, no tracks going uphill backwards or any trails running in circles around the mountains.

'What we did find around the largest glacial fed lake in the Rockies,' continued Mr. Westwood, 'were chipmunks which had left their trees and

lived in the ground like gophers, and seagulls which had forsaken the sea for this far inland retreat. But perhaps our most remarkable discovery was to come upon the nesting grounds of four rare birds, the Arctic horned lark, the rosy finch, the golden crowned sparrow and the timberline sparrow, all within a radius of one square mile in a meadow above the lake.'"

Mr. Westwood and friends must have been suspicious about the existence of a sidehill gouger or a wampus, but they simply could not allow someone else to be the first to document their existence had they been real.

Some other examples of early-day humour, and perhaps many of the funniest events, took place in the 50s, when we used to hit the bars and parties so much. I'm thinking of a Saturday night after the bars closed and two lads named Jackie English and Catsy Hooker went with me for Chinese food. I believe the café was called the Purple Lantern. When the three of us arrived at our booth, we decided to have a little fun. All three of us sat on the same side of the table and no one on the opposite side. There was barely enough room for our elbows, but we managed. Believe me when I say that we got the undivided attention of all present. Sometimes there were two or three heads in the kitchen window at the same time. Obviously these Chinese cooks had never seen anything like this before, and it was not an every day occurrence in their café. If these cooks had any doubt about the sanity of white men, I think they worked it out that evening. We also heard a lot of snickering going on at the other tables.

Another evening four of us went out to a Chinese café and after we had finished our meal, we just sat there, killing time. At one point, the man attending the till left and went into the kitchen. This was what we had been waiting for, so we all rose as one and ran out the door. As we ran away down the street, the till-tender came flying out the door, shouting, "Boys! Boys! You forgot to pay for your meal."

We stopped and shouted back to him, "Did you check under the plates?"

He spoke to someone inside and then called back, "Okay, Boys, Goodnight!"

It must have been about two weeks later when we went back to that café. The same man was at the till and he recognized us at once. He didn't say a word, but he shook his finger at us, and I took that to mean, "No more funny stuff!"

There was no more funny stuff.

I attempted to put this next story in my last book but the publisher put the brakes on it; I'll try once again and see if I can sneak it through. This story began when my older brother Clarence started school. I was absolutely crushed because I wanted to go too. Since I no longer had someone to play with, I had to make my own entertainment. Sometimes I would go down by the barn and talk to our horse—Barney, but Barney wasn't very talkative and when he did say something there was usually a bad smell associated with it.

One day I was playing near Barney when he took a dump and I noticed a peculiar thing: After he finished with his dump, his bum opened wide before closing; this spurred me to action. I bided my time until I caught him in the act again, and this time I was ready. As soon as it opened wide, I threw in a rock, then watched it slam shut. Apparently it liked the taste of rocks, though, because it opened up again. That time I threw in a couple rocks and watched it slam shut again. We carried on like that for a time until I realized that the back end of a horse could eat almost as much as the front.

The following day we were in the house when Dad came in with a serious look on his face. At once he confided, "There's something wrong with Barney; he's eating rocks." Several of us went down to the barn to check, and sure enough, there was a pile of rocks mixed with Barney's droppings. Dad puzzled on it for a while and finally decided that something must be lacking in Barney's diet or else he wouldn't eat rocks. He further concluded that we might be able to compensate for it by feeding him more oats. Well my Dad sure must have been a smart man because we doubled the ration of oats—just like he said—and sure enough Barney stopped eating rocks.

While I'm dealing with humor, there are a few stories I simply have to relate. The first concerns a retired mechanic named Doug, who has just a fringe of hair around the back of his head. The first event took place when Doug went to his barber for a haircut. After the haircut was finished, the barber informed Doug that the price was $8.00 instead of the $6.00 he had previously charged. When Doug offered that the price was a bit high for cutting a few hairs, the barber replied, "It's only $6.00 for the haircut; the other $2.00 is a search fee."

As if he hadn't suffered enough indignity already, Doug went back to this same barber for another haircut. As he worked away the barber suddenly exclaimed, "It looks like you used to have wavy hair years ago."

"Yes, I did!" Doug agreed.

At that point a First Nations gentleman that was waiting in line spoke up, "It looks like it waved good-bye."

Amid the howls of laughter from all present, Doug asked in his good-natured way, "Why does everyone have to joke about my hair?"

Doug has another story—this one from his youth in Alberta—that I thoroughly enjoy. It concerns two bulls that they had on their farm. Anyone who has been brought up on a farm knows that it is not a good idea to keep two bulls in the same pasture, as they will almost certainly fight. This is what happened in Doug's story.

These two bulls started fighting one afternoon and kept at it until evening when they decided to rest and recuperate. The next morning they went at it again, and all the while the farm billy goat watched intently. Finally, as the afternoon wore on, the billy goat, obviously not impressed, decided it had seen enough. It attacked the two bulls and gave Doug's family a delightful show. When one of the bulls would attack, the goat would jump to one side and then rush in and strike the bull under its neck, then rush out again before the bull could respond. For a couple hours they carried on in that fashion until the bulls, completely exhausted, gave up. Together they went to a nearby creek where they settled down in the water, leaving the goat the decided victor. Talk about David and Goliath!

Of all the witty people I've known in my life, one stands out above the rest—Jack Fowler was his name, and great humour was his game. Often called the Camp Inspector, Jack earned this title by being in almost every logging camp in the country. When questioned, he would prove it by describing the various camps, and knowing the bosses by name. He may have only been there for a day or so, but he had been there.

Jack had a rather tough childhood, as his mother passed away when he was born. I've heard it said that she was an exceptionally intelligent woman and that she knew when it was time to leave.

Just how far Jack was prepared to go with a joke was established when his father decided to remarry. Shortly after the honeymoon, Jack paid two women to knock on his father's door. When Steve answered the door, they called him by name and said, "Hi, Steve, we want to buy another bottle."

With that they produced some money. Just how Steve talked his way out of that one is unknown, but it must have been difficult because they even knew his name.

When asked what he did for excitement on his visits to town, Jack once replied, "Sometimes I go down to the old folks home and yell 'fire' and then I stand in the doorway and trip the pensioners as they come running out. You wouldn't believe the response—sometimes there's glasses, canes, false teeth and hearing aids flying in all directions!" This was simply a joke, because Jack really wasn't a mean person.

One story had Jack in a Prince George beer parlor drinking with the boys, when a sawmill owner came in looking for workers. He hired Jack on the spot, loaded him into his pickup truck and took him out to his camp where he was put to work. After an hours work in the office, the boss returned to town and decided to stop for a cold one. Imagine his surprise when he entered the beer parlor only to find Jack there, drinking with the boys again. He walked up to him and asked, "What the hell are you doing in town?"

Jack's response, "Same as you, I like a cold one now and then too, you know."

This prompted the boss to reply, "Well you're fired."

Quick as a wink Jack came back with, "Okay, but I have to tell you that you're not getting a virgin; I've been fired before."

No matter what the situation, Jack always had witty replies; unfortunately some people didn't see the humor in them.

Perhaps one of his funniest stories concerned the time he went to a doctor to be treated for a hydrosele or swollen testicle. During the preliminary talk the doctor asked, "It's pretty big, is it?"

Instantly Jack responded with, "Well let me put it this way—I showed it to a stallion yesterday and he cried like a baby." Apparently the doctor lost his professional dignity and simply howled.

If Jack liked something he would often state, "It's got sex beat all to hell and you don't get hair in your teeth." I didn't ask him to explain that statement.

Several people have told me that Jack was one of the three men who cut through the wall of a hotel room. Apparently they used a chainsaw to get access to an adjoining room where one of their buddies had a woman. Another story had Jack and a buddy up in a hotel room arguing about which one of them could put down the most trees in a day. After a brief arguing session, they attempted to settle the argument by dropping a power pole outside the hotel. That little joke cost them $50, which was no small sum at a time when a glass of beer sold for ten cents.

One of my favorite memories of Jack concerns a Halloween night back in the 50s. A group of us were out terrorizing the town when we stopped at the sawmill boiler-room to warm up. There was Jack, loaded up with booze, and totally covered with muck. In fact, we could smell the stink several feet away. We asked what he had been up to and he informed us that he had been down at the pig sty, painting the pigs. Sure enough, the next day the company hogs were the most colourful hogs imaginable—in fact, one of them was so colourful it died and the sawmill cookhouse was short one pig.

Some of the camps kept Jack on the payroll because he kept everyone in stitches. He was capable of telling jokes for hours, day after day, without repeating the same joke twice. I firmly believe that if Jack were a young man today, he would not only be a standup comedian, but he would also be among the very best.

Alan Ward, who was a logging contractor for many years, often kept Jack on his payroll. On one occasion I was present when Jack was skidding in trees for Alan up at the Grand Canyon on the Fraser River. Jack had gone into the woods for a drag of trees, and when he didn't return after four hours, we reported the situation to Alan. Suspecting that he may have been injured, Alan hurried into the woods to check on him. A short time later he returned and amid laughter, told us that he had found Jack sound asleep on his machine, sleeping off a drunk. One of the log-scalers present asked Alan why he employed someone so unreliable. Alan explained that he kept him around because he entertained the crew and kept them happy.

Just a few years ago Jack passed on, and I'm prepared to bet that he went straight to heaven. It seems logical to think that God would need his services up there. Who can deny that God has a great sense of humour? I mean just look at the rest of us.

I can think of no better place for a story about fishing than under the banner of humour. Certainly there is something about fishing that brings out the best, or rather, the beast in people; perhaps this fault has been with us since time began. On November 21, 1929, a Barkerville writer named T. A. Blair wrote an article for the *Prince George Citizen*. This story revolved around a Barkerville guide named Roy Thompson, and I warn the reader to be prepared because this story is not at all what it first appears to be. An edited version of Mr. Blair's article follows:

"Ever since the morning that Jonah swallowed the whale there has been a popular conception that fishermen are justified in exaggerating; an unwritten law existing that even justifies them in telling stories that are not true. But this is wrong; nothing in the scriptures justifies any such practice.

"There are men of the highest integrity who view with scorn anything that savors of an untruth in respect to their private affairs, yet who indulge in, or wink at, shady or loose stories in respect to the size of a fish catch, particularly in reference to their dimensions. Nevertheless this is a sacrilege that should not be tolerated in these days of a higher conception of a moral responsibility of those who broadcast their fishing experience. A falsehood is as much a falsehood in describing the size of a fish as it is in the falsification of accounts for the sake of a private gain.

"As a matter of fact truth is a moral fiber in the fabrication of a society, without it nations crumble and society disintegrates. Nothing can be more demoralizing to the plastic minds of the adolescent than irreverence for the sacred truth; the basic and moral foundation of either the human or empire. Any disrespect for its sanctity reverberates its unrighteous influence on the innocent, and should not be tolerated by respectable people.

"But it is a tribute to the present generation that there are some, at least in these days of mass psychology, when it requires so much real stability of character to stand alone against mass opinion, to know that there are men, at least in the Barkerville district, who refuse to condescend to any such evil practice. And none are there who deserve more credit than Roy Thompson, the well-known sportsman and big game guide of Bowron Lake.

"It was early in September of this year that Roy, with two big game hunters, went into the Lakes District in search of grizzlies and other big game. About mid-afternoon they landed on the shore of Sandy Lake. In order to enhance the evening meal, Roy put out a setline and proceeded to prepare camp. The big game hunters happened to be Chechakos [novices] on their first trip into the wilderness, who hung close to camp, prompted perhaps by some primeval instinct that in the loneliness of the hills makes men herd together for mutual protection against the unknown.

" . . . Roy worked at high speed to get his house in order, and failed to take notice of his setline. Had it not been for one of the big game hunters who noticed the line had taken great tension, it is altogether likely it would have broken, and the world would have passed on without ever becoming wise to the cannibalistic qualities of the fish that abide in these waters.

"Roy proceeded immediately to examine his line when he discovered that a minnow had swallowed the bait; that a four-inch trout had swallowed the minnow; that an eight-inch trout had swallowed the four-inch trout; that a sixteen-inch trout had swallowed the eight-inch trout. Then he found that a thirty-two-inch trout had swallowed the sixteen-inch trout; and to be accurate a trout 64.731 inches had swallowed the thirty-two-inch trout, and that a much larger trout had swallowed the bunch, but it was tough going.

"Whether it would have succeeded or not, Roy said he would not like to say, however as he attempted to pull in the line the big fish disgorged and got away. Just how many more fish would have come and satisfied their appetite in the same manner, providing the line would have held, was a matter upon which Mr. Thompson refused to express an opinion. However it is altogether probable the limit had nearly reached its maximum when Roy pulled in his catch. Mr. Thompson did say however that only the minnows get down into Sandy Lake, that the big fish are all up in Isaac Lake.

" . . . For fifty years preceding the advent of the highway, the Bowron Lake country, then called Bear Lake, was the domicile of two solitary individuals. Kenneth McLeod and Swamp Angel, who, like Robinson Crusoe and Friday were the monarchs of all they surveyed in the entire region. Occasionally an adventurous hunter or trapper from Barkerville percolated the forest to their domain, where they always received a cordial reception from King Swamp Angel and Kenneth, particularly if they brought along

liquid refreshments. But this happened on rare occasions only. As a conse-quence the fish in these lakes were seldom disturbed and therefore grew big . . . "

What stands out in the preceding story is that fishing may have changed lots throughout the years but fishermen have changed very lit-tle. What are my own feelings after 60 years of fishing? Well, I have arrived at the conclusion that fisher-people are a strange lot; what they are willing to endure for a few lousy trout is beyond belief. Possibly no one can verify this with more authority than a fishing fiend named Herb Metzmeier. Herb was still a young man when he arrived in Canada from Germany, yet within a short period of time he turned into one of the most fanatic and successful fishermen I've ever known.

He was first introduced into the hazards of fishing just a short time after his arrival when he decided to try his luck at fishing a fast-flowing mountain stream, famous for its rainbow trout. As he followed the stream, he came to a long, quiet pool that suggested the presence of sev-eral fine fish. A thick growth of willows along both banks would not allow casting, so he continued on to the top of the pool where a down-tree spanned the creek. Six feet below this tree the water foamed around large rocks and boulders—a fall there could have been fatal. Herb worked his way out onto the tree, then casted to the bottom of the pool and began to reel in. Almost at once his hook snagged, and he spent a bit of time jerking and twisting his line this way and that. After the usual amount of whipping his line around in a futile attempt to dislodge it, he lost patience and gave a solid tug, intending to break the line, then retie and continue fishing. But the line didn't break, instead the hook straightened out and the sinker came back with tremendous force and struck him on the forehead. Several times he rocked back and forth before regaining his balance enough to crawl safely back to shore.

After relating this story to me, Herb asked, "Wouldn't that have been a stupid way to die?"

"It sure would have been," I replied, "just imagine what your epitaph would be, 'Here lies Herb Metzmeier, sunk by his own sinker.'"

Late that same fall, Herb was back fishing this same stream. It was cold and clear, with a blanket of snow covering the ground. As he attempted to cross the stream on a slippery log, he lost his footing and plunged into the icy water. Quickly he got out of the stream and then made a run for an old trapper's cabin about a quarter-mile away. When he arrived at the cabin, he found that part of the roof had caved in and the stove had long since rusted away. Some previous traveler had left an abundant supply of firewood, though, so a short time later Herb had a roaring fire going in the center of the floor-less cabin. At that point he undressed and hung all his clothes to dry. A few minutes later as he was soaking up the warmth, he glanced up to find the cedar bark remnant of the roof was on fire and spreading rapidly.

Picture if you can, a would-be fisherman standing naked in the snow, throwing snow up onto a burning cabin roof and you have a portrait of a desperate man. The fact that this story was ever told testifies to the fact that Herb managed to get the fire out.

It was in the late 50s, that I spent ten days fishing with Herb at a remote wilderness lake. To prevent the fish from spoiling we kept them alive by submerging them in a crate someone had left in an old cabin at the lake. The morning when we were to go home, Herb waded out to this crate and picked it up to carry it to shore. Just as he went to put it on the bank, the bottom fell out of the crate and all the fish landed in the water with a big splash. Without doubt, I can honestly say that never before or since have I seen that many fish in one spot at the same time. As all the fish slowly swam away, Herb reached down and picked up one rainbow that was stupefied by the sudden brightness. This little gem we took home—not a great catch for ten days of fishing—but infinitely better than no fish at all.

Fourteen weary, footsore miles later we arrived home, where the first person we met asked, "Did you have any luck?"

I told him all about the fine trout we had caught and how the bottom had fallen out of the crate, and he responded with, "Haw! Haw! Yes, I'll bet!" Then we heard his laughter as he walked away. Why is there such distrust of a fisherman's word?

Another trip to this same lake occurred in the 60s, when a friend named Guenther Peemoeller and I went in to try our luck. We worked our way along the stream between the two lakes, and noticed many fine salmon lying in the riffles in preparation for spawning. As we watched, Guenther decided that he was going to have some fun, because as he put

Eric Klaubauf with two small rainbow trout, Slim Lake, 1950.

it, "There's nothing like a salmon for a good fight."

After several futile casts, he laid his hook into a big one and the show got under way. Instantly he shouted, "I've got one, see, look at him go!" Down the stream the salmon went, to the tune of a singing reel, then there was a loud snap, and Guenther's voice rang out, "That blinkity blank salmon took all my line and my best lure." The rest of the afternoon was spent watching Guenther patrol the stream in a futile effort to find a salmon with a shiny lure hanging from its dorsal fin.

Of all my fishing memories, perhaps my favorite was the time I went stream fishing with a guy who spent most of his time talking about women; his second favorite pastime was playing tricks on his friends. As I had been the victim on several occasions, I still felt that I owed him, even though I had got him several times as well. About midday we stopped and built a fire, boiled coffee and began eating lunch. My friend took a bite out of a sandwich, then turned to pour a cup of coffee from the billy can on the campfire. I had already noticed that he had been carrying the worms in the same sack that contained his lunch, so this spurred me to action. While he had his back to me, I tore a worm in half and placed it in his sandwich. He took a sip of coffee and was just going to take another bite from the sandwich when I said, "Hold it, is there something moving in your sandwich?"

He opened the sandwich to behold half a worm moving away from where he had taken a bite just seconds earlier. His mouth came open as he gave me the most hopeless look imaginable; then he whirled around and got sick. Many times in the months that followed I tried to convince him that he never ate that worm, but he refused to believe me. In fact, he still doesn't believe me to this very day.

Fishing paradise—the Parsnip River in 1970.

People can play all the games they want, but honesty demands we admit that it is a war out there. Nothing ever demonstrated this to me with more clarity than the following story about two fishing friends named Ed and Al. On one of their many fishing trips, things started out bad for Al when Ed caught the first few fish. By the time he had caught five, without a bite for Al, the tension could be cut with a knife. By the time Ed had caught eight, Al had turned his back and refused to talk. Then Ed caught his ninth, with only one to go to his limit. At this point he could no longer contain his joy and couldn't refrain from laughing.

Finally Al caught his first fish, then a second. By the time he got to five, he started talking again. Then he caught his sixth and seventh, at which point he started to see the humour in this situation. But the best was yet to come, for when Al caught his tenth before Ed, he got right into some knee-slapping laughter. Fisher-people truly are a strange bunch.

My sister Evie complained to us one day that she was tired of catching small fish, and just once she would like catch a big one. I took the few small trout she was holding and said, "If it's big fish you want, then it's big fish you're going to get. We'll do like the bear hunters and get you to stand back behind the fish about five feet, then see what happens." With that I took the fish and hung them up, next I got Evie to stand back behind them. When the pictures were developed Evie was more than satisfied with the size of her fish.

Speaking from my own experiences, I have found that if I get my limit before the other person gets a bite, then they usually find it extremely difficult to hide their anger. Some people go to great lengths not to show it, but that's when I offer my lure in a sympathetic way. This will almost always push them over the edge; I mean everybody has a breaking point somewhere.

It has become apparent to me that I must be the world's worst fisherman. How else can it be that I am only able to catch two-pound fish in a lake where other people catch ten-pounders? If others catch twelve-pounders, I'm lucky if I can catch five-pounders. Is it possible that some people exaggerate?

Sooner or later, fisher-people manage to sink their hooks into a lot of things besides fish. Some of the things I have known people to snag, are: a wild tomcat that tried to steal a piece of bacon off a hook that was left outside overnight; a loon that grabbed an imitation fish and then tried to fly in one direction while being pulled in another; an unsuspecting dog that got too close to an amateur fly-fisherman; a

Fishing is a tough and thankless job.

Author with two five-pound rainbows. (Fishermen's weight: 10 lbs; pub weight: 20 lbs.)

beaver that turned on a burst of power and speed that would have made it number one pick in the NFL draft; a human eye that was being used by a young fisher-woman at the time, and a rubber raft that almost made shore before going flat.

I don't know. The more I think about it, the more I think that fishing is just a stupid waste of time. What do we get out of it? I've been stung by bees, wasps and hornets; eaten alive by flies and mosquitoes; nearly perished from hypothermia; had bad words over the best fishing hole; had a triple hook buried to the hilt in my temple; fought my way through miles of devil's club and stinging nettles; fallen off a slippery downtree and sprained my wrist, and all for a few lousy trout.

Personally I've had it. I think a person has to be soft in the head to continue . . . "WHAT'S THAT YOU SAY? THE RAINBOW TROUT ARE RUNNING BOULDER CREEK? JUST HOLD ON, I'LL BE RIGHT WITH YOU!" . . . been lost in the woods overnight; got treed by a bear; lied shamelessly about the sizes and number of fish I caught; almost had an affair with a bull moose; lost a bloody fortune in fishing tackle . . .

Some people may disagree with my putting bootleggers in with humour, but I see a definite connection between the two. While the fines levied against these entrepreneurs were outrageous, some of the events were noteworthy. Since the law was so determined to stop this trade, enormous resources were utilized, however wastefully.

Sometimes the media got so upset that they attacked the police and openly suggested collusion. The first article I found which suggested that bootlegging was becoming a problem in the Interior of BC, was carried in the *Fort George Herald* of November 12, 1910:

"Major Tucker, of the North West Mounted Police, appears to be doing good work along the line of construction of the Grand Trunk Pacific Railroad. He is at present at Prairie Creek, with a force of four picked constables and a small army of plain-clothes men, who are not only enforcing the Dominion liquor regulations, but likewise driving out all the tinhorn parasites who ply their trade along the line. At Edson recently a large quantity of liquor, valued at $1000, was confiscated and destroyed within sight of the public. Liquor in almost every conceivable shape is taken in by bootleggers of all degrees. Some pack it in suitcases and others label it GTP [railroad] supplies. The greatest law-breakers in this respect are the keepers of roadhouses who, in most instances, have made tall money selling to road gangs 'high wine' dope, an article of their own manufacture . . . "

A similar story was carried in the *Fort George Herald* November 18, 1911:

"An amusing newsletter has floated down upon the bosom of the mighty Fraser from Tête Jaune Cache [head of navigation on the Fraser River]. It concerns two of the drove of blind pigs [bootleggers] that peruse their mud-wallowing careers in the construction camp area.

"It appears that two adventurous spirits left Kamloops for Tête Jaune, loaded to the gun-whales with a $1200 stock of booze for the ready, though illegitimate, market, found where Dagos and Swedes labor at the raising of a railroad in fever-infested camps at so much a day.

"They came to the Cache by the back-door route up the North Thompson River, the easier to escape detection. When near the Cache they held council together and decided to cache the bottled joy and hie themselves to the center of local activity to spy out the lay of the land. The wind was blowing up the little McLennan River Valley as they cached the cases away in a rock crevice and covered the pile with brush to hide it from prying eyes.

"The wind was cold and the bootleggers were in a hurry to reach the

cache. They did not endeavor to hide their tracks, or to note whether their activities were under observation, but rushed the job through, blowing on their numbed fingers and drinking deeply from a bottle of their stock-in-trade. Across the little McLennan Valley two of their ilk watched and waited.

"Their tireless efforts were now to be rewarded. The cold and the privations of the long trail of no account now with so much remuneration for those trifling inconveniences at hand, thought the Kamloops booze-peddlers as they beheld the Mecca of their hopes. They staggered and groped their way back along their tracks by night, prepared to transmit the cache to a distributing centre arranged for, only to reach the spot and find the cases gone. The silent watchers had looted the spot and are now peddling the dope along the grades."

No mention can be found of how the news media got wind of this dirty trick, but it is probable that the blind-pigs followed the grade in an effort to find the perpetrators, and heaven help them if they were caught.

An editorial in the *Fort George Herald* of April 27, 1912 gives another view of bootleggers:

"Blind pigs cannot thrive in Bulkley Valley, and it is all owing to a way the local police have of scenting game of that kind and running it to earth. Recently a man named Christianson undertook to operate in a quiet way in a secluded nook under the edge of Hudson's Bay Mountain [Smithers, BC] a short distance back of Chicken Lake. But he had no more than got his pig [still] nicely in shape to produce some easy money when along came Chief Calkin and Special D'Egville and confiscated the whole plant. Next day Christianson came up for trial before Justice Murphy, who, upon finding him guilty, promptly imposed a fine of $300, or in default, nine months' imprisonment for daring to introduce the industry into the valley. After a little hesitation the $300 was paid into court. And that was the last of the first blind pig caught in that part."

When A. K. Bouchier was acting Justice of the Peace at Tête Jaune during railway construction, he sent about 10 people a week to Kamloops for trial on charges of bootlegging. The courts saw no humour in this form of law breaking, and many perpetrators were sentenced to six months in prison.

The first mention I found of the public attacking bootleggers in the press was in April 1909, when one resident became so perturbed by the goings on in Fort George that she wrote the following letter to the editor of Quesnel's *Cariboo Observer.*

" *Sir: Following are a few facts concerning Fort George. For the past two years illicit liquor has been sold by the glass, bottle, or just as you like it. A person can get one or two cases any time, as long as you have the cash in your pocket, or you can even get it charged up for you, for it comes upriver in wholesale quantities, consequently there has been no danger of a drought here.*

"*This illicit selling is an every day occurrence. At night the howls of the red man intermingle with those of the whites, and occasionally to break the monotony, you can hear the reports of a pistol or shotgun, and it's all in dead earnest. The trail between upper and lower Fort George, in the wintertime, is tramped down 20 feet wide and there you can see the resting places of many poor victims of excess. This is perhaps old news to your readers, but as you say 'Why? Who will answer it?'*

"*Of course our officials could stop this, for are they not aware of it? It is the boast of some here that we have no law in this place; does it not look that way? Many times I have heard the boast 'the brotherhood' but I do not think any fraternal order would shield those who perpetually break the law in many other ways besides the selling of liquor. Lately some evil-minded person has put out poison around this end of the place, and the result is poisoned dogs for two miles along the banks of the river. Yours Truly, Francis Hoffercamp.*"

During the night of August 21, 1913, a railway boxcar was broken into at Tête Jaune siding, and 27 cases of liquor were stolen. The thieves were not as smart as they may have thought, though, because their load was too heavy to carry any distance. When the police arrived they suspected that the amount of weight involved didn't allow the thieves to be far away. A search of a nearby sandhill produced the booze, but the thieves—who may have been watching from a safe hiding place—were never caught.

Sometimes the would-be booze seekers got more than they bargained for, such as in the following case taken from the *Citizen* of March 19, 1919:

"*A keg exuding a very powerful odor arrived at the office of an Alberta*

Express Company recently, and two thirsty teamsters promptly bored holes in the top and inserted soda-water straws, with the intention of enjoying a refreshing draught. The arrival of the police, however, cut short their drinking bout, and the keg, on being opened, was found to contain a human head preserved in alcohol. It was being sent to medicos at the University of Toronto for anatomical reasons."

You win some and you lose some.

The animosity displayed by the general public and much of the media toward these bootleggers was plainly exhibited in this editorial taken from the *Citizen* dated August 27, 1919:

"The prescription provision in the prohibition act cannot be blamed for the drunkenness witnessed in this city and district, as Prince George druggists do not handle liquor for that purpose. The 'bootlegger' who is becoming increasingly numerous hereabouts is undoubtedly the source of supply, as judging from the odor of some specimens seized by the police the vile liquid is of home manufacture and composed largely of cheap drugs.

"The Citizen has no intention of criticizing the local police in their vain endeavors to put down the iniquitous traffic. We know from personal investigation that they are doing all in their power to obtain proof of the bootleggers' activities, but the quest is largely a disheartening one and almost invariably leads to a blind trail.

"Someday an over-zealous imbiber will be found needing the services of an undertaker; then the public will wake up.

"The 'bootlegger' who peddles this brain-destroying concoction to weak, drink-craving men is the most despicable creature on earth. No punishment short of hanging fits his crime and the time is now ripe for a roundup of this detestable bunch. The police can depend upon the support (and assistance) of the decent element in rounding up the purveyors of liquid poison."

Sometimes it seemed that the police were overzealous in their pursuit of people breaking the liquor laws. Such as the time they charged Chow Ying with having liquor on his business premises where he sold soft drinks. One would think that he would have been allowed to keep booze as he had a room and slept in the premises. The magistrate didn't think so, though, so he imposed a fine of $75 and costs.

For the owner of the local laundry, Christmas 1919 was indeed bleak. Mah Moon had laid aside four cases of rye whiskey with which he intended to have an open house at the laundry on Christmas day. Word got out, though, and Alex Stewart, the chief cop, took the booze and poor Mah Moon was fined $75 to boot.

The news media was totally dissatisfied with the slow progress of the police and forgot their promise not to find fault; this was attested to by an editorial in the *Citizen* on November 19, 1919:

"Who is responsible for the recall of the notorious characters ordered out of town a few weeks ago by the chief constable? Have the police recently taken a census of the tinhorns, bootleggers and other undesirables?

"If the police commissioners who have sworn to carry out the laws do not act, isn't it up to the law-abiding element to see that they are fired out?

"Are the police commissioners aware that ugly rumors are afloat in connection with their refusal to clean out the tinhorns, bootleggers and prostitutes?

"Does a club license include the privilege of fleecing the unwary logger and married laborer, also the untutored youth of Prince George? Does it give the holder unrestricted license to carry on public gambling dens?

"Can the rate-payers wake up sufficiently to demand the Attorney General to have a strict investigation into conditions in Prince George?"

During the 1920s, the police, frustrated in their efforts to catch the blind pigs, complained that they were unable to catch many bootleggers because they were readily recognized when they entered establishments. The Liquor Board responded by sending undercover agents into Prince George. Then their luck improved dramatically. In October 1922, an undercover policeman entered the home of a colored woman named Velma Mathews, where he purchased a drink of whiskey with two marked one-dollar bills. Moments later, the agent called to the waiting policemen to come in and make the arrest. After a lengthy search the two marked bills were discovered in a spittoon where the woman had hidden it. Velma was convicted on the bootlegging charge and sentenced to six months in prison. At the same time, two men were found guilty of the same offense with the result that Chew Ah Ling and Nick Mardalj were each sentenced to eight months at hard labor in Oakalla.

Obviously stung by the media attacks, the Liquor Board sent two undercover agents named Dickson and Harrison into the city where they quickly made five arrests for the illegal sale of intoxicants. Once again Velma Mathews was caught in the net. After getting her bondsman to put up $500, she skipped bail and left town, leaving her bondsman to pay the $500 plus costs. Three other women charged were sentenced to six months each. A man that had been charged for selling beer was only fined $75; apparently beer was not considered as harmful as hard liquor. One should also take note that the arrests came as a complete surprise to the local police who were unaware that the Liquor Board had sent the two men to town.

The hiring of "dry squads" (Liquor Board operatives) to get convictions against bootleggers, backfired on one occasion. Four liquor spotters got drunk and created a disturbance, then demanded to be supplied with beds. The end result of this was that the police had to be called out to arrest the men. For some strange reason their names were never released.

During the process of making another bust, one of the Liquor Board operatives bought a citizen a drink for his assistance in the bust. At court it was learned that the receiver of the drink was underage. This left the magistrate with no choice but to dismiss the charges laid by the operative. The operative, who was fined $300, left town in disgrace and also left a mess in his wake—because when his partner went to testify against others charged with the same offense, it was just his lone word against theirs. Result? The magistrate threw out the other charges as well.

Early in January 1924, the police sent two special agents to the nearby community of Giscome, where rumors abounded that liquor flowed as free there as it ever had in Prince Rupert—whatever that meant. These two officers took jobs in the local mill and proceeded to get acquainted with the townsfolk. After a ten-day stay, six people were arrested and taken to jail.

It is difficult to comprehend just how severe these fines were, such as the fines levied against James Bowe and Phil Turner of Longworth. Upon conviction for bootlegging they were sentenced to a fine of $300 or six months' jail. At a time when wages were 40 cents an hour, a $300 fine would probably equal at least $10 000 in today's currency.

When the United States entered the prohibition era, it became obvious just how serious a problem bootlegging and rum running had become. This sometimes resulted in deaths, both to the "runners" and the police as well. On September 22, 1922, the Prince George newspaper *The Leader* carried this headline:

OFFICER SHOT BY ESCAPING BOOTLEGGER

"Fernie BC—When Provincial Police Sergeant Stephen Lawson attempted to stop Emil Picarello's son from crossing the boundary line in a car, the latter drove past him at full speed, and Lawson shot him in the hand. Emil Picarello, father of the wounded boy, when he learned of the shooting, drove to Lawson's home at Coleman and shot him dead. The murderer has not been seen since.

"Mounted police, BC and Alberta provincial police and Montana State authorities are searching for Picarello."

Picarello was eventually captured along with his girlfriend, Florence; both were found guilty of murder and executed.

Perhaps the strangest bootlegging story occurred at the Canada-USA border in 1922, where the police realized that a great amount of booze was finding its way into the States. The case was finally solved one day when an official happened to walk by a car with a flat tire. The car, being used by two Sisters of Mercy, was not under suspicion until one of them was heard to say, "This is certainly a hell of a place for a blowout!" The official checked the car and found it loaded with booze. The nuns were in fact two men who had moved a considerable amount of booze across the border. Being Sisters of Mercy, they had been above suspicion.

During the Great Depression many people started making their own moonshine, and among them was my father who kept his still in constant motion for a few years. Mom loved to tell us children stories of the goings on that happened through those years, when the men had no jobs and lots of time for drinking. When someone's brew was ready, the gang would all converge on their home and most likely stay until the still ran dry. Mom claimed that when they got gassed up, they would attack the government with great vigor, often arguing until the wee hours and pounding the table with their fists for emphasis. The person that would make the table jump the highest usually won the argument.

One night after an especially heavy drinking bout, several of the men got sick. A few hours later Mom went outside to check on them and saw the sight of a lifetime: hanging over the fence were four baldheaded men, all sick and moaning and groaning. To make matters even more ridiculous, there was a full moon overhead and it reflected off their heads. Mom said that was the craziest thing she'd ever seen in all her life.

8 Prospectors and Miners

THERE IS A BOUNDLESS AIR OF OPTIMISM THAT SURROUNDS PROSPECTORS. Perhaps it is a necessary part of their makeup without which they would throw up their hands in despair and move on to something with a more definite future. For a short time back in the 1950s, I tried my luck at prospecting by walking the mountains with a Geiger counter. At that time I received a prospecting newsletter from Menlo Park, California, which stated that the odds of hitting it big in the prospecting game were one in two hundred among full-time prospectors. Staggering odds to say the least, yet not great enough to deter these eternal optimists. Every one of them knows that just behind the next hill or in the headwaters of the next stream lies the best strike since Klondike. Much like a gambler at the card table, there is a never-ending excitement in their lives that only they can understand.

It was often tough pickings for the would-be prospectors. Some were lucky enough to get a business man to grubstake them, while others tried to put the bite on a friend that happened to luck out and come into some money.

One of the early prospectors to work the Barkerville area as well as the Cariboo Mountains, was a man named John "Jack" Pinkerton. Born in Ontario, Jack felt the pull of the Cariboo Gold Rush and although still a young man, he joined a group heading west. This group became known as The Overlanders of 1862. They left Eastern Canada in May and after a hazardous journey, entered BC where they split into two groups: one group followed the Thompson River while Jack went with the other group down the Fraser River.

Jack explained that they had no knowledge of astronomy, no maps and no comprehension of the canyons and rapids that lay ahead. During their trip down river the groups spread out and lost track of each other. In Jack's group was Capt. McMicking, John Bowron, who later became gold commissioner at Barkerville. As well, Archie McNaughton and the Wattie brothers were among those present on the raft. Several members of the advance party were lost in the Grand Canyon, and two members of the trailing party murdered and ate a third member when the three lost their canoe in this same canyon and were stranded on a sand bar. As these trapped men had nothing to make a raft with and were unable to swim, they could not escape and so the two cannibals perished. Their remains were reportedly found and buried the following spring.

Jack made it to Quesnelle in late September and then walked to Barkerville, arriving just in time to beat the heavy winter snowfall. During the ensuing years he became very successful in his venture, as he owned and operated claims on William's Creek, Jack o'Clubs Creek and Sugar Creek.

In 1875, he returned to his hometown and married his childhood sweetheart; he then brought her back to BC to share his good fortune in Barkerville. In all, he spent a total of fifty-five years prospecting and mining in that area. He not only made several successful strikes valued at over $50 000 each, but he also managed to have a lake named after him. One of the original pioneers of this country, Jack was laid to rest in Vancouver on a sunny day in March 1920. He had reached the age of 81—an exceptionally long life for prospectors of the time.

Of the many stories of hardships faced by prospectors, few stand out more vividly than the tales of the gold rush of 98. One of these stories was carried in the *Yukon Sun* on June 6, 1899:

"John Crowley, agent of the Ladeau Company at Dahl River during the past winter, brings the information of the death of three men from starvation and cold, while attempting to make the headwaters of the Koyukuk last winter. The victims are Michael Daly, Providence, RI. J. Pronoun and Victor Letare, two Canadians, who were members of a large party who attempted to cross from Dahl River and started on the trip in January. After some two or three weeks the main party returned and reported their three companions as lost.

"Nothing was heard from the missing men until some time in March, when the Bresler party of Cycle City reported the finding of the remains of

the three bodies on the North Fork of the Bonanza, near the headwaters of the Koyukuk. In a tent was found the dead body of J. Pronoun, sitting by a stove, on which was a kettle in which Pronoun had been trying to boil the moose-hide thongs from off his snowshoes. The body was buried and about four miles below this tent they found the fragments of the body of Daly, and a short distance further down, the body of Letare, nearly devoured by wolves. In a few places on the back trail the Bresler party found notes penned to trees by the unfortunates, begging their companions, if they were on the trail, to hurry along, because they were starving . . . "

This story is but one of many that tell of the dangers faced by prospectors that wandered into the remotest areas of the wilderness.

Many touching stories concerned prospectors who often endured extreme loneliness. Some of these people spent endless months in the forests, often being driven to madness or suicide. For this reason I found the following story so touching. It was copied from the *Vancouver Sun* and appeared in the *Fort George Herald* on December 31, 1913:

CHINESE MINER SEEKS CANADIAN CITIZENSHIP
Ah Luk, Well Known in Cariboo, Arrives in City
Loaded with Gold Dust

"Vancouver, Dec. 27—Among the applications for citizenship papers, which will come up for consideration during the next few days, is one of a Chinaman. Ah Luk by name, he is probably one of the most interesting characters in the province. Until a few days ago few persons knew that Ah Luk ever existed. But he came into the city loaded with gold dust, nuggets and furs, and a story strange in these days, for he had not even seen a street-car, electric lights, motor cars, nor anything at all modern. For 34 years he lived in the Cariboo and Omenica mining districts, much of the time absolutely by himself. And his object in making the long trip to civilization at this time is to become a Canadian citizen, as he never intends to return to China.

"Perhaps some of the most binding ties which made for his decision never to return to his native land was the fact that 11 years ago he was smitten with the charms of Josephine of the Babines, and Josephine fell in love with the lonely Chinese miner. So they hurried them to a priest and have since lived in a log cabin at the mouth of Germantown Creek, in a cabin

built by Ah Luk on placer ground which he has mined every summer for the past 11 years with more or less luck.

"Luk came to Victoria when he was 17 years old, remained in Victoria for ten days, then started for the Cariboo. He toiled along the old Cariboo trail to the mouth of the Quesnelle River, where he lived for 12 years and then crossed into the Babine by way of Stuart and Takla Lakes. He first mined on Tom Creek, then went to Vital Creek, here taking out in one season $11 000 in gold. This ground is now owned by a local syndicate. He was on this creek for 11 years, and seven long years he put in absolutely alone with no company but a dog. Now he is settled on Germantown Creek and says he will remain for 'I mally Siwash,' as he expressed it yesterday.

"When Luk starts back home sometime within the next few days he will go to old Hazelton, then start on a long mush of 187 miles to his cabin and family. He will carry on his back food enough to last him over the hard trail. Asked how long he expected it would take him to mush the distance, he replied, 'him sloft snow tak'm long.'

"Luk, since arriving in Vancouver, has fairly reveled in the low cost of living. Bacon, where he comes from, costs 75 cents a pound; sugar, three pounds for $1; flour, $26 per hundred—and this is the worst of all the high cost of living for him, Luk says. It costs 20 cents a pound to get supplies to Germantown Creek, and that explains why things are so high when they get there. The settlement where Luk lives has a population of eight white men, Luk, Mrs. Luk, a young Luk and 19 dogs.

"During the summer months Luk mines the gravel and extracts in the primitive way the glittering grains of gold. He doesn't remain idle in the winter and really makes more money then than in the summer for he is a skillful trapper. For bear he gets $3 to $15; mink, $4 to $7; marten, $8 to $10; otter, $12; beaver, $6 to $7, and fox from $100 to $200.

"Therefore Ah Luk expressed great satisfaction with Canada and for many reasons he wants to become a citizen and has had his papers duly made out."

People who have knowledge of the Manson Creek area may be pleased to know that Ah Luk was the mysterious Chinese miner who is reported to have worked the claim on what is known as Ah Lock Creek near Manson Creek. It is said that he walked away with about $50 000 in placer gold. Somehow it seems so fitting that he married in that endless wilderness, and that he didn't have to spend all his days alone.

One prospector came into a bit of wealth without hitting pay dirt; and no, he didn't win the Irish sweepstakes either. This unusual event occurred to a man named J. C. Catlett and it started back around 1900 when he met a friend that he worked with for many years in the Barkerville area. In 1912 his friend hit on hard times. As Catlett had done very well in the timber staking days of 1906—having staked thousands of acres in the Moose Lake area—he loaned his friend $2 000 to tide him over until he got on his feet. Well, his friend disappeared and was not seen again until 1933—21 years later.

During January 1933, a letter arrived from his friend that contained a hard luck story—one with a surprise ending. It seems that after he left the Cariboo, he had taken a crack at everything in a speculative way and had met failure after failure. But he finally met with success when he got involved with an oil gusher in Texas. His transfer from pauper to prince had been rapid from that point on, and he did not forget his friends. After relating the story of his success, the friend asked Mr. Catlett to come to eastern Canada, which he did. Once there, he was treated like royalty and eventually handed an envelope that contained the $2 000 plus compound interest. Mr. Catlett remarked, "He looked the part of an oil millionaire, his air of prosperity topped off with a shiny automobile."

There is something remarkable about this story—it lifts one's spirits to say the least. Just why Mr. Catlett would not name his friend was not mentioned; perhaps his friend did not wish to be bothered by a great number of not-so-good friends.

Some stories involving prospectors are so inspiring that they must never be allowed to die. Stan Hale, who was born along the upper Fraser River in 1915, told one such story. This story revolved around a family named Blangy, who were pioneers in the Dome Creek area. In their later years, this couple went down to the river and built a covered loveseat out of willows. For the next few summers, this old couple whiled away many a day by sitting in the loveseat and watching as boats went by on the river. Stan pointed out that it warmed the hearts of many a passer-by to see them sitting in the loveseat, holding hands and waving to the river travelers.

There were moments when these prospectors knew an excitement that the rest of us can only wonder about, such as that caused by news such as a brief summary of the Barkerville area carried in the *Citizen* November 26, 1918:

"... *Stout's Gulch is a small stream just above Barkerville. The yield of gold from the gulch, first by drifting and later by hydraulic, amounts to $2.5 million. The width of hydraulic pay (more than 600 feet) is extraordinary for such a small stream.*

"... *F. J. Tregillus, T. A. Blair and Pat Carey are sinking a shaft on the nine-foot gold-bearing vein on their Warspite claim at Proserpine Mountain, four miles from Barkerville. At the present depth of 14 feet, the shaft discloses an excellent showing of visible gold, while the rock in which no gold can be seen shows a nice string of flour-gold when mortared and panned. The vein on which this work is being done has been exposed at intervals by trenching and open-cuts for a length of more than 8000 feet. It is believed to be the mother lode from which the $20 million placer of William's Creek and the $2.5 million placer of Grouse Creek had their origin.*"

The mention of these sums of money back in 1918 was beyond the comprehension of working people. It is no wonder that these strikes caused such a sensation worldwide.

Often prospectors faced trials that would discourage any ordinary mortal—such as cave-ins, slides, extreme privation as well as death in the wild rivers they had to negotiate in order to reach their destinations. Because so many of them worked alone, their fate often remained unknown. Surprisingly, to me at least, a great many women traveled with their men on their prospecting ventures. This meant that they often shared in the bitter trials and misfortune that beset their husbands. On June 4, 1919, the *Prince George Citizen* carried this story:

"*Tidings of another tragedy of the North Land were brought to town from Giscome Portage on Monday last. Mr. and Mrs. B. Hatch, well known in this district, left here last fall on a prospecting trip into the heart of the vast country north of Summit Lake. Taking supplies calculated to last through the winter, they were accompanied by J. Grey, who resided in Prince George for some time. All were experienced pioneers, and though no news of them had come through since the party left Giscome Portage, no anxiety was felt on their behalf.*

"Now comes the news that Mr. Hatch and his partner were taken sick in March just as their supplies were running out and they were planning to return. First Grey died, then Hatch, leaving Mrs. Hatch alone without supplies. She was found in the last stages of weakness, having supported life alone for two weeks on the flesh of a cat and two squirrels, and she is now at the store of Seebach and Huble at Giscome Portage slowly recovering from her awful experience.

"No details of the grim tragedy are as yet at hand, but it would seem that since all the party were experienced in woods life, and all possessed the unconquerable spirit of the pioneers, that the dreaded Flu, which claimed so many lives in the wilderness, has added two more to its list of victims."

As well as all the physical problems faced by prospectors, they also faced loneliness, perhaps their biggest enemy. For after spending too much time alone, people became set in their ways and were often unable to get along with others. The following story illustrates how the wilderness can close in on people and at times drive them to madness. This story was taken from the *Citizen* dated June 25, 1919:

PROSPECTORS FIGHT DUEL ON NORTHERN TRAIL
Bodies of Two Mexicans Who Left for Hudson's Hope are found in the Mountains

"Peace River. June 15—Passengers downstream from Hudson's Hope this week bring news of the gruesome discovery of the bodies of two copper prospectors, Stewart and Rigoletto, who left Peace River some six weeks ago to locate claims in the new copper district beyond Hudson's Hope.

"From the meager information obtainable, the bodies were found by a party under the direction of J. H. Johnson of Peace River, who is engaged in work in that district. Mr. Johnson's party had proceeded about 180 miles from Hudson's Hope, and were reaching an altitude where the snow still covered the ground to a considerable depth. At a camping place on the trail the bodies of the two men were found a short distance apart, each bearing several bullet wounds, the cause of death being plainly apparent. Beside the bodies lay the guns of the two men with from four to six empty cartridge shells lying beside each body, giving evidence of a duel that must have been fast and wicked, both men having apparently fought to the last and dying where they stood.

"Mr. Johnson immediately sent an Indian runner to Hudson's Hope with a report of the discovery, and from the information given by this man the police department has undertaken to recover the bodies and make a thorough investigation.

"Chief Taylor of the BC Police at Fort St. John, went to Hudson's Hope on Sunday, and on Tuesday left with Constable Beatty, of the latter place, for the scene of the tragedy, 180 miles into the mountains. Chief Taylor stated to passengers of the D A Thomas [sternwheeler] that the trip would require from four to six weeks, depending on the depth of snow to be encountered.

"Stewart and Rigoletto were Mexicans, the first known of them here being when they arranged for the trip to the copper country some six weeks ago. Before leaving they made arrangements to locate claims for a syndicate comprising fifty to sixty men, and expected to return in three months, this being the estimated time required to visit the field and return to file at Hudson's Hope."

A coroner's jury went to the scene and after completing their investigation decided that each was responsible for the other's death. It was believed that the final quarrel was over provisions, as their camp showed they were lacking enough food to get them to the nearest supply. There were also witnesses who testified that the two men had previously threatened to kill each other. Further evidence was gained that Rigoletto had formerly been responsible for the deaths of two men in his native country. The bodies were buried close to where they had been found.

The foregoing is ample proof of the mental state that people can slip into when they spend long periods of time in isolation. Many of them got to the point where they were convinced that they owned a huge chunk of wilderness, and woe to any trespassers that happened by. Often the smallest incident would set off a chain of events that ended in tragedy. Sometimes referred to as bush fever, I prefer calling it cabin fever for the following reason. Many times while interviewing woodsmen, they pointed out the constant need to keep active while in the wilderness. As long as they were up and about and kept active, their mental state remained positive. On the other hand, if they sat around the cabin for any length of time, they would find themselves sinking into depression—therefore cabin fever seems so much more fitting.

Sometimes the report of a strike, whether there was any truth in it at all, was sufficient to start a stampede. Such a report drifted out to the outside world in June 1915, when there were reports of a gold strike that went between $100 and $140 per pan. This supposedly occurred along Antler Creek near Barkerville, BC. Though often never realized, these reports were often enough to bring an abundance of gold-seekers into an area. When several men shared a cabin or a small claim, disaster sometimes followed. This next story appears indicative of a severe case of cabin fever. It took place along a stream known as Glass Creek, a tributary of Antler Creek about 10 miles from Barkerville.

This altercation started over possession of a cabin owned by Mike Kopok and a man named Witold Nowokowsky, both of whom were prospecting in partnership along Glass Creek. In April 1932, a man named John Assortin discovered the body of Kopok lying in the trail about 75 yards from the cabin. He had a bullet wound in his throat. He left the body and proceeded to the cabin where he knocked on the door. He received no response, although he did hear movement inside the cabin. He then returned to his own cabin and told his partner, Barney Landyga, who in turn went to Barkerville and notified the police.

Constable Vickers of Quesnel made the trip to the cabin and found Nowokowsky dead of two bullet wounds, one of which had severed his jugular vein and broken his neck. There was also abundant sign that a battle had been fought. The police learned that before leaving Barkerville, Kopok had visited with Nowokowsky's estranged wife and had told her that he was going to take sole possession of the cabin, as he considered it his property. He further added that when all was said and done that one man would be dead and the other in jail. The police finally concluded that Kopok had shot his partner and then committed suicide rather than stand trial for murder.

When one takes a good look at this story, there appears to be something wrong. John Assortin claimed that when he approached the cabin he heard movement inside. Yet the police report stated that Nowokowsky had suffered a broken neck from one of the bullets. Obviously a man with a broken neck didn't make any noise, so who did? Possibly there was much more to this story than indicated by the police reports.

This story or similar ones were told and retold throughout the wilderness. When two people got on each other's nerves it was only a matter of time until something dreadful happened.

A similar example of this occurred when a prospector took a friend along on one of his trips. Each evening as they sat by the fire, his friend went on and on about his many achievements. After about a week working the claim, they were sitting by the campfire when his friend got into another long discourse, making it plain that he ranked up with the best. "I was looking at him across the fire," the prospector said, "and all of a sudden I realized that I really hated that son of a bitch." The prospector shook his finger for emphasis and then added, "The next day I made an excuse to leave; I figured we had better get the hell out of there before something terrible happened."

I do not mean to imply that several prospectors working together could not get along. There is ample proof that this is not true. Al Thorell, who prospected the upper Willow River for several years with a group of close friends, once told me that they got along perfectly. He explained that they were working for a common cause which all stood to gain or lose from. But when people working together could not get along, the wilderness seemed to amplify and inflame their problems.

Swen Sansen (old Sampson) on left with his dog, "Growl," circa 1920.

How prospectors managed to keep their sanity through endless years of being alone, is beyond my comprehension. Swen Sansen (Old Samson) is a good example. He prospected the McGregor Mountains from the 1890s until 1913 when he retired to a cabin on the bank of the Torpy River. He passed away in his cabin in 1921.

Realizing the tough situation that faced prospectors in BC, the government moved to action. During the month of May 1926, a special estimate was brought before the house that allotted the sum of $2 million to assist prospectors in BC. Where it was found that a prospector had opened up a claim that showed signs of good value, an expert would be sent to investigate the property thoroughly, and if acceptable, the government would assist in constructing roads and trails to enable the claim owner(s) to get ore out. The government was prepared to pay up to one half of the cost of constructing such roads and trails. This assistance was greatly needed because the costs of development were often beyond the means of the claim owners, especially those in remote northern areas.

People who delight in following the life stories of colorful old-timers, should get a lift out of this next story; verbose past belief, it is interesting to note the flamboyant style of the writer. It was taken from the *Citizen* of November 27, 1924:

DEATH VALLEY SCOTTY NOW IN CARIBOO
Famous character of Western Mining Days Prospecting in Barkerville Country Strikes Rich Float on Cunningham Creek and Hopes to Locate Source of Riches

"If 'Death Valley Scotty' can unearth the mother lode of certain rich float he recently discovered on Cunningham Creek, his name will blossom forth into world prominence again, as on many former occasions.

"Death Valley Scotty, the most interesting and widely advertised of the picturesque characters of western mining camps, is liable to stage another comeback. No writer of fiction, with a mind at liberty to penetrate into the remotest corners of the unfathomable world of imagination, has been able to picture a character whose life has contained so many thrilling and interesting episodes. No schoolboy, with an innate passion for adventure, has read more interesting literature than a plain and unadulterated statement of the facts in Scotty's career.

"*Born and bred in old Kentucky seventy-two years ago, his age is most deceptive, and he appears more like a man of fifty. If trimmed of his title—received when he was knighted many years ago according to the traditions of Wild West knighthood for his adventures in Death Valley—his name appears as plain Walter Scott. After an illustrious ancestor, Sir Walter Scott, so far in his career he appears to be doing his bit to immortalize his common name. Although quiet and unassuming around town, it does not require a close student of human nature to pick Scotty out as a distinctive character. But to pay him a visit at his native haunts at the mouth of Crazy Creek, almost 16 miles from Barkerville, is to find him in his true element. Here with his only companion—a terrier whose genealogy he can trace back for over 80 years—within sound of the angry waters of Cunningham and Crazy Creeks, where the music of the roaring streams murmur a perpetual lullaby, Scotty has erected his domicile. An eight by ten structure amid the jungle, and like Robinson Crusoe, he is living close to nature. Here, away from the glare of civilization, surrounded by his only neighbors—moose, caribou and grizzly bear, which occasionally call and after an inquisitive look, pass along, no doubt under the impression that Scotty is some sort of herbaceous animal.*

"*But it is the rich float [free-running gold] that has set Scotty's brain on fire, and following his prospector's clue he puts in about 14 hours a day uncovering bedrock, living in happy anticipation of what is just ahead, dreaming also of making just another splash before he passes over. To visit this well-known prospector, one will find him true to tradition—the soul of hospitality. Endowed with a pleasing personality, keen intellect, kindly eyes, and a jaw that denotes tenacity and determination, Scotty impresses one with his distinctive attributes. He once weighed 240 pounds, but as a result of having been riddled with bullets his weight has been reduced to about 180 pounds. Another bullet through his spine clipped off four inches from his height.*

"*It is just forty-seven years since this veteran prospector left Barkerville, where he spent six years in his early manhood days and made a fortune. In the meantime he has made four fortunes and spent them with a lavish hand. It is said that Scotty always traveled in the van of prosperity, and that his entrance into a mining camp was always followed by a boom. Whether this has been a succession of fortunate coincidences, or is due to a canny* shrewdness that enables Scotty to see a greater distance into the future than his contemporary prospectors, is a matter of opinion. But if he succeeds in finding the mother lode that has left the trace he is now pursuing, most people will come to the conclusion that Scotty, like most successful men, makes his own luck.

"Although Scotty has made history in nearly every mining camp in the world, his exploitation's in Death Valley, Colorado, would furnish the fundamentals for a novelist. His disappearance into that inferno of heat, and his return laden with gold, furnish an enigma that defied the ingenuity of the most daring of prospectors, while his wit and nerve served him faithfully in defending his poke, once it was in his possession. On one occasion on his return from Death Valley laden with treasure he was surrounded by sixteen bandits, and ordered to throw up his hands. But these desperadoes soon discovered he was no novice at the cool art of self-preservation. No feint, however swift, hoodwinked or baffled his nerve for a moment, and in the skirmish he managed to bag eight of the robbers, the others getting away. But in fighting against such desperate odds he got badly riddled himself, one bullet taking part of his scalp, another passing through the spinal column in his neck, while a sheep's bone displaces part of his anatomy in one of his legs. This sent Scotty to the hospital for a period of five years and constituted his most desperate fight for life. After leaving the hospital, he got scent of some of the remaining bandits, followed two of them to their lair and bagged them, and says he will get the others yet.

"The above is only a passing incident in Scotty's life. Although faithful in love, dauntless in war and despite the fact that Scotty can seclude himself and live contentedly devoid of a vestige of human association, still he has a certain love for society. Once, after landing a fortune, he hired a special train at a cost of $39 000 and set out over the Southern Pacific from San Francisco, accompanied by a brass band and a bunch of his associates, for New York City, and proceeded to paint Broadway in characteristic western style. While in the metropolis his entertaining expenses, added to the subsidizing of the train, amounted to over a quarter-million dollars. Although Scotty spends his money in princely style, he was canny enough to cache away a nest egg to be drawn upon in case his flow of fortune ceased. As a result of various investments he owns a ranch in Death Valley 1800 feet below sea level, on which he grows several crops of alfalfa a year. He also *owns a large sunflower ranch in California and a walnut ranch in Oregon. But back-to-the-land is not the kind of life that appeals to Scotty's imagination. Like most prospectors he is an extremist, with an abnormal love for either the bright lights or the seclusion of the prospector.*

"Recently Scotty struck a rich stringer literally peppered with gold, and he thinks this will bring him into the main lead. Just how prominent a part the God of destiny takes in directing prospectors is a secret apparently not intended for all, but that there is a wise or unwise dispensation, a directing hand, a guiding motive that shapes their ends, and sometimes seems to apportion unfairly, the ages have disclosed. Many that work hard and think logically fail, while others, apparently reckless, but as if under the influences of a guardian angel, rise to the top at will. That Scotty is one of the favored few is self-evident, and it is in the cards that this veteran prospector, although now past the allotted three score and ten years, will live to give Broadway another coat of paint . . . "

It is almost unbelievable that this reporter could have been so hoodwinked by this prospector who pretended to be Scotty. However I must admit that I was taken in until I reached the part where Scotty had four inches blown out of his spine, yet managed to keep on trucking. In truth, the real Scotty never set foot in Barkerville. Possibly one of the most famous con artists in history, the real Death Valley Scotty never did find a gold mine in Death Valley or anywhere else for that matter. He was at his best when he was mining other people, which he did with repeated success.

Today, Scotty's Castle in Death Valley National Park is a famous tourist attraction; although claimed to have been built by himself, it was in fact built by his friend Walter Johnson, a wealthy Chicago insurance executive.

The real Scotty passed away on January 5, 1954, and he was buried near the castle next to his dog, Windy. In retrospect, perhaps there is a bit of ironic justice in the fact that another man pretended to be Scotty; after all he was only emulating the man he obviously took to be his hero.

A prospector, trapper and fur trader that won respect far and wide was a man who went by the name of Twelve-Foot Davis. A man of many talents, he made history by being one of the first 'free traders' to run competition with the Hudson's Bay Co. in BC. He also won enormous respect by delivering food from Quesnel through to the lower Peace River during the Riel Rebellion in the 1880s. For many years he made the present site of Prince George one of his ports-of-call. In December 1924, *Maclean's Magazine* carried the following story:

"... *Davis was an illiterate man to whom the signing of his name was more painful than a major surgical operation, but as a riverman it may be doubted if the Fraser River has ever seen his equal. He was first heard of in the mid-1860s when the famous Williams Creek placers were in flower. Davis was making his living as a baker, when Cariboo Cameron and the other argonauts [adventurers] were mining on Williams Creek, which was fast becoming known as the richest gold creek in the world for its size—a mile and one-half of it being credited with returning the miners $20 million.*

"*Davis had struck camp too late to secure a claim but he knew how long they should be. He got to sizing up the Cameron claim and was impressed with the idea that it was too long. Early one morning he paced the claim out and was convinced he was right. He then got a tape and put it on the ground to learn that Cameron had twelve feet more in his location than he was entitled to. Davis located the vacant twelve feet and from that day until his death he was known throughout the country as Twelve-Foot Davis.*

"*He made a steak out of his little claim, and then started out on a prospecting trip through the northern part of the province. Eventually he drifted into the business of trading with the Indians for their furs, and was one of the first 'free traders' with whom the officials of the Hudson's Bay Co. had to contend. As the prospect brightened for making money in the fur trade, Davis formed a partnership with the late Peter Dunlevy of Soda Creek and Victoria. By 1887 he was fairly well established, operating posts at Cust House at the western end of Peace River Canyon, as well as at Fort St. John and Vermilion. Davis used to bring all his stores up the Fraser River from Soda Creek, and he made a practice of bringing in horses as well, for packing across the portages. He was the first man to make use of the Crooked River for commercial freighting. A number of the Cassiar miners went into the northern district by this route, but they did not make any attempts to improve the waterway. Davis had to make improvements to use it, and hundreds of the boulders which he dragged out of the channel, were still lining it when the Federal Government undertook the further improvement last year.*

"Davis has been referred to as the first of the bootleggers of Cariboo, but this is hardly fair. He always carried a keg or two of rum with his supplies, but it was largely for house consumption, and while he was not averse to selling watered spirits to the Indians in exchange for skins, he thought too much of his rum to force the sales.

"This story of Davis goes back to 1890, when his post at Cust House was in full swing. At the same time, Walter McDonald was in charge of the Hudson's Bay Co. post at Hudson's Hope. McDonald was due to leave for Dunvegan to bring in the Christmas mail, and not being imbued with the company's hatred for 'free traders' he did the polite thing of writing a letter to Davis at Cust House and sent it forward by an Indian carrier. Not being able to read, Davis was stumped. There were none but Indians within miles of him, and he was too proud to call upon them for assistance. He studied his letter painfully, but the only thing he could decipher was the figure '3', and figures were his long suit. From this lone figure the illiterate trader undertook to construct the entire letter, and in the end he hit upon a solution. The figure '3' could refer to nothing but Three-Star Hennesy, [liquor] which loomed larger in the minds of the traders than the Star of Empire on its western way. Recovering himself, Davis asked the Indian whether he would like three bottles of whiskey, gin, rum, brandy or alcohol. The Indian stated his preference and in due time the three bottles were delivered to the mystified Hudson's Bay agent at Fort St. John. The Indian was closely questioned but he could offer no explanation, and in the end the three bottles were accepted as a peace offering from the 'free trader.'

"Weeks later Davis was visited by an Englishman. He complained of poor eyes and asked the visitor to read McDonald's letter, and this is what it told him: 'Mr. H. F. Davis, Cust House. I am leaving for Dunvegan to bring in the mail. Wishing you a Merry Christmas and a Happy New Year. Yours truly, Walter McDonald. Fort St. John, Dec. 3.'"

"Twelve-Foot Davis did a large trade with the Indians, but it was not a profitable venture for him or his associates. The 'free traders' made a serious inroad into the Hudson's Bay Company's business along the Mackenzie River, but in New Caledonia [Interior British Columbia] the distances were so great and the cost of transport so heavy that individual traders could make very little headway. Davis was a good Indian trader but the men he engaged to look after his posts were neither efficient nor careful, and the

earnings he made were lost in the posts. All that Davis got out of his twenty years of strenuous life as a trader through Cariboo and the Peace River was the six feet of earth that comes to most. His grave lies 700 feet above the present town of Peace River within sight of the spot where Sir Alexander Mackenzie camped in his memorable trip across the continent in 1792. That its location is known is due to the interest taken in it by Colonel Jim Cornwall, which resulted in the rearing of a suitable monument."

The Crooked River used by Davis and so many others was a much-needed link in early-day transportation. For instance, over 300 tons of freight was moved through this river during the summer of 1927. A great deal of this freight moved along the Peace River, and was portaged through the awesome Peace River Canyon. One of the voyageurs that made his way through the portage in 1930 noted that a man named Jack Peninngton worked the portage with a team of horses. Jack moved this man's boat and supplies through the 15-mile portage for the sum of $15.

One gentleman who was often accused of having an overactive imagination was Colin "Lucky" Caldwell, possibly the first man to fly aircraft in Northern BC in search of minerals. An amphibious Vickers Viking was shipped from Three Rivers, Quebec, to Prince Rupert, and on June 1, 1929, it set off on its tour of the Far North and Yukon. Just what the men found in the way of minerals was not disclosed, but they certainly elaborated on the wonderful tropical valley they discovered there. Once again newspapers questioned the validity of his claims but again they were forced to eat crow as others ventured into the Yukon and confirmed his stories. In an issue of *Mclean's Magazine* he gave the world its first account of the phenomena:

"On the evening of August 17, we departed the head of Dease Lake and flew to Frances Lake, a distance of 310 miles north of the BC-Yukon boundary. There was no sign of human life—white or Indian—here at all, though at an old abandoned Hudson's Bay fort on Frances Lake there were several deserted log cabins and a few old caches.

"The last place we visited before coming out was the fabled 'Tropical Valley'—colored and exaggerated press accounts of which have been so skeptically received. We had heard vague accounts of the valley while at Liard Post, based mainly upon the meagre information of Indians, and also about a prospector and trapper named Tom Smith and his daughter who

had wandered overland from the Yukon. They had gone into that region two years before and had not been seen or heard from since. We decided to make a trip to see if the valley really existed and if possible to get a trace of the missing pair.

"We knew that the mysterious region was about two hundred miles from the post and accordingly took off and followed the course of the river, which is punctuated with frequent terrifying rapids. We had flown what we judged to be the distance when we reached a region of peculiar looking lakes. They were striking to us since there were no other similar bodies in the country for some considerable distance in any direction. Deciding this must be the place we made a landing on the river and tied up to a sandbar. With the machine secure we started to scout.

"Almost immediately we struck a trail, faint and apparently not used for a long while, but unmistakably a trail. We followed this for about 400 yards from the river and then surprisingly encountered a board nailed across a tree. Upon the piece of wood painted in rude characters were the words 'ABC Code' followed by a jumble of figures and signed Tom Smith. It baffled us for a little while but finally the combined wits of the party deciphered it and spelt out the words 'message in bottle at foot of tree.'

"We dug at the bottom of the tree and just below the surface struck a bottle which upon opening was found to contain two sheets of paper covered with very legible handwriting. I cannot remember the exact wording of the message, but it started off, 'To any white man finding this message,' and it went on to the effect that by following the trail back for two miles, a cabin would be found near the first hot springs. And a short distance beyond, a garden we have left planted to potatoes and onions. By further following the trail, the message continued, the finder would come to a large hot spring overlooking a meadow in which moose are to be found every morning and evening during the summer months. The message was signed by Tom Smith and concluded by stating that he and his daughter had been living there for two years and had seen no white men. They were leaving for Fort Simpson, which, barring accidents, they expected to reach in the spring.

"We progressed up the trail, the atmosphere becoming more torrid and languorous as we advanced. Shortly we reached the first hot spring and just beyond that found the deserted cabin. A little farther away was the garden, rank and overgrown. From here we started out to explore a limited area of *the valley which appeared to be about ten miles in extent. Hot springs sprang from the ground all over. Some of them just bubbled up and ran straight away. Others formed the pools of varying dimensions we had seen from the air. The rich and luxuriant growth and foliage was distinctively suggestive of a tropical region. Ferns grew to an enormous height and size and vines spread all ways in a tangled mesh. Berries of many kinds were growing in profusion and of an extraordinary size. Flattened patches indicated where bears came in to dine. About many of the little boiling lakes were large patches of purple violets of a size and beauty I had never known before. Much of the growth was unfamiliar to me, and such as I had known in other parts of Canada, was of an extraordinary lavishness and production. I was brought up in Alabama and nothing has ever so reminded me of that southern state.*

"We stayed two days and then flew back to Liard. Later, when flying out, we reported what we found to the Mounted Police at Fort Simpson and they told us the rest of the story of Tom Smith and his daughter. Coming down the river in a canoe, the craft had capsized in the rapids. The girl had been taken down the river and swept up unconscious on a sandbar. When she came to her senses there was no trace of her father. She made her way to Fort Simpson and was working for the Hudson's Bay Company."

It is hard to imagine, in today's world, anyone taking his daughter into such a remote and distant land. On the other hand, there is much to be said for her ability to get herself out to civilization after her father's death. It is also worth noting that "Lucky" Caldwell wasn't really all that lucky because he died in the wreckage of his aircraft a short time later.

Another gentleman was taken for a nut when he came out of the wilderness with strange tales of wealth and oddities of nature. This prospector's name was J. C. Perry, who spent a lifetime in the prospecting game.

Perry made his first trip into the Liard country in 1917. He started his trip by bringing his dog team from the Yukon down to Vancouver; then up on the CPR as far as Ashcroft. Traveling by dog team, he came through Prince George and Summit Lake, and then followed the waterways north to the Liard.

For ten years he had prospected the upper Liard District and had repeatedly came out with tales of a tropical area as well as great mining potential in Northwestern BC. Unable to get local mining people to take him seriously, Perry went to the United States in 1925, where he succeeded in getting a group to fly into the upper Liard. What they found surprised all: a number of hot springs sufficient to alter the temperature of the immediate area; as well they found promise of considerable mineral wealth just waiting for development.

Perry's undoing had been his tales of a tropical area, which had in turn convinced people, such as a newspaper editor, that he was "queer in the head and had been seeing things." He was later recognized as the original discoverer of Liard Hot Springs—a popular tourist resort area.

There is a footnote to this story that must be mentioned; it was carried in *The Whitehorse Star* of October 13, 1933. Edited for brevity, the gist of the story tells how Mr. Perry had arrived in Wrangell complaining about the great number of aircraft that were working the Liard area:

"*Last fall airplanes began coming into the country, landing their passengers at Sayer's Creek, a tributary of the left branch of the Liard about 75 miles above Liard Post. This was one of the first creeks to be worked by Cassiar miners in the early days, and is said to have produced close to $100 000 before McDame's Creek was struck.*

"*Sayer's Creek has a peculiar history and the somber, moss-grown spruce trees which fringe the lonely waterway have looked down on more than one wilderness tragedy it is said. Sayers and Hyland, the first white men to visit the creek, worked within hailing distance of each other but maintained a grim silence. They would not speak or fraternize. Later when the creek became known, a few prospectors took up ground. A number of them died of scurvy and the creek was thereafter known as Scurvy Creek.*

"*Nobody seems to know why the creek was deserted, but it is presumed that other rich strikes such as McDame's, Thibbit's, Dease and later Dawson, drew men out of the Sayer's country. Soon its dark tales passed into legend; Sayer's Creek, for half a century, was forgotten.*

"*In 1930, the myth of rich diggings on Scurvy Creek was revived. A man named Hamilton, claimed to be a survivor of the party who had died of scurvy, made an effort to return to the creek. He cruised the country in an airplane but failed to locate the old diggings. His story started others on the quest, however, and two more tragedies [Renahan and Burke] were added to the sinister records of Sayer's Creek . . . *"

It is almost laughable when one realizes that in one instance Mr. Perry pleaded for people to go into the Liard, and a short time later, complained about their presence. The most important part of the story, though, shows that prospectors endured a hazardous existence.

In another example of the dangers faced by prospectors the *Citizen* dated July 14, 1931, noted:

"Longworth, July 12—Harold Olson has been missing in the mountains near here since Friday afternoon. In company with three companions Olson was traveling along the mountains when he ran into a severe electrical storm. Lightning struck close to them and the men separated. Three of the party came together later, but no trace of Olson could be found. A search was instituted but it proved fruitless, as the strong wind that was blowing drowned out the voices of the search party. The search is being continued in the hope that the missing man will be found in one of the numerous canyons in the vicinity."

The search was successful and Harold was found, only to die later in an attack by a grizzly bear. It should also be noted that Harold was the brother of Einer Olson, also a prospector, who worked the Barkerville diggings for many years.

The dangers inherent in travelling the wild waters of the Province are described quite well in this article taken from the *Citizen* of 31 December 1930:

"Vancouver, Dec. 30—Two men are reported to have lost their lives in the Cottonwood River, about 100 miles from Telegraph Creek, while making their way out of Cassiar District following a season's prospecting. There were three men in the party, John Ensor and John Campbell, both of Vancouver, and Claude Irving. They were making their way along the Cottonwood River in a boat they had constructed, when it swamped. Ensor and Campbell were carried down with the current, and were not seen again, Irving, who managed to reach the bank. Irving made a journey of 100 miles [160 km] to Telegraph Creek to bring the news of the disaster. Of the three men, Campbell was the best known. He followed placer mining for years. He took part in the Klondike excitement, but during the past few years was interested in the creeks of Cassiar District."

During the month of June 1930, three men made their way into the Trembleur Lake area of North Central BC, intent on doing some prospecting. Carl Fredericks, Herman Peters and Max Westfall set up camp and supposedly started looking for minerals. Several days later, Fredericks made his way back from the lake with a considerable amount of the party's supplies. His story suggested that he had taken ill and had been forced to come out for hospital treatment. He then bought a railway ticket to Edmonton and disappeared.

Four months later the bodies of his two companions were found, badly mutilated, in a shallow grave near their last camp. The head of Westfall had been beaten in, while that of Peters was severed from the body. Fredericks was captured and tried for the murder of Westfall at the spring assizes in Prince George, but the jury couldn't agree, so the case was moved to the fall assizes.

Back in court, Fredericks stated that he had left camp on the night of their deaths and when he returned Peters fired a couple of shots at him. He dodged into the woods and escaped. He heard other shots and after waiting an hour, he returned to camp to find his two companions dead. His explanation was that Peters had shot Westfall and then committed suicide. He further added that he had cleaned up the camp and buried the bodies so that he wouldn't be accused of the crime.

What is interesting about the statement of the accused is that the court was supposed to believe that after committing suicide, Peters had cut off his own head.

A witness named Harry Taylor then testified that the accused had entered his hardware store in Vanderhoof on June 2, 1930, where he purchased a box of 30-30 cartridges. He had also asked to purchase a box of 45-70 cartridges but was told there was none in stock. This information was crucial because at the first trial it had been established that 45-90 bullets had caused the two deaths, although no rifle of that type was found around the camp or in the possession of the three men. The point is that bullet wounds from these two rifles would be identical.

Taylor also testified that Fredericks had told him he had been wounded in the German army, which explained the limp that had been apparent while he was in the store.

After a lengthy trial in which several people testified, and after nearly four hours of deliberation, the jury brought in a verdict of guilty.

Justice Fisher then imposed the death penalty with the execution date set for December 3, 1931.

The fact that Fredericks had asked to buy 45-70 ammunition from the hardware store in Vanderhoof should have been conclusive evidence that there was another rifle involved. But the court of appeal in Vancouver saw it differently; they ordered a change of venue and so the case was moved to Kamloops where Fredericks was acquitted.

Did Fredericks get away with murder? I don't believe there was any doubt that he committed the crimes. For his escape from justice, Fredericks owed a deep debt to the John Howard Society, as they had gone to bat for him and forced the change of venue.

And so one wonders what became of this innocent man named Fredericks. The *Citizen* of March 30, 1933, noted that he had been sentenced to 60 days in Oakalla for carrying a gun without a licence. Game warden Oscar Quesnel had arrested him at Bridge Lake for carrying a concealed and loaded .45 Colt. Sounds like a decent chap, doesn't he?

Concern about this so-called prospector grew to the point where the authorities checked with the German government regarding his past, where it was learned that he had been convicted of six serious offenses; this led to his deportation in 1933.

During the month of March 1932, 18 men were flown into the McConnell Creek area, on the headwaters of the Ingenika, about 20 miles east of Thutade Lake in northwestern BC. A gold discovery that showed great promise had been found and the men were preparing for placer mining as soon as conditions permitted. The last planeload of supplies had arrived on April 2, so by the end of May the men were desperately short of supplies. Two volunteers were asked for, to walk out to civilization and notify the stockholders of the situation. To this end H. Henry and Mike Miller agreed to go; as well, a man named Fred Firth asked if he could tag along and they agreed. The party left the camp on May 16, and mushed their way down the Ingenika as far as Pelly Creek. At that point it was decided that they would build a raft and float their way out.

They expected to find some trappers at the mouth of the Ingenika, but they had all left the area to bring out their furs by the time the men arrived. Left with little choice, the men pushed off and continued down the Finlay River. About eight miles further along, the raft came round a bend right into the Big Creek logjam. There was no chance to avoid it, so it was every man for himself. Henry and Miller each jumped onto the jam, but when Firth attempted to follow, he appeared to lose his balance and fell off the raft. He was instantly sucked under the jam and that was the last his companions saw of him. The two men searched for the body for several hours, then gave up and made their way to Fort Grahame where they reported the tragedy. A search party was formed, which returned to the scene but their search proved fruitless. Henry and Miller then continued on into Prince George.

Back at the claims, the men were beginning to wonder if the world had forgotten them, but that was not the case. We can scarcely imagine their joy and surprise on June 5 for this was the day they looked up to find they were being bombed with food. Flying a Canadian Airway's plane, pilot E. Wells and mechanic J. Faulkner flew low over their camp and pushed out 800 pounds of food—to the joyous shouts of the miners below. It had been two months since they had received any provisions.

Sometimes prospectors survived perils by a bit of good luck. Such was the case when Vic Williams, game warden for Peace River, happened along. Three prospectors were making their way down the Finlay River in Northern BC when they entered the Finlay Rapids. Their boat capsized and two of the men were hanging on for dear life when Vic came along and rescued them. The third man, named Fallbacker, was lost in the rapids. He had been returning to his placer operations along the Peace River when he met with his death.

A similar article in the *Vancouver Sun* of December 6, 1933 noted:
"Vancouver, Dec. 6—Word has been received here of the finding of the body of an elderly prospector named Henry Derby. He was found in the vicinity of Rainbow Creek in the Nation River district. Derby's tent collapsed with the weight of snow and the prospector was either smothered or frozen to death. The body was discovered by Jim Bird."

Thankfully, some woodsmen managed to get to safety against great odds. Such as a veteran trapper named Jack Weisner. While out in the woods in the far north, the 72-year-old man got caught in a terrible

storm and froze both of his feet to the point where he was unable to travel. One by one he was forced to kill off his dog team, in part because he
had no feed for them. A break finally came his way on January 7, 1934,
when a knock was heard on his cabin door. It was a man named Jack
Blanchard, who was a packer for a fur trader named Otto Luberg. Mr.
Weisner was assisted by a great number of people—passed from one to
another—until he eventually reached Fort St. John, 500 miles and
almost two months later. Not only did they save his life, but they also
managed to save his feet—minus some toes.

For people who have followed the many stories of Headless Valley
along the Nahanni River, the next story should prove interesting. It gives
an account of events that at times are at variance with accounts in many
books and articles written to date. This information was taken from the
Citizen dated May 24, 1934:

"*The Nahannie gold field in the Mackenzie District around the headwaters of the Nahannie River, which enters the Liard at a point about mid-
way between Fort Simpson and Fort Liard, is not flowering as quickly as
was expected. Hundreds of prospectors have made their way into the district
from British Columbia and points to the east. They have gone in on foot, in
boats and the favored ones in planes, but if any substantial finds have been
made the discoverers have kept the information to themselves.*

"*Just like many mining fields, the Nahannie had its lost mine, and the
legend has woven around its tales of violent deaths. Placer gold is said to
have been discovered at the headwaters of the Nahannie back in 1905 by
William and Frank McLeod, who were natives of that country, having been
born at Fort Liard. They came out to Fort Liard in the fall of that year, but
started back to the Nahannie the following spring, accompanied, so the
story goes, by a Scotch engineer named Wier. That was the last that the residents of the Fort Liard section heard of any of the three men.*

"*The chapter of tragedy was not completed, however, as some years
later a Yukoner named Jorgenson made his way into the Nahannie. He
came upon pay gravel at the junction of the Flat River with the Nahannie.
He evidently got a message through to his partner in the Yukon and asked
him to join him. When the partner came to the junction of the two rivers he
found the place where Jorgenson had been working but no trace of the man
himself. He followed a number of trails from the camp and eventually came*

upon the body of Jorgenson, from which the head had been severed. The manner of Jorgenson's death remains a mystery.

"Phil Powers, another venturesome Yukoner, sometime later added his quota to the tragedy of the Nahannie. The news of lost mines, the locations of which are buried in the graves of their discoverers, travels into most mining camps. Powers found where Jorgenson had been working and made his way up both the Flat and Nahannie Rivers. Whether he came upon anything worth while is not known. His body was later found in the ruins of his burnt camp.

"Jack Hammell was the next man of note to resume the search for the lost mine of the McLeods. He was well equipped for the search, and had the advantage of having Charlie McLeod along with him. As well, they came into the area by plane. His party spent the summers of 1928 and 1929 in an intensive search but failed to find anything.

"The lost mine remained lost for 27 years. One of the reasons was the fact it was some 75 miles distant from the point at which the remains of the McLeod brothers had been found. The discoverer is said to have been a resident of the Fort Liard district. The story goes he learned William McLeod had given the Roman Catholic priest a map of the district in which his find had been made. While the other searches had been going on, the priest had been in France. He is said to have turned the map over to the unnamed prospector."

"In the summer of 1908, Charles McLeod, a brother of the two missing prospectors, started on a search. He found the skeletons of his brothers lying on the ground, covered with their blankets and came to the conclusion that they had been killed while they slept. He buried their bones, marked the grave and the following spring the RCMP commenced an investigation; but this was one of the mysteries the Mounties failed to solve. Then there followed some intensive prospecting of the area in which the skeletons had been found, but no notable discoveries were made. It was evident, however, that the McLeod brothers had not met death at the point at which they were working, as there was no evidence of a place of habitation, nor of equipment such as prospectors carry with them. There wasn't much known about the McLeod discovery, and after considerable fruitless prospecting in the district, interest died down."

Again there was an interesting footnote to this story. It seems that by early 1934, a group of Liard Indians had staked a number of claims along the Nahannie River, and they were for sale at $3 000 per claim. The RCMP was so impressed with the new gold strikes that they made arrangements to re-open the post at Fort Liard. Newspaper reports stated that many trappers were leaving their lines and heading toward the new rush.

I suppose that at one time or another most of us have imagined what it must have been like to be the first person to find and explore an area unknown to the rest of the world. Now perhaps, you can be that person. Just sit back and pretend that you were at the controls of the airplane in the following story. This story took place in 1939, when famous northern bush pilot Russ Baker was on a flight with Game Inspector Thomas Van Dyke aboard.

Russ Baker's story was carried in the *Citizen* dated February 2, 1939:

"I left Fort St. James for Whitewater on January 19 under fairly good flying conditions, took on gas and supplies and set out for McDames Creek (near Cassiar) far to the northwest of Whitewater, with fuel enough for about four and a half hours of flying.

"Out of Whitewater flying conditions were very bad. Snow was falling and a dense fog partly shrouded the country through which we were flying. We crossed the Turnagain River and finally approached Deadwood Lake. In an attempt to fly above the weather, I was cruising at 9400 feet at about 120 miles per hour. I flew due west down a big river which seemed to be about twice as large as the Nechako River. By its size and my position, I thought I must have been flying down the Dease River, but I soon realized that I, or my map, was in error. For suddenly out of nowhere great hulks of mountains emerged out of the fog in front of me—like giant icebergs on the sea.

"I was surprised—amazed. To be flying at 9500 feet and suddenly to be confronted with huge mountains towering above me gave me a feeling that is difficult to describe. Never in all my years of flying have I had such an experience. All the peaks were glaciated and must have risen to 11 000 feet. I knew my altimeter, which registered our altitude at 9400 feet, didn't lie, but it was apparent that my map did.

"This big river then took on a new meaning for me, for it was evident that I was not on the Dease at all, but was taking my course from some big unknown stream that wasn't shown anywhere on my map. I followed this

Winter
1935/36,
first plane at
Penny, forced
down because
of bad
weather.

river for about 50 miles, until it began to peter out, and then I followed another river back northward again and finally came back to Deadwood Lake. After flying for two hours I had arrived at the same spot from where I had started. It was evident that the two rivers along which I had flown were branches of the Rapid River, which is itself a branch of the Dease River.

"By this time our fuel supply was becoming low, so we sat down on Deadwood Lake, where we stayed the night. In the morning we took a northwest course out of Deadwood Lake and reached McDames Creek in a short time, following the Rapid River. From the time we left Whitewater until we landed at Deadwood Lake we were three and a half hours in the air, yet the normal flying time for that distance is forty-five minutes. From Dease we cut back to the Stikine River, where we encountered that second geographical phenomenon. From my observation it was evident that the two brothers—Chuckichida and Caribou Hide Lakes—are somewhat misplaced on the map of northern BC."

Just what happened to Russ Baker is a subject that will no doubt be debated for many years, but Prince George pilot Don Redden offered one possible explanation. After 40 years of flying as a bush pilot, Twin Otters in the Arctic, and Lear jets, he knows whereof he speaks. Don told me how he experienced a similar thing in 1971. He was flying north of Takla Lake at the time at about 7200 feet elevation when he suddenly looked ahead and didn't recognize the country he was flying through. The mountains looked strange—some of the peaks appeared to be mesas, while other peaks appeared to be farther away and much higher than they should have been. Puzzled, he checked the instruments and all were in order. Then he dropped the Beaver to a lower altitude and everything returned to normal. Again he climbed up to 7200 feet and it returned. At that point Don called to another Beaver aircraft that was following at a lower elevation and told him to climb up because he wanted to show him something. When the other pilot approached his elevation he freaked out and suggested he was lost.

And what does Don attribute this phenomenon to? He feels certain that they had flown into a major inversion. This may also be what happened to Russ Baker because there are no mountains 11 000 feet high in the area where he was flying.

These pilots were every bit as fearless as the woodsmen they flew with in all kinds of weather, but there are many books that detail their exciting lives so I will leave them be.

Getting back to prospectors, the June 8, 1944 edition of the *Citizen* gives another example of what perilous lives they endure.

FIND SKULL, BONES, SOUTH OF QUESNEL

"Discovery of the bones and skull of a man in the Nazko area, south of Quesnel by a man employed by the Quesnel Light and Power Co., has launched an investigation by provincial police. It is believed the bones are the remains of William Chenall, Clinton man, who came to Quesnel six years ago on a prospecting trip with a partner named Stewart. They went into uninhabited country and some weeks later Stewart's body was found. The search for Chenall's body had been unsuccessful."

These two men were but a sampling of the great number that met with tragedy.

Perhaps there are many people who, like myself, consider Robert Service to be the "Voice of the Yukon" and one of the best writers of poetry that ever existed. Not long ago I read an article in which it was stated that Mr. Service manufactured the story of Dangerous Dan McGrew, that he in fact never existed. Since I hold Mr. Service's work in such high regard, I am always on the lookout for information about it, as well as him. For that reason I was pleased to find this next article about Dan McGrew which appeared in the *Citizen* dated January 21, 1937:

"Philip Gershel, a man of 71 years is at present a traveling salesman for a New York grocery house. He has been attracting much attention in the press recently by reason of the claim put forth that he was a witness to the shooting of Dan McGrew described in the widely-read ballad by Robert W. Service. Gershel says he narrowly missed the slug that the murderer of Dangerous Dan intended for the lady known as Lou.

"Gershel, according to his story, has been something of an adventurous wanderer. Born in Melbourne, Australia, he left home for South Africa when he was 21 years old . . . Three years later, Gershel arrived in Dawson City, in the Yukon, flat broke. Here he landed a job as piano player in the Monte Carlo saloon and dance hall. The place was run at the time by a Negro, Jim Dougherty, and it was run on the rip-roarin' plan.

"Gershel's duties were to keep the piano going from early night until dawn, and for this he says he was paid $50 nightly in gold. His wages he deposited daily in the Dawson bank in which Robert Service was the teller. In this way he became acquainted with the poet of the Yukon. In time Gershel says he became known as the 'Ragtime Kid.' He had a free hand with his piano playing and made a hit by feeding the company 'the bird in the gilded cage' and like tunes; but by the time Dangerous Dan was bumped off the shooting habit had become too fixed for comfort. The men often did not shoot where they were looking, and the spectator hazard went up. Gershel's closest call to becoming a casualty came on the night Dangerous Dan was shot down when he got a bullet through his hat.

"On the night of the shooting which Service tells about, Gershel says he was operating on the piano when a man known to him as 'Siwash Bill' came in. He was known to have fallen hard for the 'lady known as Lou' as Service called her. This night 'Siwash Bill' was even more drunk than usual. He called for a drink and then told Gershel to scram from the piano. He could play, and for a minute or two he hammered out a tune until he happened to spot 'Lou' sitting with Dangerous Dan. 'Siwash Bill' started cursing and getting up from the piano, drew his gun and went into action. His first shot was fired at Dan and killed him instantly. He then turned the gun on 'Lou' but missed her completely, the bullet going through Gershel's hat. The murderer then ended his own life and an ordinary barroom tragedy became an epic of the frontier with the ballad by Service.

'Gershel says Service misnamed the dance hall in his verse. At the time

of the shooting it was known as the Monte Carlo, but the name was after-
wards changed to the Malamute as Service gives it. He says Service must
also have known the woman in the case was known as Lil and not Lou, but
this does not matter very much. Gershel says Lou was the best looker in
Dawson, and in the north she cut quite a figure. She would be described
now as a gold-digger. Possibly she was one of the first of the modern gold-
diggers, but she certainly could dig.

"After pulling out of the Yukon the 'Ragtime Kid' eventually settled
down in Minneapolis, got married and raised a family, but he says he does-
n't play the piano any more."

Several added notes about Robert Service were found in Edmonton's
Evening Journal during the months of May and June 1911; these notes
stated that Mr. Service was on his way back to the Yukon. He was at Fort
McPherson in the last dispatch, and intended to follow the trail traveled
by Inspector Fitzgerald and his men when they perished. Mr. Service had
already written *The Trail Of 98* and was hoping to gather material for
another book. Unfortunately I was unable to find out if he reached his
destination.

Another article that relates to Mr. Service was carried in the *Citizen*
of August 4, 1938:

"Sam McGee of Great Falls, Montana, immortalized by Robert Service
as the inspiration of the poem The Cremation Of Sam McGee, was a pas-
senger aboard the CNR steamer Prince Rupert on July 25, going north for
his first visit to the Yukon in 20 years. He left the north in 1909 but was back
in the Klondike for a visit in 1918.

"Sam McGee, grey, grizzled and getting along in years, is still hale and
hearty and continues actively in the road contracting business today as he
did in the days of 98 at Whitehorse where Service wrote about him. His
home these many years has been at Great Falls, Montana, and it is from
there that he now comes.

"McGee is going north with Dick Corless Sr. of Prince George. They are
heading for the country near the headwaters of the Liard River, about five
miles beyond the British Columbia border, where they have placer ground.
From Whitehorse they will be flown into the Liard by Corless' son Tom of
Prince George, in a three-place seaplane."

I have always found Service's descriptions of the north to be outstanding. Sometimes when I am listening to his poems I just have to close my eyes and it seems I am right there in the midst of the action. Perhaps that is why I am so intrigued by these articles, whether they are fact or fiction.

Getting back to the dangers faced by prospectors, sometimes they got into trouble much closer to home, such as the miner that died right beside his cabin. In January 1934, a miner named J. Irvine was heading up Hixon Creek (forty miles south of Prince George, BC) with two bags of flour in his pack. He was wearing hip-waders when found, and had frozen his left foot quite badly, yet he had continued on until all the flesh was worn off the heel. As well, he had badly twisted his right ankle. Just a short distance from his cabin he had given up on the pack and had placed it in the crotch of a tree. Only about 20 feet further along he had dropped by the trail.

Since he dropped right beside his cabin, it was assumed that he arrived under cover of darkness, because from where he cached the flour he would have seen his cabin, had it been daylight. This was the conclusion reached by the attending police officer.

When one takes a good read on this story, one wonders if perhaps Mr. Irvine may have become snow-blind. That could explain him falling in the creek and consequently freezing his one foot. It may also explain why he twisted his other foot. Most important of all, though, it explains his inability to find his cabin.

During the month of May 1936, a group of prospectors were making their way up the Nation River (southwest of Williston Lake) when they ran into trouble. Upon arriving at the third canyon, they were forced to line the boats through. The leading boat got safely through the canyon but when the second boat tried, problems ensued. Two men, John Merkos and Gust Evans, stayed in the boat to hold it off the canyon wall, which they did by using long poles. Right in the worst part of the canyon, the towrope parted and let go. In an instant the boat swung out of control and started back down the rapids, while the men frantically raced along the shore in an attempt to assist. The last they saw of the boat was when it went rapidly tearing around a bend in the canyon. A few miles down the river, the searchers came upon the upturned boat, but no trace of the two men could be found.

The task of reporting the tragedy fell to Felix Mazilius, so he made his way down to the mouth of the Nation River and waited, hoping to hail a passing boat. Luck finally came his way when J. Jorgenson, boat-builder and freighter of Summit Lake, happened along and gave him a ride to Summit Lake. From there he walked to Prince George to report the accident. A few days later Provincial Constable Frank Cook and Coroner Skinner started for the river, and along the trail met a man named Delmar Miller, who told them that he had found the body of Merkos floating in the Parsnip River. Together, the men made their way back to the scene. After the investigation was completed, Coroner Skinner issued a permit and Constable Cook took the body down the Finlay River where he interred it on the riverbank about 26 miles below Finlay Forks.

Such was the experiences of the early-day prospectors and police-men; certainly theirs was a hazardous existence.

Not all prospectors' adventures ended in tragedy, far from it. Some stories told of fortunes made and the unimaginable excitement of hit-ting it big. During the month of August 1938, the following story appeared in the *Citizen:*

"Prospecting in the country east of Barkerville last week, Ted Ossipa was flabbergasted when he found himself the possessor of a 14-ounce nugget. When he first noticed the shine of the gold in the clay where he was working, he was more than delighted at the idea of finding a $2 piece, as it then appeared to him to be. On digging in and picking up what seemed a chunk of clay, he was attracted by the unusual weight, and on washing away the dirt, discovered in his hand a nugget of unusual beauty, weighing approximately 14 ounces."

One would-be prospector with an unusual story was a man named Toby Mogeson. An employee of the sawmill in Penny during the 50s, Toby was talked into this venture by a friend who claimed he knew his business about panning for gold. Off they went on a Sunday, along Red Mountain Creek, where they found a spot that looked promising. Toby spent the whole day shoveling the gravel of the creek-bed onto a blanket, while his partner kept pouring pails of water to wash the gravel away and leave the gold adhered to the blanket. When they played out, his partner suggested they leave the blanket in the sun to dry while they went home to eat. He insisted that by the time they returned the blanket would be dry and they would be able to shake the gold from it. That same evening they returned to their diggings only to find that someone had stolen the blanket. I don't suppose it surprises anyone that Toby never made it as a prospector.

Al Hamilton knew the excitement a prospector feels after finding a rich strike. Back in 1962 he was out on a trip with two friends—Steve Wlasitz, Al Hamilton and Sid Goyer—when he lucked out. What he didn't know at the time was that the creek had been salted. His buddies (if I may call them that) had melted down some welding rods, allowing the drops to fall into water where they assumed many unusual shapes. After seeding the creek, the men made certain that Al was the one to check the spot first and apparently they got their money's worth. Many fantastic dreams were elucidated, and a letter was forwarded to Noranda Mines detailing the find. When the news was finally broken to Al, rumor has it that he took the joke rather well. He apparently told one person that "I'm one of the few people that struck it rich and never had to pay any taxes."

Up until a few years ago, I was generally unaware of the enormous contribution made by engineers and surveyors throughout the early years. The sacrifices they made and the hardships they endured are a testament to a hardy breed of individuals. In July 1932, J. Leighton, known as the "Scribe of Savona" wrote the following letter to the *Ashcroft Journal*:

"*In 1871 the Dominion Government sent out several survey parties in BC to select the best route for a railway. It was known as the CPR survey party, and most of them made their headquarters at Kamloops. One of the parties was under J. Mahood, as chief. They went up the North Thompson to Clearwater River and then began their location work. This was carried on until they came to a good-sized lake that was the main feeder of the Clearwater River. The lake was unnamed, so the party called it Mahood Lake after the chief . . .*"

"*Late in 1871 Mr. Mahood's party reached Barkerville to survey a line through to Fort George. He wanted to make that point [Barkerville] his winter headquarters. He had a good-sized party, and supplies for six months or more. A pack train was engaged from Barnes and Brink who farmed near the present site of Ashcroft, with Mr. J. C. Barnes in charge.*

The contract called for delivery of the party and supplies at Barkerville.
When they reached there, Barnes would not engage to go any further with-
out a guarantee that if they got caught in the snow, he would be paid for his
outfit.

"*The writer was telegraph agent at Barkerville at the time and well*
remembers the circumstances. After two days' telegraphing to Ottawa,
Mahood and Barnes came to terms and the outfit started off. The reputed
distance between Barkerville and Fort George was 90 miles. After a few
days' travel breaking trail—slow work and some snow falling—there came
a heavy fall and they found themselves blocked with fully three feet of snow.
There was no feed for the animals and they could not move, and at the time
they were 60 miles from Barkerville. Barnes gave the thing up and with his
men headed back for Barkerville, which he reached after several days' buck-
ing snow.

"*Mahood made a winter camp there but the animals soon perished.*
Barnes was paid for his pack train as per agreement—$125 for each animal
and the rigging. He went down home by the BX [sternwheeler]. I know of
only one man alive today who was with that party. His name is Alex
McLean. He lived at Kamloops and vicinity for several years and then
moved to the coast."

The Mahood party was just one of many that went through trials
that should have broken the strongest people; his party just one of many
parties of surveyors and engineers that got trapped by heavy snowfalls in
the mountains.

Much could be written about the early-day engineers and surveyors.
The hazards involved in their work were numerous, and often they
worked far beyond the reach of medical help or any semblance of civilization. There were men such as L. C. Gunn and Frank Swannell whose
exploits were well documented. But there were others who received little
attention.

One such man was A. Sprague, also a surveyor for the GTP
Railroad. During the summer of 1905 he surveyed the area west of Fort
George where he found a satisfactory grade. During the summer of 1906
he set off to find a suitable route from Tête Jaune Cache to Fort George.
With him was E. Kepner, acting as guide. These men took an abundance
of supplies with them—so much so that they were prepared to spend a

A successful J. B Hooker hunt. Hooker is second from left, circa 1940.

winter in the woods if necessary. Though they may have survived such a winter outing, it is certain that their horses would not have survived and would have faced lingering starvation unless they were mercifully taken down.

Another such man was T. A. Groat, a guide for the GTP Railroad. By March 1907, this man had been through the Rockies in four different places. He had traversed the Yellowhead Pass, the Sheep Creek Pass, the Wapiti Pass and the Pine Pass as well. It becomes readily apparent that some of these individuals spent the greatest part of the year in the forests.

At that time, people were taking bets about which route the railroad would take, with some suggesting the Goat River Pass and others betting on the Slim Lake Valley. Still others were certain the railroad would follow a more direct line and cross the Willow River just below the canyon. This led to a rush of homesteaders acquiring property in that area. When the railroad took a more northerly route near Eaglet Lake, many of the settlers moved so they could be closer to transportation.

9 Memorable People

THIS CHAPTER IS DEDICATED TO SOME OF THE OUTSTANDING PEOPLE THAT walked this land before us. While many individuals are well known, there are others who remain virtually unknown. One individual that is worthy of mention for dedication and bravery is Father Coccola; a man who proved that men of the cloth could be just as brave and tough as anyone else. In March 1912, Father Coccola made the trip between Fort St. James and Prince Rupert, BC. He accomplished this by a combination of snowshoes, dog team and pony. This trip constituted a journey of about 700 miles.

In a tribute to this man, the Fort George Herald of May 24, 1913, wrote:

"Father Coccola, the big kindly pioneer priest of the Northern Interior country, who for years past has been ministering to the needs of the Indians at the Stewart Lake Mission, was a visitor here this week. The name of Father Coccola is associated in this country with deeds of kindness and with deep respect from all religious denominations. Father Coccola is always welcomed everywhere he goes. He came into the north country long before the Grand Trunk Pacific surveyors ever planted a hub in this country. Amongst the pioneers he performed many kind acts, and, being learned in medicine and surgery, Father Coccola often helped the sick and wounded in the days when there were no doctors in this region . . . "

Even among the many exceptionally brave and talented people that came into the Interior, Father Coccola was a light that shone brightly for all to see. He earned the complete trust of the Indian people and whites as well. Part priest, part doctor and part surgeon, his work throughout the wild country that he served stands as a monument to the strength and courage he possessed. He was one of a special group of priests that would go anywhere and perform any task, no matter how difficult. Often he mushed, walked or snowshoed miles through the wilderness to attend sick or injured trappers or prospectors in their isolated cabins.

Father Coccola first arrived in British Columbia in 1879 and located the silver-lead mine at Moyie. From the sale of this property sufficient funds were raised to build the first hospital at Cranbrook, BC. Then the good Father moved north to Stewart Lake where a big mission was founded. During the years he spent in the Interior of the province he traveled all the old trails, going by horseback, dog teams or snowshoes into the remotest areas which were only inhabited by a few Indians. For many years he covered a huge piece of wilderness, which included François Lake, Teslin Lake and all the Babine country. As well, he traveled to Telegraph Creek, the Stikine River, Bear Lake and territory east to the Alberta border.

In an article regarding the influenza epidemic, the January 14, 1919 edition of the *Citizen* noted:

"The epidemics course was ran with exceptional severity on the Stony Reserve near Vanderhoof, and but for the splendid work of Rev. Father Coccola, many more would have died. Affectionately known throughout the north, Father Coccola has spent the greater part of his life in this section of the province, and his success in this instance was due to the implicit trust placed in him by the Indians."

Everywhere he went he was greeted as a long lost friend, and he earned and carried with pride the title of "Friend of Humanity." Perhaps an early resident of Prince George paid him the greatest compliment when he stated, "Father Coccola didn't need a monument; he was a living monument."

In truth, this person's dedication and service stand as a timeless reminder of a life given to the service of others—a hero in anyone's book.

Another person that begs remembrance was Joe Merrienne, also known as Sousa Thapage. Since Sousa played such an integral part in the history of the Interior, I want to reprint an article carried in the *Citizen* on January 30, 1920:

"There appears to be a vast difference between people who like to call themselves 'old-timers' and people whom the few that know term pioneers.

This was brought home to the writer one day recently when he heard an introduction couched in the words, 'Shake hands with Mr. So and So; he's an old-timer; he came in with the steel!'

"There are a great number of men in this country who came in with the preliminary surveys of the GTP [Grand Trunk Pacific Railway] about 1907, and there are the old settlers of Lower Cariboo. These men may be called old-timers, but when we speak of pioneers let us go back to the men who survive from the days of the Cariboo gold excitement. These old servants of the Hudson's Bay Company and the pioneer trappers and prospectors who remember the Cariboo country when Gus Wright's famous road crossed the Fraser River canyon at Spuzzum.

"Such a one is Joe Merienne, better known here as Sousa Thapage. This name clings to him from the days when Joe was a great boatman and packer for the Hudson's Bay Company. It means 'big packer' for he was once renowned for his strength in carrying great weights over the portages and at the unloading of the 'brigades' when the boatmen would vie with each other in the carrying of the heavy loads, for their vanity took the form of physical prowess.

"If you look at a map of the town-site area here [Prince George] you will find a little triangle of land in the South Fort George town-site which is marked 'Thapage Homestead.' At one time the whole of the South Fort George site was Thapage's pre-emption. He sold it and there sprang up about his log home on the Fraser River at 'South' the bustling little pioneer community, which was filled with such a hectic and vigorous life in the days of construction. Then came the steel and the founding of the real town Prince George, and the life went out of the old town and moved over here. Now there is nothing but the skeleton of the wonderful little boom city left there, and old Thapage sits there by the river bank again in the summer time and casts his mind back over the 70 years that he has spent here since his birth at Fort George.

"Sousa Thapage is a French Canadian half-breed. His father was a servant of the Northwest Company under Simon Fraser, the explorer of the great river here that bears his name. Simon Fraser established the Northwest Company's post here in 1808. In the spring of the following year, accompanied by John Stewart, Jules Maurice Quesnel, a crew of 19 men and two Indians, they embarked at this place in four well-furnished

South Fort George, circa 1912. Picture taken near the present Simon Fraser Bridge. The road across the River goes up to the L. C. Gunn homestead and starts at the reaction ferry that became redundant after the arrival of the railroad.

canoes to explore the unknown waters between this point and the Pacific. Stewart Lake and Quesnel are named after his two companions. Thapage believes that his father was one of the party under Simon Fraser on the historic expedition to the Pacific. They left Fort George on May 29, and reached the mouth of the river on July 1, establishing the fact that the Fraser was a separate and distinct stream, and not the Columbia, as had been believed to be the case.

"Thapage was born at Fort George about 70 years ago. He is not sure of his dates, but the writer thinks that he is nearer eighty than seventy. He entered the service of 'the Company' as a boy and worked on the brigades that took out the skins to Victoria over the river and trail routes, which used to stretch between here and the seaport of the company. On the return they would bring in food and trade goods. Sometimes the termination of the long journey was Langley, in the Delta. In time, by reason of his strength and usefulness, Thapage became captain of a boat, and one of the right-hand men of the Factor.

"*The Factor here, when he entered the Company' service, was Manson, and following him came Charles Ogden, a descendant of the great discoverer who came up from Oregon. Then came Alexander Peters, who is now sheriff of Cariboo, Ed Kepner, who for many years ran the Occidental Hotel at Quesnel, 'French Joe' Reid, James Cowie and Armstrong. The latter three factors are within the memory of most of the men who worked on the GTP surveys.*

"*Thapage's memory is clouded. He is an old man. He speaks French patois better than he speaks English, and so it is difficult to piece together a really comprehensive narrative of his remarkable life in this country. He speaks only in generalities. 'In de sommer,' he said, 'we all de time feesh; feesh de salmon; follow him way up de river.' 'In de winter,' he spat, 'cut cordwood for de company. Maybe hunt a leetle. Dat is when we don't go on dat Brigade.'*

"*He can remember the days of the gold rush and of the Klondike excitement, when scattered expeditions tried to go over into the Yukon over the terrible trail of the Yukon Telegraph and the Hudson's Bay Company, which stretches for the hundreds of miles between here and Dawson. He was one of those who went out in search of Sir Alexander Curtis, whom, in company with Mr. Roger Pocock, left here bound for the Yukon many years ago. Sir Alexander Curtis was never seen again after the party had broken camp one morning on the trail near the Mud River.*

"*The surveys of the CPR through this country he recalls quite clearly, and he relates having helped to pack their supplies out to the cache which still stood in the woods near the old trail to Quesnel about ten years ago. He recalls Sir Sanford Fleming, who was appointed engineer-in-chief of the CPR in 1871.*

"*Sousa Thapage has never crossed the mountains. In the old days the Edmonton Brigade would meet them on the Fraser River in boats. In those days canoes were not used for transport. Big boats were built which were tracked up the river by many Indians. This method of transportation was in vogue even up to 1909 between Quesnel and Fort George, and in 1907 the writer made several trips with the 20 Indians who tracked scows up the river from Quesnel to the Post here. The trip would take about 14 days, and about 20 000 pounds would constitute a good load.*

"*Asked if he can remember any of the Indians here who were older than himself, he mentioned two—Freddy Bascar— 'Old Freddy,' as he is called, 'was a beeg boy when he was very li'll.' Old Freddy had two brothers killed by a grizzly bear, and Freddy only barely escaped with his life on the occasion. The other man Thapage mentions is Seymour, one of the finest Indians in the whole Interior. His son is now chief of the Fort George Indians.*

"*He tells of the time when the old Hudson's Bay Post was at the mouth of the Nechako River, and of the year of the great flood which inundated it. The water on this occasion came to within a few feet of the top of the bank at the point where the present disused Hudson's Bay post is located. He states that Indians can yet point out marks high up on the big trees where the water reached in the flood he tells of.*

"*Thapage married a daughter of the redoubtable Bouchier, who is referred to in Father Morice's book,* History of the Northern Interior of British Columbia, *as the 'Avenger.' His father-in-law was the trusted half-breed of the company who used to be sent out to track down marauders and bad Indians in the old days of H.B. rule.*

"*Now the old man has fallen upon evil days. His relations are dead or have scattered. He can not properly come under the care of the Indian Department, for he is a half-breed and a pre-empter [homesteader]. 'All I want is some wood,' he told the writer, 'just some wood. My leg, he's bad now; I can't cut no more, I am too old.'*

"*The Citizen commends this case to the Provincial Secretary for some relief. It is distressing to think of a man who has spent a long lifetime here, suffering for the ordinary needs of existence at an age when he cannot help himself. Friends may give him temporary relief, but some reasonable relief should be afforded him for the balance of his life.*"

Another story about Sousa's life was carried in the *Fort George Herald* on March 23, 1912. Since it adds touching memories of the way of life at that time, I will include part of it:

"*. . . In those days the home of the old half-breed was, besides the old Hudson's Bay post, the only house in Fort George. The surveyors and trappers were ever welcome. On occasions Thapage would give a dance—something the stranger never would forget. Indians, half-breeds and white men would gather under the old man's roof and long into the morning the revelry would go on. The music was that of the fiddle—Hudson Bay jigs,* *accompanied by the dull monotone of a deer-hide drum. Thapage would smile and welcome everyone, ceaselessly guarding his reputation for hospitality. His wife, a great good-natured woman, would echo his welcome. Half-breed girls would shyly dance the 'square dances' or huddle together in groups, bedecked in calico dresses and startling-colored handkerchiefs, whispering and laughing low. There were times when boisterous revelers would hammer on the old man's portal in the middle of the night, but never would his reserve of hospitality allow unwelcome guests to peer beneath the mask . . . "*

If people take a drive down Queensway Street in South Fort George, and carefully watch the street signs, they will notice "Thapage Lane." This is the only reminder that this entire area was once the homestead of this incredible pioneer.

Worth expanding on are the lively parties held by Sousa and his wife. It is impossible for someone in today's world to understand the importance of these parties in a remote wilderness area. In the days prior to radio, music was virtually unknown in many areas. Gordon Solmanson, who was raised near the Torpy River back in the 1920s, told me a story about music and its effect in those days. An elderly trapper came out of

the mountains for Christmas and during the festive season he was invited to a party. During the evening he stared in amazement as music was played and people danced and laughed. This trapper later told Gordon's family that when he went back to his

Joe and Bessie Beaudreau playing the piano and fiddle, 1966.

trapline he had a terrible time; the music kept going around in his mind and he felt more alone than he ever had before. It took about a month before things got back to normal for him.

I was always aware of the effects of music in a rural setting. Certainly when we were children our home was an endless source of music. Both of our parents played instruments, and not many weekends went by without a party in our home. Many times in the intervening years people have told us how much those parties meant to them.

While I'm on the subject of the early history of Fort George, it seems appropriate to consider the price of staple commodities compared to prices in Eastern Canada. The following list gives some comparisons made during the month of April 1911:

Western prices—eggs, $1.50 dozen; butter, 50c/lb.; pork, 40c/lb.; potatoes, $8 bag; hay, $60 ton (wild).

Eastern prices—eggs, 16c/dozen; butter 21c/lb.; pork, 8c/lb.; potatoes, 50c/bag; hay, $16 ton.

These prices show that people coming to Fort George needed an extra bundle of money in their socks, although it must be added that these commodities were hauled in over the Blackwater Trail during the winter months. With the arrival of the first sternwheeler after the river was clear of ice, the freight prices dropped an average of 6c/lb.

Many readers will recognize the name of the following pioneer, as he was highly regarded throughout the Province and known worldwide for his big game hunts. The *Fort George Herald* of October 4, 1913, stated:

WELL-KNOWN TRAPPER BADLY MAULED

"Barkerville, BC. Oct. 10—Word was brought into town Wednesday evening by George Shaw, a member of a party of surveyors working at Bear Lake, 20 miles north of this place. Frank Kibbee, the well-known trapper and guide, while engaged in following up a large bear that had been caught in a trap and had broken it away from its fastenings, had been set upon by the enraged animal, and frightfully mauled about the face and body.

"Dr. Callanan immediately left for the lake, but up to the present time no further word has been received as to the condition of the wounded man. According to Shaw's story, Kibbee and his companion—Frank Conners, set off to visit the spot where the trap was located, but on arriving there found

Frank Kibbee with moose, circa 1920.

that the bear had been caught, and owing to its enormous size had been able to drag the trap from its fastenings. The two men immediately set out to follow up the trail, and after going some distance, Kibbee, who was in the lead, was suddenly sprung upon by the infuriated animal and borne to the ground. Before his companion could come to his assistance he was frightfully bitten and clawed about the face and body. Conners, hearing the noise of the scuffle, rushed forward and shot the bear with a revolver, killing it instantly. On rolling the animal off his companion, Conners discovered that he was bleeding profusely, and was unable to walk. He managed, however, partly by carrying him and partly by dragging, to get him to his home, a distance of four miles. Fortunately, Mr. C. Baker, the surveyor who was working around the lake, had a first aid outfit among his effects, and was able to render temporary assistance to the wounded man pending the arrival of the doctor.”

Just how tough a man Kibbee was, was shown about a month later by an article in Quesnel's *Cariboo Observer,* which noted that Kibbee had been in Quesnel to visit the doctor, who had pulled out the remains of several teeth that the grizzly had broken off. It further noted that he was picking up supplies and heading back to his trapline.

The third newspaper article I found about him was taken from the *Fort George Herald* dated January 13, 1915:

HUNTER HUNTING WIFE

“With every desire to be obliging and assist Dan Cupid in his missionary activities, says the Victoria Colonist, *the press will no doubt courteously comply with the request 'other papers please copy.' Trapper, hunter and*

guide Frank H. Kibbee of Barkerville appends to an 'appeal to the girls for a wife' which this well-known Cariboo frontiersman published in the Ascroft Journal.

"'I am a bachelor,' declares Kibbee with positiveness in his matrimonial prospectus, 'by occupation a trapper, hunter and guide; am the owner of a ranch 20 miles from Barkerville, BC, aged 40, height five feet eleven inches, habits strictly temperate. I should like to correspond with a nice young lady between the age of 25 and 40—object matrimony.'

"'My home camp,' the lonely and lovelorn one continues, 'is at Bear Lake, which is 21 miles by horse trail from Barkerville . . .'

"'My hunting territory takes in Bear Lake, Bear River, Swan Lake, Three-mile Lake, Sandy Lake, Long Lake, Isaac Lake and the Iron Slough, a distance of approximately 150 miles. The portages between the lakes are very short, the longest being less then a quarter of a mile. The hunting is mostly from boats. Will gladly meet any parties at Barkerville with horses.'

"'My territory is pre-eminently bear country, particularly the habitat of the grizzly, but there is also moose, caribou and some deer—although not many. The fishing, too, is splendid—rainbow and Dolly Varden trout, char and salmon . . .'"

Included in his advertisement were the names and addresses of several prominent people who were willing and able to vouch for his character and reliability. The most interesting part of this gamble was the fact that it appeared to bear fruit. Just a short time later Kibbee was on his way to Vancouver to claim his bride-to-be.

Sandy Phillips of Wells, BC, who has followed the life of Kibbee with endless zeal, tells the story of Kibbee's trip as related by Jean Speare, who remembers hearing it during her childhood:

The marriage of Frank Kibbee and Anita Juanita, 1912. Photo courtesy Barkerville Archives.

"Kibbee was somewhat of a bashful man who did not know how to knot his tie. So he got a friend named Joe Wendle—after whom Wendle Lake was named—to knot it for him just before he headed off to the city of Vancouver to meet his wife-to-be. He rode his horse to Barkerville and then traveled by stage to Vancouver—which took a couple days. All throughout the trip he wore his shirt and tie, because he was afraid that he would never get the tie knotted properly again if he took it off."

We can only imagine what the shirt and tie looked like by the time he met his bride-to-be, but obviously it wasn't bad enough to deter her because a short time later they were married.

Kibbee truly was one of the old-time woodsmen—just as rough and tough as the country he inhabited. It is nice to know that his memory will live on with a lake named after him.

Sometimes great adventurers seem to meet and marry people with the same adventurous spirit, and the next two stories certainly prove this point. As good a place as any to start is during the Yukon Gold Rush, when George Snell, formerly of Australia, arrived to try his luck at hitting the mother lode. Within a few years things went so well for him that he ended up with a company and fifty employees. One day George was inspecting his cookhouse when he found the cook using bacon strips to make the fire burn hotter. The cook was immediately fired and George went looking for a new cook. It didn't take long, though, before he came up with a very attractive young lady named Mary Jane McLeod, who took over the cookhouse as well as his heart. Janey, as she was known, had arrived from Prince Edward Island along with two brothers, and the cook job was just what the doctor ordered. In 1906 they were married in a lavish wedding in the Yukon.

A couple years later they moved to Seattle, but not for long. The pull of the north tugged at them and drew them into another adventure. They made their way north through the province until they reached Quesnel; this is where the tough part of their journey began. Following the old Telegraph Trail with packhorses and a cart, they found the going slow and tiring; sometimes they covered only a short distance in a day's travel. At one point, possibly the Blackwater Hill, they had to take their cart apart and pack it and all their supplies up the hill.

For a month and a half they labored along the trail until they

The wedding of George and Jane Snell at Dawson City, 1906.

reached the Nechako River at what is now known as Vanderhoof. This was to be their new home. The first white settlers in the Nechako Valley, their daughter Louise, the first of eight children, was the first white baby born in that area.

The devotion of family life at that time was shown when Janey's sister passed away. George and Janey took her sister's son, Alec, and raised him as their own.

During the years that followed, George became a first-class farmer; but prospecting was in his blood and throughout the years it continually called him back into the forests. He hired some men to run his farm and went back to his first love, looking for the elusive pot of gold just behind the next mountain. Newspaper articles from the 1930s are rife with sto-

Chuck Williams and George Snell, Manson Creek area, circa 1930.

ries about his claims; they repeatedly describe his crews sinking shafts on this or that stream, always upbeat and sure that they would hit pay dirt. During those years George freighted for Bob McCorkell who also had claims in the area.

Their daughter, Olive Snell, was also involved in these ventures, as she cooked for the crew of Bob Adam's mine along Manson Creek back in the 30s. Olive has some wonderful stories to tell of their adventures in what was then a wilderness area. One of her stories concerned the 40-man crew that worked at the Adam's mine. Apparently they would gladly stay after their evening meal to help Olive and her sister Esther do the dishes, so they could come out and play ball in the evenings. "They were perfect gentlemen out there in the woods," she said, "but some of those boys would turn into animals if you met them in town." And what made the difference in their behavior? A thing called booze, which made many a good man turn into an animal.

Famous pack train owner Skook Davidson was a frequent visitor to their camp, as he packed all over the northern part of the province during the 30s and 40s. It was common for people travelling through the forest to find him sitting by a campfire waiting for a stream to drop out of flood stage so he could cross it and get on with the job. According to Olive he did not drink alcohol while he was working but he sure made

George Snell freighting across the Omineca River, circa 1930.

Bert Goderich and his wife in the cab; they were later lost in a plane crash. Olive (Snell) Williams on right. Old Hogem Road, 1935.

up for it when he came to town. Then it was bottoms up and the devil could have tomorrow.

There is a story about Skook that simply must be told. Ray Mueller of Sinclair Mills, who was present when the event occurred, related it. The year was 1933, and Skook had just came off his trapline in the upper Herrick Creek to Dome Creek, for a little B&P (Booze and Partying). Just a short time earlier he had ordered a few bottles of booze, which were in the Dome Creek Post Office, waiting for pick-up.

It was a Sunday when Skook and Ray dropped into Postmaster "Scotty" Stewart's home to pick up the booze. Disappointment awaited them, though, because "Scotty" informed them that he never opened the post office on Sundays. At this point Skook lost patience, picked up a fry pan and klonked "Scotty" over the head with it. Result? That was the only time in the history of Dome Creek that the post office opened for business on a Sunday.

This is the same Andy "Scotty" Stewart who was minding his store back about 1920, when someone rushed in and asked if he would assist a woman in labour, because her husband was absent and there was no one else around to help. After agreeing to give his assistance, "Scotty" added, "Sure they call for me when they're calving, but they sure never call for me when they're bulling."

Skook Davidson, Manson Creek, 1936.

Before I leave Skook, I must mention that he spent many years packing and guiding with a fellow named Frank Cooke, who eventually bought the guiding territory when Skook retired. There is a story about how Frank found a human skull, and instead of notifying the police, he placed on a stick at his camp. Rumour has it that the police were not amused.

Getting back to Manson Creek, much of the hardship and often overwhelming problems they faced is detailed in the excellent book *The Goldseekers* by Ralph Hall. As an example of what they had to deal with, Ralph tells how he worked seven days a week for an entire summer without finding a trace of gold.

On one trip into Manson Lakes, Ralph was left alone to guard a large amount of food that was to be picked up by pack train a few days later. In his book he reminisced:

"After the plane's third trip, and with all the grub under canvas, I made my bed for the night. With a cheerful campfire blazing and a good feed under my belt, I leaned back against a pine tree and relaxed. It was good to be alive! I shall always remember that night. Not because of the things that happened, but—on the contrary—because of the solitude and magnificence of God's handiwork. Only when a person is alone and at peace does he really take time to appreciate his environment."

Good stuff from a man barely into his twenties.

I asked Olive if Ralph's book told it like it was and she agreed that it most certainly did. She went on to say that she knew most of the people mentioned in the book.

Frank Cooke's tent along the Hyland River, 1946. Apparently the police were not amused.

Somehow it seems appropriate that the daughter of the adventurous Snell family, Olive Snell, met and married Ted Williams of Prince George. For Ted was the son of one the great pioneers of the Interior of BC. Just a small example of his incredible life is contained in the next story.

Many of the most-needed pioneers were those who first traveled the waterways and opened the country for others to follow. One such man was George Williams. I believe that George was one of the finest rivermen to ever grace this country. Although in fairness I must say that he became so, in part, because of his ability to pick the right people to assist him. When the Europeans first arrived in this area, many of them had little or no experience with wild water. George had already had such experience because he had delivered the mail from Prince Rupert to Hazelton during the years of 1907-08. In the summer he delivered some mail and other commodities by canoe, and in the winter by dog-team, coming through from Kitimat. In 1909 George came to Fort George and went to work for the main railway contractors—Foley, Welch and Stewart (FWS); this is when his wild-water days really began. During the summer of 1910, he made several trips between Fort George and Tête Jaune, 315 miles upriver, where he picked up surveyors or writers such as Stanley Washburn who wrote *Trails, Trappers and Tenderfeet*, an excellent book.

Just a short time later he again returned to Tête Jaune where he picked up a writer named Fred Talbot, who wrote two books—*The New Garden of Canada* and *The Making of a Great Canadian Railway*. These two books describe so very well the Interior of the Province at that time and the many sacrifices that were made by all concerned.

During the following years until late 1913, George Williams moved scows along the river for the contractors and Fort George merchants, and he earned fame as being among the greatest of these rivermen or "River Hogs" as they were often called. To his fellow rivermen he was known as "The Wizard of the River," a title that stuck with him for many years thereafter.

Much of the secret of his success was due to the fact that he mainly hired Fort George Indians to man scows as well as pole and paddle canoes with him. Many of these Indians had years of experience on the rivers and were as George's son Ted described, "The best of the best."

This is where George Williams really shone—he had the ability to spot talent in others and then was able to get the best from them. He treated the Natives with a great deal of respect and won their respect in return. His record speaks for itself: he brought countless thousands of tons of freight down river without any loss of men or material. In short, he lived up to his title—"The Wizard of the River."

George Williams bringing second dugout canoe up through the Upper Canyon, assisted by Fort George Indians. They are on their way to get author Fred Talbot in Tête Jaune, 1910.

After his freighting career was over, George became a businessman who successfully operated Williams Meat Market in Prince George. At the same time his knowledge of the wilds was put to good use by the government when he was appointed to the Game Conservation Board. After his appointment the *Citizen* noted:

"On numerous occasions his services as guide have been sought by hunters of international reputation, and his knowledge of this country's game and fur-bearing animals and the measures necessary for their protection will doubtless prove of inestimable value."

Perhaps it was inevitable that someone with such a craving for adventure would become a treasure hunter. This started in April 1927 in Panama, where he turned up some old coins and pieces of jewelry. But it got into full swing during the winter of 1927, after he purchased a new-fangled metal detector. Mid-November found him going through the ruins of old Puerto Bello, which had been sacked by the famous pirate Henry Morgan. Then it was on to Cocos Island where it was rumored that $50 million in pirate gold was hidden. From the ruins of Castillo de

Assisted by Fort George Indians, George Williams (black hat) takes author Fred Talbot (on left) down river from Tête Jaune to Fort George. Grizzly Bear Mountain is in the background.

San Geronimo, where the Spanish governor fought to the death against Morgan's buccaneers, some church plates of silver were found; this included a silver bell seventeen inches high. There was also a miniature altar of solid gold two feet three inches in height and a crown of silver set with gold. Other finds included silver vases, jugs and trays.

After returning from his treasure hunt, George made an interesting and challenging trip during August and September 1928. Along with Mort Teare and Tom Griffiths, they took a 26-foot riverboat down river to Quesnel; then had it hauled to Bear Lake. Their quest was a fabled lost mine along the river, which they spent about a week searching for before they gave up and returned home via the Fraser River. At least four large logjams were encountered along the Bear River where the men had to portage their boat through the forest. As well, several other spots gave them trouble because of low water levels.

The endless adventures that George was involved in give us an idea of the insatiable hunger that possessed this man; perhaps it was this inherent love of adventure that brought him to this area in the first place. Rugged adventurer that he was, there was also a human and humble side to this man. This was shown by the manner in which he treated other people. I have it from several different pioneers that he was held in the highest regard by his peers.

If ever the City of Prince George was to honor a former member of the community, they need look no further than this man, for he will always stand as a shining example of the courage and tenacity of our forefathers.

Another Interior riverman that demands mentioning was Bob Alexander, who also moved vast quantities of freight along the river during the days of railroad construction. Throughout the early years Bob became a famous freighter on many of the northern rivers. For instance, during the months of September and October 1910, he piloted two men named Craig and Horne through the Giscome Portage and Peace River route to Edmonton and return. This boat trip took 32 days, and on his return Bob noted that "Edmonton is growing into a beautiful city which will some day be compared with Fort George."

Mort Teare mentioned above was also a great adventurer. There is a story about him and his brother traveling far from the haunts of men

Wild water expert George Williams in later years.

when one of them got an infected tooth. After the suffering became unbearable, they found a railway spike and put it to good use. One of the brothers held the spike against the infected tooth while the other struck the spike with a large rock. The tooth came out and the brothers continued on with their travels. It should also be noted that Teare Mountain near McBride was named after this mountain man.

When we turn back the pages of time and look at the pioneers who walked this land before us, there are some that stand out as the true movers and shakers of their time. I feel that Frank Freeman is one such person, in that he blazed a trail well worth remembering.

Born in Hilton, Nova Scotia, Frank first came to this area in 1909. Employed by FW&S, the railway contractors, he used his skill as a powder expert to clear the Grand Trunk Pacific right-of-way between Fort George and Fort Fraser, a distance of about 120 miles or 190 km.

In 1912 he started down the Fraser River from Tête Jaune, where he blew out many rocks, boulders, logjams and river obstructions. He worked on the Goat River Rapids, the Grand Canyon, as well as the Giscome Rapids. When this work was done he headed up the Nechako River where he cleared a channel through the Isle de Pierre and Mud River rapids.

The number of lives and the value of equipment saved by these "blasters" cannot be known, but it was substantial; yet even when their work was completed there was still a great loss of lives and equipment.

With the onset of World War 1, Frank enlisted with the Canadian troops, but later transferred to the Imperial Forces and saw service with the water transport in Mesopotamia and in Egypt, where his knowledge of water transport was put to good use.

After the war, Frank worked in the forest industry for a time. This included a stint in Penny, BC, where he became a close friend of my parents, Joe and Bessie Boudreau, who held him in high esteem. Among his many achievements was that of overseeing the building of the first road to Willow River—a project of great significance as it opened the area to vehicular traffic for the first time.

Perhaps the most fitting tribute to Frank's life was written long before his death in the following article, edited for brevity, that appeared in the *Fort George Herald* dated August 24, 1912:

"There arrived in town this week from the upper river a big fair man in a green shirt that was rent by a flying rock up in the Grand Canyon. There he is driving a gang of rock men in his job of clearing obstructions to navigation out of the river, and tearing out a steamboat channel with dynamite and steel. His name is F. C. Freeman, but among his familiar friends he passes muster under the name of 'The River Hog.'

"He is a silent person—this "River Hog"—speaking only when you ask him things, and then not answering at any length. He works for FW&S, the railway contractors and his task is to free the river they want the great sternwheelers to navigate, from the rocks that threaten their safety on the rivers. A few weeks ago the S. S. Operator, *a boat that can load 300 tons of freight, smashed on a rock in the Goat River Rapids and her crew jettisoned about 150 tons of freight in order to save the vessel from total destruction. Since then the "River Hog" has visited the Goat Rapids with a crew of his men and a load of dynamite, and a clean channel has been blown in the living rock of the riverbed. No longer are the Goat Rapids a menace to navigation; or a place to whiten the hair of the river captains who gamble their skill against the rocks that lurk in ambush beneath the muddy waters of the great river that flows so swiftly on toward the sea.*

"In the Grand Canyon, Freeman is tearing the land to pieces where it crowds the water too closely. From the riverbed, with steel and dynamite, under his direction, men are clawing the hungry rocks. The great walls of the canyon give back roaring echoes as huge charges of powder in the

Frank Freeman, centre, with Josie and Frank Hinsberger, Penny, circa 1925.

coyote holes shatter the rocks, and the waters close quietly over the scar in the canyon's jaw. Where, since time began, the great hungry tooth has gnashed and torn at every sign of the coming of the multitude and their fleets to conquer.

"The 'River Hog' is now commencing operations up the Nechako River. The White Mud Rapids, and the Isle de Pierre, both dangerous chutes of rock strewn, white water, will be harnessed and broken, and made to run smoothly through a wide, deep channel.

"And so we leave him to his task, this 'River Hog.' He has a big task in these northern waters, but he is used to handling big jobs. When he passes along there will be many a placid chute of water where the river has lain in wait, with death at hand, to trap the unwary as they run the gauntlet."

Frank spent his last several years in Willow River, BC, and suffered a great deal from pneumonia and other lung problems. Some suggested that his lung trouble was brought on by staying too close to the powder blasts throughout the years. Whatever the cause, Frank passed away in the Prince George Hospital in 1931; a pioneer who gave much of himself so that life would be better for those who followed.

While I'm on the subject of rivers, I must repeat a story that created disbelief throughout the Interior for many years. This event took place during the months of May and June 1921, when Monte Fraser, a well-known McGregor River guide, and Thomas Corno, also a guide, completed a sensational trip. They set off on this trip by having their canoe hauled by mules from Prince George to Summit Lake, where they began their water journey. With them were three miners, M. Kerr, R. Kerr and W. Aubin, bound for their mineral claims near Rocky Mountain Canyon on the Peace River. From Peace River the guides carried on to Edmonton, a total of 750 miles.

What made this trip remarkable was that a three-horsepower gasoline engine driving an airplane propeller powered their 19-foot canoe. The propeller, which produced a speed of seven miles per hour, was stationed four feet ahead of the stern. Included in its clever design, was a rope system for controlling the steering rudder in the stern of the boat. This meant that the pilot could sit in the front of the boat where he was positioned to read the water, and yet have full control of the craft.

Their trip started at Prince George on May 9, and they reached Peace River on June 4. From there they went to Edmonton and returned to Prince George. A short time later they took another group of prospectors to Peace River. The surprising part of this story is that these men managed to make this air-propeller system work. Others who tried it quickly gave up because of lack of control on narrow streams; in fact, I had one riverman tell me that he didn't believe the story because he had tried it and found that he had almost no control of his craft. Another individual suggested that these men must have had both a water and air rudder.

Another individual that had a profound effect on the Interior of BC, was Roy Spurr, a man of many talents. Just like many other settlers of that time, Roy came from a family that had roamed the earth before he finally settled in this area. For that reason, I want to present a brief summary of his family history.

Robert Spurr was born in Somerset County, England, in 1611, where the Spurr family had held land since early in the 12th century. In April 1635, he sailed to America, where he settled in the area of Dorchester, Mass. Here he became a prominent man who was said to be more liberal in his religious beliefs than most. In 1676 he was called before the church "to make acknowledgment for entertaining at his house loose and vain persons." The power of the church was again demonstrated in 1678, when he was again censured.

In 1759, his grandson, Michael Spurr, moved his family to Annapolis Royal in Nova Scotia, where they took a free land grant of 500 acres of land. Five generations later, on December 22, 1885, Albert Roy Spurr was born in Deep Brook, Nova Scotia.

As a young man, Roy started out as a bookkeeper, working for the Dominion Coal and Steel Company at Sydney, NS. He was the son of a sea captain, and perhaps there was restlessness handed down through generations. At any rate, Roy felt the urge for adventure and headed west. His dream was to be a fur trader, and he dabbled in it for a time.

In 1911 he arrived in Tête Jaune, BC. The Grand Trunk Pacific Railroad was heading west and Roy spotted an opportunity: he opened a small café and thus began his second love—cooking; at the same time he also did some fur trading. By winter 1911, the railhead had passed Tete Jaune and the town was dying. Once again Roy saw an opportunity—he moved down river in June 1912 and built a small café and rooming house at the head of the Grand Canyon, 106 miles upstream of Fort George. He operated in that spot until Fall 1913, when the railroad constructed low-level bridges that halted steamer traffic on the river.

As the river traffic came to a close, Roy moved down river once again—to the new community of Willow City, later called Willow River. Here he had another go at fur trading when he opened and ran a stopover place and store. A few years later he moved once again, this time to the tiny community of Penny. Ever the opportunist, in 1917 he built a sawmill at Penny, in partnership with Tom Wall and Hugh MacKenzie; this mill operated until 1921. Then Roy started the Red Mountain Lumber Company in Penny. My father and mother moved to Penny in 1923, and my father was employed in this mill, which was capable of cutting 50,000 board feet per shift. For several years Roy boarded with my folks, and they had great respect for him: first as a person, and also as a man who showed great devotion to his dream.

Ever a major worry was the threat of forest fire, and in 1927 it became a living nightmare, for that year a fire roared through the area, through the incredibly thick and aged coniferous forest that prevailed. Only at the last minute the wind changed, and blew the fire back into itself. By some miracle, all the buildings and the sawmill were saved.

My mother used to enjoy telling us about how they released the chickens and other animals so that they had a chance to escape the fire. Several days later, after the fire had cooled down, they went looking for the animals, and this led to a humorous incident. Just before dark one evening, while clamoring over the remaining debris in his search, Roy Spurr stepped over a burnt log only to come down on top of a hog that had taken refuge there. There was a mighty squeal, quickly followed by Roy in full retreat for home, while the hog went the other direction. A few days later it returned home.

In 1928, Roy sold this mill, and the following year a major change occurred in his life—for fate moved him to Vancouver, where he met and married Margaret Mann. In 1932, along with friend Don McPhee as a partner, they purchased the Winton Lumber Co. at Giscome, BC, which had gone into receivership. Many say that the Eagle Lake enterprise thrived when others didn't because of Roy's devotion to the thing he knew best—hard work. Others say it was his willingness to accept change that created prosperity in the tiny community which was so dependent on the mill. When asked if he had any hobbies, Roy responded with, "My work is my hobby."

Shortly after their mill purchase, Roy and Don McPhee built a sawmill at Upper Fraser; then purchased another at Sinclair Mills. All three operations were very successful.

Roy was not one to use abusive language, so when he was faced with a problem he would exclaim, "Gracious"; when faced with a serious problem, "Goodness gracious"; when faced with a crisis, it was, "Oh my goodness gracious." Always one to get involved, he showed an example of this when he became the first president of the Northern Interior Lumberman's Association in 1940.

Several people told me the fact that Roy had an unusually dry sense of humor. This was vividly displayed the day a workman cornered Roy and went into great detail complaining about the way things were going. After several minutes of listening to the complaints, Roy very slowly turned in a complete circle, then faced the man and softly said, "You know, everywhere I look around here I can't find anything tied except

Left to right, Harold Mann, Fred Spurr, Roy Spurr and Margaret Spurr, June 1947.

the horses." It was a very diplomatic way of telling the chap that if he didn't like things, he was free to move on.

In the early 40s, several carloads of air-dried lumber were shipped from Giscome to England. Some time later a telegram arrived from the receiver of the lumber, "Received the knot holes. Stop. Please forward the knots!" This story caused a great deal of laughter along the line for many years after.

Not long after Roy took over the Eagle Lake mill, he hired his brother-in-law, Harold Mann, to run the woods operation for him. On his arrival in Giscome, Harold went to the cookhouse for his evening meal. As soon as he walked in, he noticed a vacant seat at the end of one of the tables. He sat down and was in the process of reaching for the potatoes when a big hand grabbed him by the neck and lifted him out of the seat. Then a stern voice advised, "This is my seat; don't you ever sit in my seat again." Harold often told this story and used to end it by adding, "That was my introduction to Giscome."

With Harold's input and assistance, Roy went about dismantling the company's logging railroad. With its two engines, 23 flatcars, and seven miles of grade, it had been much too expensive to operate. Instead, they replaced it with machines and built all-weather logging roads, then put trucks on strict timetables that made or broke the drivers. They drove pilings to support the major tramways—pilings that would heave with each winter's frost, requiring them to be leveled again each spring. They also built over 15 miles of plank roads over swamps and muskegs. Roy's camps were the first to install showers and electric lights in the Interior of BC; he also went to great expense to build houses for his employees and their families.

The old adage that history repeats itself came true for Roy in 1938, when another huge forest fire came close to his Giscome operation. Once again the winds moved the fire in a direction that caused it to miss the community.

Roy Spurr's Giscome operation was very successful; but after building the mill up to where it shipped 22 million board feet of lumber per year, Roy and Don McPhee sold most of their shares in Eagle Lake Sawmills, as well as the Upper Fraser and Sinclair Mills operations. The Milner Interests purchased the shares in 1947 for what was reportedly "a considerable sum." But this did not mean retirement. Roy carried on running the operation for the new owners, who advised, "The

Left to right, Roy Spurr, Bill and Gordon Spurr with Don McPhee, 1938.

Giscome railroad for logging, circa 1925.

company's policy is to continue the good reputation that has been built up by the former owners in the manufacture of good lumber and the maintenance of good labor relations."

At this same time, Roy built the Giscome Farms. This company, with its subsidiary Northern Dairies, supplied a large percentage of the milk consumed in Prince George.

One story that I found quite compelling concerned a cook named Joe Read who was employed at Giscome during the late 40s. At this same time there was a comptroller named Bill Hine who had been left by the Milner people to keep an eye on things. One day Joe turned in a list of supplies needed at the cookhouse, and when Bill saw it, he took it upon himself to delete many items that he thought were unnecessary. When the supplies arrived at the cookhouse, it didn't take Joe very long to realize that the list had been tampered with. A few minutes later he arrived in the office with the list in one hand and a meat cleaver in the other. He threw the list on Bill's desk and stuck the meat cleaver right through it and left it buried in the desk. Then he shook his finger under Bill's nose and said with much emotion, "When I order supplies I expect the orders to be filled." According to Roy's son, Fred, Joe never had any problem getting his orders filled after that.

There's another cookhouse story that should be told. It occurred the

Giscome fire,1938.

day a voice rang out in broken English, "The camp's okay, but the cookhouse is all the time too much not enough grub."

Roy Spurr was one of those individuals who seem to appear when and where they are needed, the kind of person who has a profound effect upon the lives of so many other people. Industrious to the end, he suffered a heart attack on August 13, 1954, while on duty at the mill; he died on the way to the hospital in Prince George.

Among the souvenirs left after Roy's passing was some information concerning an inaugural trip he took on the Pacific Great Eastern Railroad—now BC Rail. On November 1, 1952, an inaugural train with Premier W. A. C. Bennett aboard arrived at the CN Depot in Prince George. It marked the completion of the northern extension from Quesnel to Prince George—so long overdue.

The train made a special stop at Ahbau Creek 56 miles south of Prince George, where L.C. Gunn, famed surveyor from the building of the Grand Trunk Pacific Railway, drove a silver spike.

Down through the years, the PGE had taken on many descriptive names—some of them not at all flattering: there was Prince George Eventually, Please Go Easy, and Past God's Endurance. But when BC's Minister of Railways, Ralph Chetwynd, addressed the crowd of 5000 gathered at the depot in Prince George, he added yet another twist by

Foreground - Giscome dairy; background - Giscome and Eagle Lake Sawmills.

exclaiming, "Prince George, Egad!" This brought a response from some wise guy in the crowd, "Prince George Especially."

I believe that Roy Spurr's memory will live on, and rightfully so, because he played such an integral part in the development of the Interior. Perhaps long-time employee Buster Brown of the nearby community of Willow River summed him up best when he described him as "a man of his word."

The L.C. Gunn mentioned above was another legend in his time—a man who surveyed much of the Interior. A very colorful and outspoken chap, he and Roy Spurr were involved in another story that demands telling. This occurred on a CN passenger coach near Jasper, Alta., when Mr. Gunn decided to pull the leg of an American reporter named Cy. The story was carried in an American magazine—*The Pycolog*.

LINCOLN NH {USA} SEPTEMBER 1945
MOOSE

On the recent trip to British Columbia, it was just outside of Jasper Park, Alberta, that I made moose mistake No. 1 when I innocently asked the Conductor if there were any moose around. Up to that time the conductor had been a pleasant, genial old chap and full of stories about the West which I had swallowed with complete gullibility. At the mention of moose, his hair, what there was, lifted, his eyes took on a glassy stare and his breath came in the gasps of a hay fever victim. Finally he was able to gasp out, "Are there any moose?"

"Listen son; just below here in a stretch of 12 miles with the train going so fast I could just count the poles, I counted 52 moose." And with that he settled back as if he had just made his last will and testimony. To this there was nothing to be said, but I made up my mind to find an honest man before mentioning moose again.

"This man seemed to be Roy Spurr, Manager of the Eagle Lake Operations at Giscome, BC. Mr. Spurr is a man of the highest ability, integrity and sincerity, but at the mention of moose his old felt hat lifted about two inches. Then his features took on a shocked expression, that a new saw hitting a railroad tie plus a forest fire on Williams River could never duplicate, and I could see moose mistake No 2 coming up. Mr. Spurr was going up his driveway to lunch one noon when a big bull moose jumped out of the woods and blocked his way. For one-half hour Mr. Spurr tried to get by the moose, but when he tried to get by, Mr. Moose moved over. Finally Mr. Spurr, thinking of his dinner getting cold, got hot under the collar, went back to the mill and had the boys come up and kill the moose with cant hooks. At this point I decided to become a victim of the other sex.

"When Mrs. McCall, the housekeeper of the Guest House at Giscome and a sincere and gracious lady, was asked about moose she made a grab for her broom. At this move I prepared to get out, but discovered the broom was only to demonstrate moose mistake No. 3 just ahead. On many a morning, with a howling blizzard going on and the temperature at -40, she had stood on the back porch brushing moose aside with her broom in order that her cats could partake of their milk in steam-heated saucers without moose interference.

"After this one, I vowed never to mention moose again and I didn't until introduced to Mr. Gunn. After talking to Mr. Gunn I decided that any man who had surveyed the country as he had and laid out the course of the Canadian National Railroad would not be bothered about the moose question. What Mr. Gunn went through on my question, "How's the moose?" is impossible to describe. Even after a five-minute interval he had not recovered sufficiently to tell his moose yarn and went onto a bear story while recovering. Mr. Gunn was returning from a surveying trip in his 'Lizzie' when he came upon a tiny mite of grizzly bear in the road. Not wishing to

harm the little chap, Mr. Gunn stopped his car, got out, and planted a gentle kick on the rear quarters. The young fellow squeaked a bit, and Mr. Gunn was immediately faced with 15 feet of Ma Bear. He made the car and got underway, but as he went by, Ma reached out a paw and took off one rear tire. Pop Bear appeared at this time on the other side of the car and took off a front shoe. For 10 long miles Mr. Gunn rode for his life. At the 10-mile post, with all tires gone, all glass out and with Pop Bear just about to pull off the gas tank, the 12 little bears who had been following on behind, played out, and Mr. Gunn was spared the inconvenience of winning the greatest hand-to-paw bear fight that ever threatened to take place in British Columbia. What Mr. Gunn's story on moose is, he alone knows, for at the conclusion of this true story, I remembered I had to telegraph my aunt Hattie in Calais, Maine, about her heart trouble.

"Moose mistake No. 4 was sure a beaut. I decided to take a chance with a young chap at the mill for moose mistake No. 5. It seems that he and his wife were taking a shortcut through a virgin strip of timber one night with the aid of a flashlight when an enormous bull moose charged them. Quickly this chap hurled the flashlight over his wife's shoulder striking the moose between the eyes and shouted to his wife to climb a peach tree that happened to be in this virgin stand of spruce. He luckily had his spikes on (they had been to a dance) so took refuge in a four-footer. Looking down from a height of 100 feet he discovered a miracle had happened. The ring of the flashlight had slipped over a small horn and the light, which never went out, was shining in the eyes of the moose and blinding him. Reaching ground again, they pushed the moose out of the way and went unhurriedly home. To help out, Mr. Moose, unable to see, but going by hearing, followed them to their front steps where he was promptly dispatched into small hunks without points.

"I found the people of the Northwest Pacific to be industrious, able, sincere and honest until moose was mentioned. Just mention moose, brother, and you've got something on your hands you'll remember for a long time. Anglers are good, but moosers are better, believe you me."

The article was continued in the *Pycolog* just two months later:

MOOSE APOLOGIES

"After reading yesterday's mail, I made myself this promise. If ever again I have the good fortune to pay a visit to the Canadian Northwest, especially to the community of Giscome, BC, I will believe to complete entirety every moose yarn that is presented. If told that a young bull moose walked into the lumber yards of the Eagle Lake Lumber Co. and walked out with an 80-foot boxcar full of white spruce on its antlers with plenty of horn sticking out on either end, I am just going to consider it was fortunate that Pa and Ma Moose didn't come along and walk off with the whole mill with the lake thrown in.

"To the conductor who plies the rails between Jasper Park and Giscome, who told me that he counted 52 moose in 12 miles and which I disbelieved at the time, I humbly apologize. With my own eyes, I have counted in a picture I received, 47 moose in a huddle on the Fraser River just ready to start out for the Community House at Giscome for breakfast. On another picture received, 26 moose were counted heading for a Mrs. McCall handout. My conductor friend should have his eyes examined, for as things stand right now, he must be missing half the flock. Fifty-two moose in 12 miles to me now is just chicken feed.

"Two months ago I wrote an article on moose, published in the Pycolog, *in which I intimated that some of the yarns had been stretched to the breaking point and beyond. Since that time I have received enough literature on moose to start a library. This has been donated by my back-door neighbors 3000 miles away and includes pictures, stories, Habits and Care of the Moose, Moose History and Moose Calls. The only possible addition that can now be received is a bull moose himself, and I wouldn't be surprised to have one show up any day now by parcel post.*

"From now on I'm believing every moose yarn that's told and do believe to some extent all those told in the past except one. I refuse to believe now as then, the yarn of Jim Crump and Henry Waldo: that on their air cruise the moose were so thick that the horns sticking up in the trees bothered their estimation as to the number of trees per acre. That, brethren of Vancouver and Giscome, BC, and Lincoln, NH, I refuse to swallow now or ever. —Cy."

The above stories plainly show that insofar as humor and exaggeration are concerned, there was plenty to go around—even years ago.

Not all of the above stories are exaggerations, though, for I have seen a picture taken in the 1940s near Hansard Bridge: it shows at least 36 moose bunched up waiting for the ice to freeze so they could cross the Fraser River to their winter feeding grounds.

The type of people descending on the Interior of the province in the early days was demonstrated once again by a Prince George alderman named T. Griffiths. During an interview in 1928, he recalled the Klondike days, as well as the hardship and frustrations endured by many. He recalled how a great number of people left cities along the West Coast and made their way north. Some came by way of Skagway, while others sought water access by way of Atlin and Teslin Lakes. Then came plans to build a railway to the Eldorado from BC; this caused the towns of Glenora and Teslin to spring up overnight. Griffith and a partner took a chance on the Teslin route and they decided to capitalize by affording transportation to the many across the 90 miles of the lake. They built a large scow on which they placed a tubular boiler; with this they intended to make their fortune. As well, they plied the lake with large nets and then sold the fish to men going to the goldfields.

For three months they cleaned up, and then word arrived that the proposed railway would not be built; this news caused people to desert the Teslin route and use the roads in from the coast.

This is the way things stood in October 1898, when Norman Lee of Hanceville in the Chilcotin, arrived at Teslin Lake with 175 head of cattle. Lee knew that beef was selling for $1.00 a pound in the Yukon, and so he set off on this 1500-mile journey, which, had it been successful, would have guaranteed his pension. He also intended to sell to the crews building the proposed railroad. When Lee learned that the railroad idea was bust, he realized he had no option but to take the herd to Dawson. After an incredibly tough trip that lasted several months, he arrived at Teslin Lake where he purchased lumber from Griffiths to build scows. Assisted by Griffiths and his partner, Lee had the remaining cattle butchered and loaded on scows for the trip to Dawson. On October 17, the barges were loaded and Lee started along the lake, but after two days they encountered rough weather. Beaten by the continuous waves, the scows started shipping water and the seams took to leaking so badly that the crew attempted to beach the scows. By the time they got to shore, the scows had settled and the beef was all under water.

Discouraged, Lee returned to Teslin seeking help to assist in raising some of the beef. They returned to the sunken scows and raised a considerable amount of the beef, but by then freeze-up was upon them and there was no chance to get the meat through to Dawson. The venture was a total loss, and Lee who was flat broke, decided that he had his fill of the northland. With winter upon them, Griffiths and his partner left Teslin by dog team and made their way down the Stikine River to Wrangell; then caught a steamer back to Vancouver. A few weeks later Lee followed in their footsteps and returned to Nanaimo and then back to the Chilcotin. His sense of defeat somewhat lessened when he learned that another Chilcotin rancher had similarly failed. Named Harris, this chap had also driven a couple hundred head of cattle to Teslin where

they were slaughtered and placed aboard scows; after a successful trip through Teslin Lake his scows got frozen in along the Yukon River and most of the meat was lost.

Photo taken by Ernie Micks in 1938. This grave is located going over the old road going to Baldy Mountain, north of Fort St. James to Manson Creek, BC. Gillis received a letter from his sweetheart, telling him that she married some one else, so he killed himself.

Such was the stuff these pioneers possessed—if they lost at one venture, they simply moved on to another.

I doubt that there are people more deserving of recognition than those that were involved in the Monkman Pass Highway. This epic adventure really got public attention in August 1936, when two members of Alex Monkman's crew arrived in Prince George in mid-August. Along with a crew of volunteers, they had succeeded in blazing a trail from the Peace River area of Alberta, through the Rocky Mountains to the North Fork of the McGregor River, then called Herrick Creek. This meant that they were only about 35 miles north of Hansard, which is on the CN Railway line, only 50 miles east of Prince George, BC. From that time until December 1938 a great number of people threw their weight behind the project. One newspaper described it as the greatest piece of work ever attempted in Western Canada on a community effort basis.

Alex Monkman had first discovered this pass in 1922, while he was on a hunting and trapping trip. Alex was surprised when he ran into other trappers who informed him that he was in the McGregor watershed. On his return to Alberta, he informed the railways that he had found a new, low pass through the Rockies. Surveys taken in the following years confirmed that it was in fact the best route through the Rockies. As the years went by Alex realized that here was the answer to getting Peace River grain through to the ports of Vancouver or Prince Rupert. A distance of only 132 miles would join up with the CN Railway at Hansard. This would cut off the 800 miles required to go through Edmonton.

YUKON CATTLE DRIVE

Norman Lee left his ranch in this valley in 1898 with 200 head on a 1500-mile "beef" drive to the Klondyke gold camps. Five months later, winter forced him to butcher the herd. He loaded the meat on scows, which were lost on Teslin Lake, 500 miles short of Dawson City. Lee returned, undaunted, to help in the development of the cattle industry on Chilcotin's productive grasslands.

PROVINCE OF BRITISH COLUMBIA

This sign near Lee's Corner tells of his cattle drive.

Lorne Lyle, a merchant from Aleza Lake, was a staunch booster of the Monkman project and got directly involved. At the same time another group was busy promoting the Yellowhead Highway from Jasper to Prince George. Its president, Arthur Read of Longworth, wrote the following letter to the *Citizen* dated September 2, 1937. It was addressed to the Secretary, Monkman Pass Highway Association (MPHA):

"As you have at times published open letters to me in regard to the opposition of the Yellowhead Highway Association, I would like to respond. You can hardly expect the residents of the upper Fraser Valley, who have waited for highway communication for 25 years, to sit idly by and see a new project sidetrack our outlet. Your road will traverse a difficult and unin-habited country, while the Yellowhead is opening a settled valley with the largest industry and payrolls in northern BC.

"I would suggest to your association that instead of taking the longest route through the uninhabited McGregor valley [Monkman Pass] to Aleza Lake, that you look at once into the shortcut [east fork of the McGregor River] that will bring you out on the CN Railway near Kidd or Dome Creek. Boats have been portaged across this route to headwaters of McGregor for many years. It will shorten your route by 50 to 70 miles, and your project will more likely be endorsed by public bodies along the CN Railway . . . "

Mr. Read's concern was that the Monkman Highway would in fact isolate the community of Longworth, whereas the Yellowhead Highway from Jasper would run right by their doors.

At this same time another group, mainly pushed by the US govern-ment, was considering the possibility of putting in the Alaska Highway through the Pine Pass. Understandably, the end result was that govern-ment officials were pulled in all directions, a course of action that was detrimental to all groups.

With more and more people joining the force, the Monkman proj-ect was advancing rapidly, and by August 12, 1937, they were able to drive a car for 53 miles along the new road. The crews involved worked their hearts out, donated the first two weeks of their labour for their board, and then received $1 per day if they wished to stay on. In August, a truck drove a distance of 65 miles along the road. This was half the dis-tance to Hansard and it encouraged all to greater effort.

By April 1938, Vancouver had thrown their weight behind the Monkman project, and calls went out to all governments to get into the act and render their assistance. As well, every imaginably method was used to raise funds with no donation, however trivial, being refused.

To bring more attention to their cause, the workmen packed a 50-pound bag of flour through the pass to the North Fork of the McGregor River. It was left with trappers Martin Framstead and Henry Hobi, who spent four days packing it through the woods to Hansard. In one instance, the men nearly drowned in the river and were forced to give up using horses and had to pack everything on their backs. Once in Prince George, the bag of wheat was shipped on to Vancouver with the clear understanding that there would be much more to follow when the road was completed.

At that same time, US President Roosevelt began pushing for a highway to Alaska. To add momentum to that project, former US President Hoover was adding his voice to that effort while he and friends were fishing in Stewart Lake at Fort St. James, BC. During their trip, some high-powered advertising came to that community when one of the group caught a 16 1/2-pound rainbow trout.

All these forces pulled governments in different directions leading to a great deal of confusion, with governments crying that they had no money for anything except maintenance.

Although some credit has been given to the McGregor River trappers for their assistance in the Monkman project, newspaper articles suggest they earned a great deal more. They were frequently used as guides, and their knowledge of the surrounding area was put to good use by the trail-makers. One of their experiences was documented in the *Citizen* of June 23, 1938:

"Four tired men, three with axes in hand and the other with a compass, are making their way through the entangling brush on the route of the Monkman Pass. They are a reconnaissance party locating a trail for the proposed Monkman Highway out of Hansard. Suddenly one of the men shouts as a huge cow moose and her calf charge toward them. Just as the moose is lunging at the men, they are surprised to see a huge bear appear from the bush and tackle the calf moose.

"Meanwhile, the cow moose has started an attack on the unfortunate

compass-man, Martin Framstead, who makes a rapid ascent up a nearby tree. Martin's face is entirely bearded and it is quite apparent that the animal's anger is aroused at the sight of the heavy whiskers. Martin, not having seen the bear, is concentrating his attention on the moose below. In an effort to save the compass, he clutches the instrument with hot hands, fearful lest it should fall.

"Meanwhile, unbeknown to the be-whiskered tree-climber, Henry Hobi is making a valiant attack on the bear with his axe. The bear releases the calf, and struggles for a time with the man with the axe. In a minute the bear gives up the fight and charges off into the bush. All this time Martin Framstead, clutching the compass, is up a tree, still without having seen the bear. And Henry Hobi, Caribou John and Ole Hanson are still laughing at the recollection of Martin Framstead up the tree with the compass in his hand—as they recount the story of their adventure."

By the end of July 1938, about 100 men were working the grade, while steady pressure was applied to governments for assistance. The Alberta government, while not financially involved, kicked in tents, slip scrapers and other pieces of road building equipment. They also supplied surveyors to locate the road in an official manner so it could be placed on maps. The work along the grade was often extremely difficult; the crews suffered from the elements as well as the mosquitoes and flies that showed them no mercy.

Encouraging news arrived in Prince George in August when two men walked through the Pass. They brought word that one crew was at beautiful Kinuseo Falls and that another crew had cut a ten-foot wide trail a distance of five miles north of Hansard.

Martin Caine, the secretary of the MPHA in Prince George repeatedly put out calls for money, claiming that $500 to $600 would be enough to push the road north to the McGregor River. The aim was to get a light car through the Pass before winter arrived because this would prove the feasibility of the road to all doubters.

The biggest obstacle to the MPHA was the American Alaska Highway Commission (AAHC) under Warren Magnussen. They held a meeting with BC Premier Pattullo, during which he promised to take the matter up with Ottawa. At this same time the people of McBride involved in the Yellowhead Pass project, a recognized provincial government project, were organizing as well. Their intent was to raise as much money as possible to push the road through to Prince George and Prince Rupert. They knew full well that time was against them, and they hoped that a concerted effort on their part would move the government to greater effort.

In need of a gimmick to further their cause, the MPHA decided to attempt to get a Model T Ford "Pathfinder" through the Pass to Hansard and then on to Vancouver. Named the Mountain Lizard, this vehicle arriving in Vancouver would be their crowning achievement and all effort was aimed at getting it through. By September 8, 1938, the truck was already at the Murray River and success seemed certain. By the end of September word was received that the Pathfinder was only 21 miles from the McGregor River and the crew felt certain they would make it through before winter.

When the Pathfinder was within four miles of the river, an appeal was sent out for assistance; the response was noted in the *Citizen* of December 2, 1938:

"On the second day of the snowstorm three boys left our camp to go down to the base on the McGregor to pack in supplies of grub and gasoline. They told the trappers of our predicament, that we were shorthanded. The

Jack Shufelt, Bill Yost, Caribou John, Martin Framstead, Mr. Duncan and Ole Hanson. McGregor River trappers, circa 1935.

next day by noon every trapper on the McGregor was one of Murphy's Pathfinder car crew. That night the car rolled into camp 39 and two days later amid wild cheers, it rolled into the base camp on the McGregor."

The *Citizen* also noted:

"We had been told that the trappers would be deadly opposed to the Monkman Pass Highway and that anyone promoting it would be unwelcome. The generosity with which they threw open their cabins for our use and the vigor with which they assisted was no inconsiderable factor in putting the first car through the Monkman Pass. In the name of the people and the MPHA we wish to thank you—Ole Hanson, Herb Cook, Caribou John Bergstrom, Bill Yost and Martin Framstead—gentlemen all."

Further word was received on November 10, when a group of men arrived in Prince George. They noted that the truck was at Henry Hobi's cabin at Moose Creek, now called Fontiniko Creek, and would be brought out to Hansard the next day. This news caused great rejoicing, and for the first time all involved really started to believe that their unremitting labor had been worthwhile.

The *Citizen* noted their arrival in Prince George:

'The men were heavily bearded, had gnarled hands, and their clothing was soiled. Francis Murphy, the 'Moses of the Monkman' who had been leading his doughty pioneers in their task, wore a bandage around his head, the result of an axe cut."

These men, along with a host of others, were all entertained at a fund-raising dance to celebrate what many had considered an impossible mission. Word flew around the world and praise came from some faraway places. In an issue of England's *Nottingham Post* it was noted:

"A new road is being driven through the Rockies and is being paid for by the 85 000 residents in the Peace River area of Alberta. It will link their land to the Pacific coast and give them a new outlet for their products. Without any assistance from governments or any outside source, they raised a public subscription fund using such means as dances, shows and whist drives. And now they are carving through the great barrier from Rio Grande in Alberta to Prince George in British Columbia."

Just how successful the dances were fund-raising was demonstrated in early December, when 46 dances were in swing on the same Saturday night.

Ben Cook's camp at Fontiniko (Moose) Creek. The Pathfinder car sat here for 29 years.

In the BC legislature, MLA H. Perry, while asking for $20 000 for road assistance, expressed his view:

"There are assets of the flesh and there are assets of the spirit. The initiative and enterprise of the Peace River people who conceived and went ahead with the enterprise are among the most valuable assets this country possesses.

" . . . The people who have undertaken this job did a very valiant and energetic thing. It was a heartbreaking job and they got a few thousand dollars from Vancouver that was highly appreciated. But they have just failed by about $20 000 to get the road through."

The piece of road referred to by Mr. Perry was the piece from Fontiniko Creek through to Hansard, which was never completed. The river froze over before the Pathfinder car could be brought out to Hansard. It spent the winter sitting in Henry Hobi's boathouse at Fontiniko Creek. Finally, in June 1967, it was taken down the McGregor River and shipped back to Alberta where it was rebuilt and put on display at the Stojan garage in Sexsmith.

And what spelled the end for the Monkman Pass Highway? The war started in 1939 and all attention was given to the Alaska Highway. The MPHA dream, and the road itself, faded away into what must have been a heartbreaking ending for those who gave their all.

There is another story that must be added to the Monkman chapter. It concerned a man who got off a passenger train at Dewey in 1949. This man had only a few supplies with him and his intent was to follow the Monkman Pass Road through to Alberta. It was mid-winter when he attempted this feat, yet the few supplies he had on a small toboggan showed that he was unprepared for the long trip. Steve Wlasitz, who was at the station at the time of his arrival, heard the section foreman advise him not to attempt the trip; that it was a 132-mile hike. He replied that he was going to follow the Monkman Highway and continued on his way. Somewhere in that endless wilderness he disappeared, hopelessly searching for the road that would have been snowed in, as well as overgrown in many places during the intervening years.

As for the Yellowhead Highway that had been worked on by many relief crews during the Dirty Thirties—it was another 30 years before it came to fruition. When it finally did, it took a different route and a great deal of the effort made by the early trail-makers went for naught.

The following story which was taken from several newspapers as well as from *Canada's Flying Heritage* by Frank Ellis, speaks of courage above and beyond what is expected of any human. It tells a story of two men that didn't know the meaning of the word "quit." This story began on October 10, 1930, when a prospector named Robert Martin chartered a float-equipped Junkers' monoplane at Atlin and flew to Lower Post in the far north. The next day Robert left Lower Post with pilot Paddy Burke and an engineer named Emil Kading, formerly of Prince George, on a flight that should have taken them back to Atlin via Teslin, Gladys and Surprise Lakes. En route they ran into a heavy snowstorm over the mountains and Burke turned back to the Liard River where he put the plane down and they spent the night.

It was still snowing the next morning when they took off and just a short time later Paddy was forced to land again when the weather socked in solid. On touching the water, the floats encountered some rocks and were torn apart. In desperation, Paddy ran the plane to the steep bank of the river where it was impossible to get the plane out of the water or to perform the necessary repair work.

The men were not worried, though, because Paddy had told his wife to notify the owners of the aircraft in Vancouver if he was too long overdue, so they expected a rescue plane within a week. They took stock of their supplies that consisted of one eiderdown and two summer-weight sleeping bags, an axe and a 30-30 rifle with 12 shells. Their total food supplies consisted of 51 pounds of beans and rice, 3 tins of bully beef, 1 pound of tea, 3 pounds of sugar, 3 tins of dried vegetables, 2 pounds of butter, 3 pounds of raisins, and 6 chocolate bars.

Throughout the first week Kading hunted every day but saw no game. Later, when they took stock of their supplies, they were alarmed at how quickly they were disappearing. With winter coming on, they considered building a raft with which to float to the nearest village many miles down river. The idea was quickly discarded, though, because two of the men could not swim, and they all agreed that the rope required to hold the logs together would not last long in the rock-strewn river. After much discussion, they decided to leave a message that they were walking out to Junkers Lake at the headwaters of the Liard River where they had left a cache of food during the previous summer. They carved a message into a tree and started their hike on October 17. The river had not frozen over so they found the going along the bank to be extremely difficult, wading through the deep snow. What with carrying their sleeping bags, food, axe and rifle, they averaged less than four miles a day.

After one week on the trail, Burke, who was less conditioned than the two prospectors, played out. At that point the men decided to camp and hope that they would be found in time. By the 24th, the last of the food was gone and during the next three weeks the men subsisted on one duck and three squirrels. During that period of time, Kading hunted every day without seeing even a single track. Finally, on November 15, he managed to bag a caribou that wandered near their camp. Near death, Burke did not respond to their efforts to ply him with soup. On November 20, in the silent campsite, with only the dull light of a campfire casting its flickering shadows into the eerie darkness, Paddy Burke gave up his fight for survival.

In their weakened condition, Martin and Kading made a coffin of logs and placed the pilot's body into it and used his sleeping bag as a cover. Then they tied his boots up in a tree and left the following note in one of them: *"Paddy Burke died November 20, 6:30 P.M. cause: sickness from lack of food, having been 23 days without same. Please pardon our poor efforts as we are in a sinking condition. Expect to leave here Saturday 23 for Wolf Lake, following the Liard River until Caribou Creek. Hope we can make same. Snow very deep and no snowshoes. Bob Martin, Emil Kading."*

The next day they set off, carrying as much of the caribou meat as their weakened bodies would allow, but within five miles they played out and gave up. During the days that followed both men spent at least 18 hours out of every day in their sleeping bags. Without hope, their strength and will-to-live quickly fading, we can scarcely imagine the despair and utter loneliness that plagued them in the silent, endless forests.

Not once throughout their terrible trip had they heard the sound of aircraft, but finally on November 24th, they sighted a plane. Totally unprepared, it took them several minutes to get a fire going to signal, and by that time the aircraft was gone. Filled with despair, the men tried to conserve their energy by spending most of their time in bed. Martin's toes had been seriously hit with frostbite; a result of the men wearing leather boots unfit for winter travel.

When it became obvious that her husband was overdue, Mrs. Burke had notified the Vancouver Office and they immediately dispatched an aircraft from the Tredwell Yukon Co. in Whitehorse. The pilot was a man named Dorbrandt and he reached Atlin on October 26. After several unsuccessful flights into the area, he was forced down on Thutade Lake because of a shortage of gas. On November 5, an Indian walked many miles to a point where he was able to report that the missing Dorbrandt plane was down on Thutade Lake, and out of gas.

After being re-supplied, Dorbrandt had to leave the area because other prospectors were dependent on him for pickup and supplies.

On October 30th, the *Prince George Citizen* noted:

"Advice from Vancouver last night stated Captain E. J. Burke, who has been missing in the Liard River district for the past 18 days, is still unreported. And the two planes that started in search of him are now also missing. It is the worst time of year for flying in the north, as there is sufficient ice on the lake surfaces to make landing with pontoons difficult, and not enough ice to permit the use of skis. The two relief pilots are Frank Dorbrandt, who passed through Prince George a few days ago on his way to Anchorage, and Pat Renahan, who started out from Vancouver . . . "

After Dorbrandt's rescue, a thorough search was conducted for another lost search plane. This plane was owned by Alaska Airlines, flown by a Canadian pilot named Renahan, and was hired by a friend of Burkes, a prospector named Sam Clerf. Along with an engineer named Frank Hatcher, they headed north along the BC coast. On November 4, somewhere north of Prince Rupert, they ran into thick fog and crashed into the ocean. One wheel that washed up on a tiny island was all that was ever found of the courageous searchers and their plane.

Then another plane got into the search. This aircraft was *The City of Prince George* and on its way to Atlin it made a fuel stop on Thutade Lake. Aboard was pilot R. I. Van der Bly, assisted by his engineer T. Cressy, and passenger W. A. Joerss, a former pilot. A thin layer of ice covered the lake and when they attempted take-off, the floats and propeller continually loaded up with ice. After several unsuccessful attempts to get off, the pilot was forced to give up. A discussion was held and they decided that Joerss would attempt to fly the plane out to civilization, even though his licence had been suspended. The reason given by pilot Van der Bly was that Joerss "knew the country better." As Van der Byl and Cressy discussed their 200-mile hike out of the area, Joerss managed to get the plane off the lake and then flew to Vanderhoof.

As soon as word of his arrival reached the police, they began investigating his illegal use of the aircraft, while at the same time they gave their attention to the stranded airmen.

After the two men were rescued, they stopped in Prince George. The *Citizen* of December 18, noted:

"Pilot R. I. Van der Byl and air engineer T. H. Cressy, who were marooned for a considerable time at Thutade Lake, while taking part in the search for the late Capt. Burke, passed through Prince George on their way to Jasper. The people of the province have waited long for their story as to how they came to be stranded at Thutade Lake, when former pilot Willaim Joerss came back to Burns Lake. There was a disposition to the belief that Joerss had treated his companions unceremoniously in leaving them. But both men are in agreement that this is well wide of the mark. Both men went the limit this morning in the endeavor to create the impression Joerss is entitled to the highest credit for the way he handled things in getting the plane out of Thutade Lake. Had he done otherwise the plane would have

remained in the lake until spring, and the province would have had another mess on its hands with missing airmen.

"Pilot Van der Byl says they ran into unexpected conditions when they arrived at Thutade Lake. They were prepared for an increase of 1500 feet in their elevation, but had been led to believe the district enjoyed very mild winters and that the lake never froze over until after Christmas. Instead of this they found there had been heavy snows, the surface of the lake had frozen, and they ran into zero weather. The intention had been to proceed to Dease Lake, but when they tried to get away they found it impossible. The chief difficulty was the forming of ice on the plane, which made it so heavy it would not rise out of the water. It was necessary to cut channels in the ice so that the plane could gather momentum by taxi-ing in the open water. This resulted in a lot of splashing and as soon as the water hit the plane it froze, and added weight.

"There seemed no prospect of getting away with all of the party and the men held a consultation. It was evident the plane would have to be lightened to the greatest extent. Not only would it be necessary to leave two men behind, but the minimum of gas should be carried, which meant reducing the flying radius. As Joerss knew the country best he was persuaded to take the plane out if he could and make arrangements for us to get out later . . . "

The end result of this was that Joerss was not chastised, even though he undoubtedly broke the law by flying without a licence.

By November 15th, five additional rescue planes were heading north—three to the Liard area and two other aircraft that were involved in the search for the Renahan plane. Often flying conditions were impossible and the men risked their lives on every flight. Yet another scare passed through the search team when a pilot lost his bearings and had to be assisted by another search plane. Eventually all of the search planes gave up except one.

This plane had been sent by the Tredwell Yukon Company under the command of a pilot named Everitt Wasson who had already attained fame in the North for his daring rescues. As soon as he joined the search, he made several dangerous trips into the area. When he arrived at Liard Post, he was unable to land in the deep snow because he had floats on the aircraft. He dropped a note to the manger of the post and asked him to write on the snow if Burke had been there. The reply read, "Yes, Burke left here October 11 for Teslin, Teslin." The message was incorrect—it should have said Atlin, but manager Osborne thought it was right because only once before had Burke failed to call at Teslin on his return trips to Atlin. This misinformation resulted in Wasson flying hundreds of miles while searching in the wrong area.

Well into winter, Wasson was forced to fly to Mayo, where he had the floats exchanged for skis. While there, he talked a famous Yukon guide named Joe Walsh into assisting in the search. Well equipped with winter gear, the two men left on November 12 to thoroughly search the area between Liard Post and Atlin. This meant flying through rugged mountains that had never been mapped, with continuous snowstorms forcing them to make landings in treacherous places.

Their first clue finally came when they landed on the Liard River near the Francis River, where the Indians told them that a plane had flown over heading upriver several weeks earlier. Heartened by the thought that they were getting near, they continued the search in earnest. At times they flew into blinding snowstorms where they were forced down on tiny lakes. In one instance they made ten attempts before managing to get off a lake after being forced to spend the night there. On one takeoff attempt, Walsh had to run alongside the aircraft on his snowshoes as it gathered enough speed for takeoff, and then had to climb back into the craft as it flew away.

In order to fully appreciate what these searchers were up against, one only has to look at a map of northern BC and the Yukon. The incredible distances flown in the search become more apparent and the heroism involved crystal clear.

On November 24th and again on December 4th, Wasson and Walsh made return trips from Liard Post to the headwaters of the river. That was when Martin and Kading had spotted their plane. It was also the time when the searchers spotted the snow-covered Junkers on the river ice. Several times they circled but were unable to land because of the broken ice surface. They returned to Whitehorse for more supplies and then returned and landed on the closest lake. This meant a 32-mile hike to and from the Junkers where the men found the note that had been hung in the boot.

Again the searchers returned to Whitehorse where it was suggested that the lost men could be with the Indians at the Pelly Reserve. On December 6, Wasson and Walsh left Whitehorse and were looking for a pass over the Pelly Mountains when they spotted a tiny column of smoke rising through the trees. They circled the spot and soon two frantically waving men let them know that the long search was over. As they circled over the stranded men, Walsh pushed a box of food out the cabin door, then thought that it had landed too far from the men, so they circled again and dropped their own supply of food. With it they left a note that they would walk in to assist the lost men as soon as they found a lake to land on.

As soon as the searchers set down on a small lake, they began the ten-mile walk to the lost men, but darkness forced them to camp for the night. The next day they set off again but missed the camp. Twice Kading fired his rifle to attract them—his last two cartridges; a short time later the searchers stumbled into their camp.

Joe Walsh immediately set to work to make a pair of skis for himself and graciously gave his snowshoes to Kading; while Martin used a spare pair of snowshoes that had been brought along. After the difficult trek back to the plane, the men had trouble getting the engine started, but it finally yielded and late in the afternoon of December 10, the group arrived in Whitehorse. Six days later, Wasson flew an RCMP officer back to bring out Burke's remains, and on December 19th, he was laid to rest.

As for the stricken Junkers, it was moved down to Takla Lake, where it was fitted with a new set of pontoons which had been brought up from Vancouver. During late June 1931, the plane was heading to Vancouver under the guidance of pilot W. R. McClusky when it crashed near Hope, BC. The pilot and his mechanic, the same Emil Kading from the Liard accident, escaped unharmed. The aircraft was rebuilt and flew until 1938 when it came to a tragic end. In attempting to land at Nation Lake in Northwestern BC, the plane crashed; the pilot and a passenger were both killed in the accident. The old Junkers had yielded to the "three strikes and you're out" rule; it found its final resting place and portions of it can still be found on the shore of this little lake.

In late December, a coroner's jury took up the death of Burke; the *Citizen* of December 24th noted:

"*Whitehorse, Dec. 23—The coroner's jury today rendered a verdict that the late Captain Burke, the Vancouver airman who lost his life on the upper reaches of the Liard River, died from starvation and exposure. The verdict carried a rider—that all airmen operating in the northern parts of Canada should receive training in woodcraft, and be required to carry a supply of food and ammunition. The body of Captain Burke will be interred at Atlin, the point from which he started on his fatal flight.*"

On December 30th, the body of Burke was interred in a coffin draped by the Union Jack, and carried to its final resting place by returned soldiers.

In due course, Everitt Wasson was awarded $1500 and Joe Walsh $500 by both levels of government, a considerable sum of money at that time. As well, both were cited for heroism. Author Frank Ellis summed up their rescue mission very well when he noted, "This concluded a rescue mission, which, for tenacity and heroism, has never been surpassed in Canada's flying history."

For those who may wonder if their heroism was noted, I must point out an article that was picked up from the *Vancouver Sun* and carried in *The Whitehorse Star* October 28th, 1932:

"*Several noted Yukoners are among those who have come 'outside' for a holiday. They are Joe Walsh, Mayo, one of the best woodsmen in the North, and Mrs. Walsh . . . .Mr. Walsh figured in the news two years ago when, with pilot Wasson, he discovered three lost flyers, Kading, Martin and Burke.*"

The *Vancouver Sun* also noted on January 22, 1931, that Everett Wasson was in the city and had taken a bride—Florence Jones, formerly of West Vancouver and of late a nurse in the hospital in Whitehorse.

Some people seem to excel at doing things that appear impossible to the average person, although it may seem quite normal to them. During the month of April 1931, the body of a man was found on the Yukon Trail about 10 miles below Fort Yukon. In poor health, scantily clad, he had attempted to walk the 29 miles from Beaver. It was suspected that his death occurred about the middle of January when the temperature had dropped to -78f. Formerly known as a first-class woodcutter, James Broderige had been attempting to walk out for medical attention. What makes this story so unusual is that James only had one arm. Somehow I have difficulty picturing a one-armed man cutting and splitting a great amount of wood.

The following photo depicting a cold day in the Yukon, was given to me by Chris Gleason. Chris trapped the McGregor Mountains between 1915 and 1924 and then moved to the Yukon where he spent many years prospecting. He never told me how much gold he found, but he did tell me that he struck pay dirt in a rather unusual way. After the completion of the Alaska Highway, much of the equipment used to build the road, was placed in several buildings and offered for sale. As Chris had a ready supply of cash available, he purchased it lock, stock and barrel, as the old saying goes. Then he sold it off piecemeal and made "nothing but money" as he put it. Didn't someone say that if we try enough crazy ideas, one of them are bound to succeed?

I have heard it said that a person should always save the best story till last; that is why I have saved this story until now. Although not taken from this area, it describes the indomitable spirit of the human race as well as any story that has ever came to my attention. Certainly this young man's adventure inspired me as a youth. The individual involved was a young man named Andy Traynor, who was employed by the Sherrit-Gordon mine, located at Lynn Lake, just north of Flin Flon, Manitoba.

One Sunday Andy decided to pass the time by walking the three miles from the camp to the mine. As it was a nice, sunny day, he worked up a sweat and a thirst as well. He knew that a small stream ran through the forest just a short distance off the trail, so he walked over to the stream to get a drink. As he knelt down to drink, a box of matches fell from his shirt pocket into the water. After satisfying his thirst, Andy walked back toward the trail, daydreaming as he went. After walking a short distance he thought that he had crossed the path, so he went back looking for it. This was his undoing, for he had not yet reached the trail. As he wandered back, he missed the stream because it made a 90° turn. Andy wandered around for a time but refused to sit and wait for help because he would have been too embarrassed to admit he was lost.

As he wandered farther into the wilderness, a search party was formed. They found the box of matches in the stream, but after five days of searching, gave him up for dead. Andy was far from dead, though, and as he made his way through the endless forests he had the presence of

Chris Gleason's picture, taken in the Yukon, 1949.

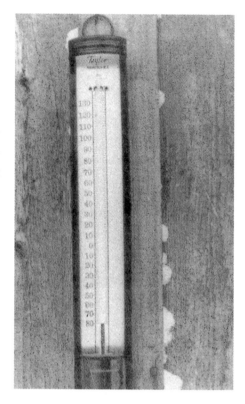

mind to make a shelter for himself every night.

Even if he had been carrying a knife, Andy would have been able to fashion some crude weapon for himself, but he had nothing, not even a fire to warm him at night. On one occasion his spirits rose when he managed to kill a few fool-hens with rocks, but that was his only solid food during his first month in the forest. Many times he found and gorged himself on berries, but this resulted in dysentery, which further weakened him.

At one point he spent three days crossing a huge area of swamps, only to give up and retrace his steps. His state of mind during that time cannot be imagined, for he must have felt a despair and loneliness that wrenched his soul. Many times he became overwhelmed when he realized that he could walk forever without meeting another human.

After over a month of wandering, Andy came to a river and followed it to a canyon. He realized that at one time the canyon had been used as a portage and he desperately hoped that it was still in use. An old cabin stood by the portage and after a search, he found a piece of fishing line with a hook on the end. He threw it into the river and immediately caught a fine trout. As he fed on the fish, he started to believe that he had a chance to survive.

The following day Andy tried fishing again. With the first strike, the line broke and he lost the fish as well as all hope. He took off the tattered remains of his clothes and tied them on a pole in front of the cabin, hoping some passer-by would find them and investigate. Then, totally crushed and at the end of his strength and will to live, he went into the cabin and lapsed into unconsciousness.

Only by a miracle help arrived, and it came in the form of a Forest Service patrol plane that happened to fly over the portage. The crew noticed the clothes hung on the pole and circled several times. Though there was no sign of life, they decided that further investigation was warranted so they landed further up the river and walked to the old cabin. What the rescuers found was almost beyond belief: inside the cabin they found a skeletal form that weighed less than 90 pounds; all that was left of what had once been a strapping young man of over 220 pounds. Andy didn't know he was being rescued.

Flown to hospital, Andy went through a prolonged recovery. Many times he awoke to hear himself screaming, believing he was back in the wilderness, hopelessly lost. When he finally left the hospital he knew one thing for certain: he would never go into the forest again.

Andy Traynor's adventure must surely stand as one of the greatest wilderness survival stories in Canadian history. Just how many miles he walked is anyone's guess, but the Forest Service checked their maps and found that the portage where he was rescued was 350 miles in a straight line from Flin Flon. Andy had been in the forest for one and a half months, and during that time had subsisted on only a fish, a few grouse and wild berries.

Index